French cinema in the 1970s

Manchester University Press

French cinema in the 1970s
The echoes of May

ALISON SMITH

Manchester University Press
Manchester and New York

distributed exclusively in the USA by Palgrave

Published by Manchester University Press
Oxford Road, Manchester M13 9NR, UK
and Room 400, 175 Fifth Avenue, New York, NY 10010, USA
www.manchesteruniversitypress.co.uk

Distributed exclusively in the USA by
Palgrave, 175 Fifth Avenue, New York, NY 10010, USA

Distributed exclusively in Canada by
UBC Press, University of British Columbia, 2029 West Mall,
Vancouver, BC, Canada V6T 1Z2

British Library Cataloguing-in-Publication Data
A catalogue record for this book is available from the British Library

Library of Congress Cataloging-in-Publication Data applied for

ISBN 0 7190 6340 X   *hardback*
EAN 978 0 7190 6340 4
ISBN 0 7190 6341 8   *paperback*
EAN 978 0 7190 6341 1

First published 2005

14 13 12 11 10 09 08 07 06 05   10 9 8 7 6 5 4 3 2 1

Typeset in Cheltenham with Futura display
by Koinonia, Manchester
Printed in Great Britain
by Bell & Bain, Glasgow

Contents

List of illustrations

Acknowledgements

I would like to acknowledge the help given in the preparation of this manuscript by the staff at the BiFi Library (and earlier the Cinémathèque in the Palais de Chaillot), the Forum des Images des Halles, the Institut Britannique and the Bibliothèque Jean-Pierre Melville in Paris, and Simone Potter at the BFI for help with the illustrations. Special thanks to Professors Celia Britton, Ginette Vincendeau and the late Jill Forbes, for their help and support.

Part of chapter 5 is reprinted by permission of Sage Publications Ltd, from *French Cultural Series*, vol. ii (1991), pp. 13–33 © Sage Publications 1991.

Thanks also for the permission to use the images: *L'Affiche rouge*: INA, Films 44. *Les Camisards, Moi Pierre Rivière*: Maître Roland Rappoport. *L'Attentat, Themroc*: StudioCanal. *Le Cecilia*: M. Jean-Louis Comolli. *Charles mort ou vif, Jonas qui aura 25 ans …*: Télévision suisse romande. *Mister Freedom*: M. William Klein. *Lo Païs*: M. Gérard Guérin. Every effort has been made to obtain permission to reproduce the illustrations in this book. If any proper acknowledgement has not been made, copyright-holders are invited to contact the publisher.

Introduction

In the thirty-five years since the explosion of social unrest of May 1968, innumerable books have been written, in France and in England, assessing and re-assessing the events and their influence. Almost as soon as the last rumblings had died away, as France settled into the comforting routine of life under the newly elected Pompidou, May '68 became a date dividing recent history into two. Little matter if any real changes took place in society, the upsurge in the desire for change seemed to mark a new direction in the consciousness of France. May '68 was a date on which change was – albeit briefly – shown to be possible. For a small number of people it brought fulfilment and challenge; as radical *groupuscules* operating largely in isolation even from each other suddenly found that they had an eager mass audience ready to consider the most abstruse political theory, but, by the same token, were obliged to confront criticism, argue their views with other factions, and face response from others with a quite differ-ent language and set of priorities. In some cases the revelation of their own weakness was brusque;[1] others found themselves influential beyond anything they had previously imagined.

For a much larger part of the French population, May' 68 brought a genuine discovery, or rediscovery, of a collective identity, where individuals could add their voice to the general shout that all was not well and, to a limited extent, inflect the methods and priorities if not of the social establishment at least of the recognised 'spokesmen of the people' – the unions or the Partie Communiste Français (PCF) – which many felt to be stagnating or not to be sufficiently sensitive to changes in perception. And, of course, for an established and even somewhat self-satisfied power-structure which had largely escaped serious challenge

---

[1] See Pierre Victor's interview with J.-P. Sartre, *On a raison de se révolter* (Sartre 1974, 148–60).

since the resolution of the Algerian war six years previously, there was the shock of discovering that the population was not necessarily content to offer approbation or polite disapproval.

May 1968 became a folk-memory which even now has resonance in French political debate; and that despite the largely undisputed fact that its lasting organisational legacy was quite slight (not, however, non-existent). As Margaret Atack (1999) has pointed out, the volume of writing about May as a phenomenon was almost unprecedented and began even while the events were still in progress. More than a political phenomenon, May '68 was a *cultural* watershed, an explosive rearrangement of the tectonic plates of French society – it was clearly a necessary climax to a decade or more of accumulating maladjustments, but at the time, and for some years afterwards, May '68 was read unambiguously as a *beginning* and not as an end. From the chaotic expression of ideas, from the creative surges it had conjured up, it was assumed that new forms of everything would spring.

It is not our intention here to recapitulate yet again the history of May and June 1968. This study aims to consider the ways in which the shake-up in French perceptions transferred itself to French cinema screens during the following decade. We should emphasise that we are not principally concerned here with the experiments in alternative, politically militant cinema which sprang directly from the activism of May and which was neither intended, nor in general able, to find distribution in even the independent mainstream circuits. This current, which rose from insignificance to a very creditable list of films by 1976 (see *Cinéma d'aujourd'hui* 1976: 200–21) before declining rapidly in profile and importance, had some influence on more mainstream production and its existence therefore needs to be taken into consideration; however, with a few notable exceptions neither the audience nor the reputation of the 'militant' films extended beyond a small circle of committed activists. Our emphasis is in the changes which occurred during the 1970s in the French output of films which could be seen by an average metropolitan cinema-goer without making such special efforts as joining a cine-club or seeking out films shown in community centres or to special interest groups.

Within that output, the traces of 1968 spread in wide and varied ways, from a genuine change in the content and manner of filming, to the arrival in the enduring genre of film comedy of new stereotypes and butts for laughter, or the relaxation of censorship which led in the middle part of the decade to an explosion in the availability of pornography and to its adoption into something like the mainstream of French production with the worldwide success of *Emmanuelle* (Jaeckin, 1974). The enormous numbers of pornographic films, both made in France and imported from such centres of production as Sweden and the USA, which were enjoying brief careers in small cinemas in Paris by 1975, caused considerable distortion in production and distribution figures. They represented a result of the disappearance of censorship which had been unforeseen, at least in its scale, and when in 1976 the government recanted to the extent of slapping punitive taxes on the showing of sex films and refusing all subsidies to them, the move provoked debate and criticism but not unanimous disapproval among the post-1968 reformers. Despite occasional exceptions such as *Emmanuelle*, the majority made no pretention to any artistic merit and certainly not to progressive politics, neither did they as a rule expect to gather large audiences, the individual films being largely substitutable for each other, and substituted after a week or so on the screens. Nonetheless, the wide availability of sexual subject matter certainly contributed to a greater freedom for all films as regards the issues considered suitable for examination on screen. The 1976 tightening of the law attracted criticism for its occasional early incoherences – such as the X-certificate delivered to *Emmanuelle 2*, which represented a potential financial disaster for the producer who had been counting on repeating the success of the first film the previous year – and for the problems it seemed likely to pose to a small number of distributors who had used porn circuits as a money supply in order to finance Art et Essai films (Lusofrance, which distributed the progressive and admired Hungarian Miklos Jancsò, for example). However, the return of the X-certificate did not mark a particularly repressive backlash to the portrayal of sexuality on the mainstream French screen. Audience assumptions and expectations had moved to incorporate an uninhibited approach to – at least heterosexual – sexuality even in the most unproblematic popular genres, as the admittedly unforeseen success of *Et la tendresse, bordel?* in 1979 indicates. The rise and fall of the erotic film in 1970s France is a vast subject which is beyond the possible scope of this study; interested readers may be referred to

Philippe Maarek's 1979 book *De mai 68 … aux films X* until further
work is produced on this potentially rich subject.

So how did cinema see its relevance to the nominally political and
social issues of May 1968? Firstly it was noticeable that in the
most coherent rhetoric associated with the events, no matter
what the political angle, cultural issues are considered to be important. The active groups on the left of the student movement
defined themselves in relation to Trotski (notably the JCR[2]) or to
the Chinese cultural revolution, (the Marxist-Leninists or Maoists
as portrayed in *La Chinoise* and exemplified by the UJCML[3]).
Although the latter groups rejected the confusion of political and
'cultural' discourses operated by their rivals in some publications, notably those directed at a student audience who were
presumably seen as too easily seduced by such things,[4] it was
essential to their political line to hold that the class struggle was
taking place on a cultural as well as a directly economic level, and
in other texts they concentrate on attacking what Louis Althusser
would term the 'Appareils Idéologiques d'Etat'.[5] Although the
latter's famous article 'Idéologie et appareils idéologiques d'Etat'
(Althusser 1970) was not published until 1970, his teaching had
been highly influential on a generation of politicised students who
studied under him at the Ecole Normale Supérieure. From the
'Cercle d'Ulm' (as this group was called), the ideas spread to a
wider audience. They appealed to a student readership in that they
attributed to the cultural apparatus, especially the educational
system as it existed, an active role in preserving the economic status

---

[2] Jeunesse communiste révolutionnaire.

[3] Union des jeunesses communistes marxistes-léninistes.

[4] 'La bourgeoisie utilise la double méthode de la répression et de la duperie: la
répression se fait par l'appareil de l'Etat et les institutions universitaires; la duperie
par les groupes trotskistes, anarchistes etc. qui exacerbent le subjectivisme et la
vanité des étudiants, mêlent les questions politiques aux questions 'sexuelles',
'culturelles', etc.' ['The bourgeoisie uses the double method of repression and deception: repression is carried out by the state apparatus and higher educational estab-
lishments; deception by the Trotskyists, anarchists etc, who exacerbate students'
egocentrism and vanity by mixing political issues with the 'cultural', the 'sexual'
and so on.'] 'Pour un travail correct parmi les étudiants', directive of the Bureau
Politique of the UJCML, avril 1968, roneotype: reproduced in Kessel 1972: 31.

[5] See the second document in Vol. 2 of Kessel's collection, 'La mainmise du
capitalisme idéologique d'Etat sur l'enseignement supérieur', *L'Humanité nouvelle*,
76 (16 novembre 1967): rep. Kessel 1978: 32–6.

quo through the inculcation of accepted socio-economic roles.

They appealed to those concerned in cultural production, including cinema, for the same reason. For politicised intellectuals, such ideas implied rethinking their own production, questioning whether it did not implicitly assume a social structure which the author might in fact wish to disavow. Such implicit assumptions were, according to Althusser and his followers, an active agent in the perpetuation of the capitalist system. Such a view clearly invested intellectuals with responsibility much greater than the simple support demanded by the traditional Communist party; writers, artists, students – and above all those concerned with cinema, with its traditionally enormous popular audience – were attributed importance and influence by a rigorous theoretical structure, which placed them at the centre, and not simply the tolerated margins, of Marxist cultural change. The attraction – but also the danger, as some of the post-May directions of action indicated – of a 'cultural revolution' was that it could apparently be made by students, teachers, writers, film-makers, who in creating a culture built on new and revolutionary assumptions, could destroy the consensus which supported the hegemony of the old one and transmit new perceptions to the population at large.

The cinema seemed to all to be an art-form with more potential than most, and it was also an art-form that students, revolutionary or not, favoured. *Clarté*, the UEC magazine,[6] included articles on Varda and the Nouvelle Vague as well as on political subjects (Hamon 1989: 16). Compared with literature, cinema was a popular medium: audiences were declining in 1968 but attendance was still respectable. For the students it equated with relaxation: culture enjoyed by choice in leisure-time, with minimal links to official education. These two advantages it shared with the mass-media, but despite the considerable limits placed on its subject-matter by the financial demands of distributors and sometimes by local or national censorship, its freedom was much greater than that of radio and television.[7]

Around 13 May, those involved in the French cinema began to

[6] The UEC (Union des Etudiants Communistes) was the forerunner of several of the political groupings of May, including the UJCML and the JCR.

[7] 1968 rhetoric was highly critical of television; among the Sorbonne graffiti appeared the slogan 'Vive la communication, à bas la télécommunication!', and several analyses located in it the vehicle of choice for the propagating of both old

respond to the rising voice of discontent. As a response to the huge demonstration which took place on that date, the Cannes Film Festival was suspended for 24 hours, while on the following day in Paris the student body of the Sorbonne began to organise film screenings on the four main campuses and also in some *lycées* and factories. On 16 May, the Ecole Nationale de Photographie et de Cinématographie, the technical film-school in the rue de Vaugirard in Paris, was established as a permanent information centre on the cinema, and it was there, on the evening of 17 May, that the first combined meeting of cinema professionals was held, summoned jointly by the Confédération générale du travail (CGT) and by the journalists of *Cahiers du cinéma*. It was a stormy occasion, but the meeting agreed to constitute itself into a permanent committee, dedicated to a complete rethinking of the structures of the cinema industry in France: in homage to the French Revolution, the committee christened itself the 'Etats-Généraux du cinéma', or EG. The next day, Saturday 18 May, while the EG was establishing its organisational structure, the Cannes jury resigned its functions, several directors withdrew their films and the evening screening was halted. The questioning of the Film Festival was born from a meeting of the Comité de Défense de la Cinémathèque, which had been constituted in February to oppose the threatened sacking of the distinguished founder of the Cinémathèque française, Henri Langlois: it included the leading directors of the Nouvelle Vague. Truffaut and especially Godard were outspoken in their demands that the Festival should be cut short; Louis Malle was one of the first members of the jury to declare his resignation; among the directors who declared themselves in solidarity with action were Claude Lelouch and Alain Resnais. Claude Chabrol, Eric Rohmer and Jacques Rivette all signed the founding document of the EG, as did Catherine Deneuve, Louis Daquin, Jacques Tati's daughter Sophie Tatischeff, and a great many names who were to become the most established values of the French cinema, such as Claude Berri, Claude Sautet and of course Marin Karmitz.

---

and new 'official' hegemonies. That criticism would surface in several films of the 1970s, and not only in profoundly revolutionary ones. However in the later years of the decade, and even more in the 1980s and 1990s, several of the radical post-68 film-makers turned to television work.

The Etats-Généraux remained in existence throughout May and June. They co-ordinated the majority of the guerilla-filming activity which resulted in numerous, anonymous *Cinétracts* recording and analysing the events of May; they arranged screenings and debates and they set up open committees to discuss the future of the French cinema. Their main meeting place moved out of Paris, to the Centre Culturel de l'Ouest Parisien at Suresnes, just south of Nanterre, and at meetings on 26 and 28 May four proposals for restructuring the industry were presented there, ranging from the idealistically radical to the cautiously reformist. A compromise project constructed from the four submitted was drafted on 6 June, but received little support. After the elections returned de Gaulle firmly to power, the EG converted itself into a semi-official association, and its members began to direct their energies elsewhere, although the body produced three newsletter-pamphlets between May and the end of the year, and offered some co-ordinated support to the similar movement of protest which erupted in September at the Mostra in Venice. Out of the EG was also born another association, the *Société des Réalisateurs de Films*, which proved much more permanent and still exists to this day as an official mouthpiece for film-makers in France.

Film-makers who devoted themselves wholeheartedly to the cause of Marxism-Leninism were fairly rare, but the implications of Althusserian Marxist theory were important and spread beyond its unconditional supporters. It was developed and promulgated notably by *Cahiers du cinéma*, which benefited from a considerable readership since its identification with the Nouvelle Vague. Its highly theoretical and political stance in the early 1970s made it hard reading, and eventually it reviewed its line in the face of falling circulation, but nonetheless its status and profile contributed to the visibility of the ideas it espoused. *Cahiers'* line demanded that, since the assumptions contained in a film were to be considered directly influential on the structures of society, it was necessary to consider them all, and not merely the explicitly political content. Not only every aspect of the content of the film, even the most anodine, but also the form of the narrative were to be questioned. From the radical challenge that was thus issued arose a number of obscure films, as well as some that made and consolidated reputations still influential today. Other film-makers took seriously the need – proclaimed in *Cahiers* but also much more generally among the 68ards of the film industry – to take the means of film production – cameras, finance, expertise – back to the grassroots and make them available to ordinary people (usually 'the workers', in the context). Chris Marker had made such moves even before 1968, and Marin Karmitz was to do so soon afterwards; the work of both these directors came to mainstream attention, although in the case of Karmitz the effect of the films which he made in the immediate post-68 period on the course of French cinema was arguably indirect.

Among the 'anarchist' elements stigmatised by the UJCML, interest in the cinema was even more pronounced. The small but vociferous and influential situationist group saw in the cinematic spectacle at once a metaphor for the state of culture in the late 1960s and the most effective way of communicating their ideas. Although their own films were certainly not aimed at a mass audience, their ideas created considerable interest among those working in film, and their influence on the ambient culture was independent of, and infinitely greater than, their own production.

However, relations between the revolutionary wing of the film world and the revolutionaries themselves, even the student revolutionaries, was not always easy. When Cohn-Bendit, an anarchist although not a situationist, considered the cinema in a chapter of his 1975 account of the events and their aftermath, *Le Grand Bazar*, he did not join the calls for new formal structures or Althusserian re-creation. While bowing to the notion that cinema could and should be politically useful and that therefore 'we should be capable of carrying out a radical critique of our taste for certain films' (Cohn-Bendit 1975: 83),[8] he expresses considerable doubt about the real involvement of film-makers in the political ideals he is defending: 'There's a hatred for the film-makers among the comrades for two reasons: jealousy – everyone wants to make films these days – and the cynicism of the film-makers towards the movement, they don't identify with it. Thus no discussion is possible' (Cohn-Bendit 1975: 88).[9] He also totally

[8] 'l'on [doit être] capable de faire une critique radicale de notre goût pour certains films'.

[9] 'Il y a une haine des camarades envers les cinéastes pour deux raisons: la jalousie – faire du cinéma, c'est l'envie de tout le monde aujourd'hui – et le cynisme des cinéastes envers le mouvement; ils ne s'y identifient pas. Il n'y a donc pas de discussion possible'.

rejects the 'style ciné-club de gauche' in practice; his preference being for a fairly traditional form and a 'revolutionary' content attached to a thoroughly conventional story.

> I'm not very liberated, I dream of making a blockbuster on the story of Cronstadt ... to get this real problem [the importance of Bolshevism] discussed through a love story between the Bolshevik sailor and an anarchist woman ... If you destroy a certain cinema, you move into a *no man's land*, while for me making a film is still showing a story. (Cohn-Bendit 1975: 84–6)[10]

In fact, Cohn-Bendit had little cause to worry that stories would disappear from the cinema, certainly not in 1975, when traditional forms were reasserting themselves even among the most committed reformers. When we move away from the direct influence of the political ferment of the May left, other factors appear in the wider landscape of the cinema which betray more diverse, polyvalent traces of change and different perceptions of the 'new' French society of the decade. First, there is the invasion of the popular screen by protagonists who reject society in the name of May, whether they be left-wing students (virtually a new stereotype pervading all genres from *policiers* to broad comedy) or criminals. Bank-robbers, for example in José Giovanni's *Les Egouts du paradis* (1979), scripted by Michel Audiard, claim to act for motives of social revolt rather than personal gain. It would seem that the memory of 1968 provided a solution to a dilemma always problematic in the popular thriller: how to make the undeniable attraction of a villain somewhat morally justifiable. Such strategies, of course, also degraded the revolutionary discourse. At best, it led to a vein of criminals-as-social-critics which sought some legitimacy in 1968 to support a pattern which had already been evident in earlier production, including even US films of the 1960s, for example *Bonnie and Clyde* (Penn, 1967). Sometimes this was harnessed to a Utopian spirit, which is one of the most engaging currents of French independent films of the 1970s, but often it led to a glorification of individual romantic revolt quite

---

[10] 'Je ne suis pas très libéré, je rêve de faire un super-production sur l'histoire de Cronstadt ... faire discuter ce problème [the importance of Bolshevism], qui est réel, à travers cet amour entre le marin bolchevique et la femme anarchiste ... Si tu détruis un certain cinéma, tu entres dans le *no man's land*; alors que pour moi, faire du cinéma, c'est quand même montrer une histoire'.

contrary to the spirit of 1968: Jean-Pierre Mocky's cynical protagonist in *Solo* (1970) is an early example. By the closing years of
the decade, the tropes of the revolutionary student and the political
demonstration with banners had been thoroughly absorbed by
the most commercial narrative cinema and could be used to
advance many and varied plots. This adjunct to the image of
French life went into temporary abeyance at the start of the 1980s,
but would appear again – as would other characteristic features
of 1970s film – in the young cinema of the 1990s (see Chapter 4).

But within the ranks of commercial cinema there was also a
more serious response to a changed climate. There was a growing
willingness to portray political action generally, and that, during
the whole of the following decade, *always* evoked the memory of
May. Political and social 'struggle', to adopt the much-loved word
of the period, provided the dynamics of plots in such varied
genres as historical reconstructions, tough urban thrillers, coming-
of-age movies and fantasies, and it was by no means always an
anecdotal element. It is this mutation of the paradigm of different
genres which will form the background for the major part of this
study.

Of course, adopting a new, perhaps politically sophisticated,
approach to subject matter and narrative did not always imply a
similar questioning of form, although the most revolutionary
texts usually demanded that this too should be reconfigured. By
the mid-1970s the phrase 'traditional form' had acquired different
implications when applied to a militant documentary and to a
commercial fiction film. The militant sector, always highly politicised, had recognisable codes of its own, usually related to
techniques of *cinéma direct*, which in its own context were 'traditional', but when transferred to the mainstream immediately
denoted the *non*-traditional and politically oppositional. Prior to
1968 Jean-Louis Comolli was observing the use of *cinéma direct* in
fiction films and its political implications; as public awareness of
this kind of cinema increased, its stylistic signs became a kind of
shorthand for a subversive ethos on the commercial screen.
Evidence of a low budget (grainy film, and minimal or natural
décor) or of direct filming of 'reality' (interviews to camera, shaky
hand-held footage, newsreel) became accepted codes for a
parallel cinema, as did the use of explanatory titles (which
recalled Brecht's approach to theatre) and graffiti and wall-art

(which recalled the walls of the Sorbonne). Such codes came to be integrated, to a limited extent, into a cinema without particular formal audacity, as politicising short-cuts which would be instantly recognisable to the audience. At a somewhat deeper level, theoretical debates about the nature of cinematic realism and its desirability did osmose from the pages of the specialist journals into film-making practice even within the mainstream. The Brechtian/Althusserian position held that true 'realism' implied incorporating into the film elements drawing attention to, and thereby destroying, the 'illusion of reality' presented by the images: at its most developed, it required a film to present not only a representation but also an analysis of its content and, ideally, of its own production. Such films were always an intellectual minority, but the contrast they required with traditional concepts of realism and smooth narrative did inflect the mainstream in different ways. The popular 'new naturalism' borrowed some of the techniques of *cinéma-vérité* for more than mere oppositional shorthand, while cinematic experiment such as had already been espoused by the Nouvelle Vague acquired an 'ethical' justification in the name of disturbing the audience and thus (notionally) encouraging intellectual engagement with the content. This second, non-naturalistic, interpretation of the formal debates of 1968 was to leave some traces on the stylish, reputedly apolitical successes of the *cinéma du look* in the early 1980s, especially in the work of Léos Carax.

Apart from these major cinematic debates, certain themes prominent in the discourse of 1968 may be identified in the cinematic production of the following decade.

First, there is the possibility of destruction of the hierarchical structures of society, and of a certain redistribution of power towards the base. The students who began the protests, it is generally agreed, did so out of a need to attain some control of their lives, and similarly in the workers' movement there emerged a nucleus of protest not only against a dictatorial management, but also against the claims of such established organisations as the CGT to speak for the grassroots without consulting them. Arguably, the disturbance and reorganisation of hierarchies was something which May '68 and its after-effects achieved, although perhaps in ways that its protagonists neither predicted nor wanted. Certainly the Utopian or carnivalesque fantasies of post-68 films such as *L'An 01* were no more than their own wish-fulfilments; however there were film-makers who made genuine attempts to overturn the hierarchies of their own profession and to put their principles into practice.

Closely related to this theme is the famous desire for a *prise de parole* on the part of those for whom others 'spoke', articulated mischievously by one of the Sorbonne graffiti: 'Je ne sais pas quoi dire, mais j'ai envie de le dire'.[11] The interpretation of *prise de parole* in a medium in practice more élitist than most took many forms. Expensive technology and the need for a minimum of expertise meant that cinematic discourse was in the hands of the few, while films had mass appeal and spoke to many. For several of those who had the power of decision, then, it was not so much a question of taking control of language as of giving it. The militant sector pioneered the notion of providing material and training directly to those who might wish to use it, encouraging them to participate in the production of films: very rarely did such enterprises penetrate into mainstream distribution, but a more equitable representation of different social groups did begin to emerge in the fiction film. Images of the young, the working class, the rural provinces, women, minority groups and immigrants all came under scrutiny; there was a demand for more frequent and less stereotyped exposure and indeed a measure of self-expression. This trend continued to grow even after other themes of 1968 were declining; several regional film centres were set up during the 1970s (although they were not necessarily successful), and the decade saw the tentative emergence of a female presence in the cinema. By the last years of the 1970s, there was even the timid beginning of a cinema recounting the experience of ethnic minority communities which continued to develop, slowly but nonetheless surely, into the 1990s and onwards.

A third influential theme from the rhetoric of May, adopted eagerly by many films of the decade, is the notion that 'everything is political', that the economic system and structures of power relations extend into cultural and sexual life and are to be combated there as well as in the workplace. These two issues, of direct relevance to student life, had played a great part in setting

---

[11] 'I don't know what to say, but I feel like saying it'.

off the initial protests: and the theory that repressive structures extend into the private domain is explicit and quite carefully theorised in Godard's work from 1973 onwards. It recurs in many forms and guises, serving as the underlying assumption of many apparently 'intimate' but profoundly 'political' films,[12] and it had an enormous influence in widening the scope of 'political' cinema and in initiating a new view of traditional situations. It was also, of course, the most vital theoretical assumption of the women's movement, which gathered strength during the 1970s and which inspired films dealing with its favoured issues. In a decade where there was an audience *expectation* that since 'tout est politique', films would have some socio-political relevance, this extension of the field of politics allowed film-makers the scope to insert their social awareness into the treatment of very varied stories. The importance of the working of wider political and social forces on apparently insignificant incidents of ordinary life was sometimes referred to as 'historical' thinking. This is a phrase to which Godard gave great importance in *Tout va bien*, and a concept which is fundamental to understanding the aims of the most ambitious films of the 1970s. In contemporary situations, it implied an analysis of the situation presented, while it also altered approaches to the representation of history and even the relation established between spectator and representation in the historical film.

Apart from themes, the cinema's inheritance from 1968 includes the manner in which 1968 expressed its protest, of which we find echoes in cinematic expression of the 1970s. Daniel Singer has observed that the actions of 1968 themselves, at least the early ones, were conducted in a spirit not unlike that informing cinema and theatre:

> Each action, whether big or small, had to be spectacular, so as to attract attention, and preferably be symbolic, so as to undermine authority either by revealing its oppressive nature or by demonstrating its impotence. Above all, the action had to be instructive, pedagogical ... Minorities, however active, had no chance of success unless they could stir up the indifferent, awaken the apathetic, spur on the resigned. The main purpose of action was to mobilise, to turn passive onlookers into actors. (Singer 1970: 63)

[12] For example those of Luc Moullet, *Anatomie d'un rapport* and *Genèse d'un repas*, exemplary essays in projecting from small-scale everyday experience to global patterns and dynamics.

These words seem remarkably apt to the aims of many film-makers of the 1970s. Certainly, a film that truly mobilised its audience was an ideal rather than a reality, but Singer's description admirably illustrates what the new socially conscious fiction film was working towards. The film as a revolutionary act – much sought, rarely achieved – remains a challenge to progressive film-makers throughout the decade. In a few rare cases, circumstances aiding, the challenge came near to being met. The story of *Histoires d'A*, generally considered to have hastened the legalisation of abortion by the spectacular audience figures it achieved while restricted to underground distribution, is probably the most obvious example. Its fame and its effectiveness actually owed very little to its intrinsic qualities as a film. Many films, however, aspired to acting as a revolutionary inspiration to their audience through their visual rhetoric or their exemplary narrative: in the most complex cases, the existence of the film-as-object or the film-as-event is itself to be viewed as a revolutionary *act*. Examples are Doillon's *L'An 01* or, more seriously and more influentially, Alain Tanner's *Jonas*.

Another way in which the form of the May events reproduced itself in the form of the films of the decade was through graffiti. Several times anthologised and one of the best-known sources documenting the 'spirit of '68', the graffiti-text of the walls of the occupied Sorbonne (and elsewhere), distilling complex political concepts into witty one-liners, naturally appealed to practitioners of an art that works by ellipsis and never has much time to make a point: besides, they rapidly acquired a great force of connotation. Marcel Hanoun's film *L'Eté* constructs a cinematic essay largely around the 1968 graffiti. Different film-makers exploited different aspects of the graffiti-text; its multiple, unattributable authorship (Alain Tanner), its visual impact (Godard and others), its slightly enigmatic nature – requiring the reader/hearer/spectator to think twice in order to seize its meaning – and its very direct political connotations in the wake of the publicity of the wall-text of May.

This book seeks to examine through considerations of specific work how the ideas and the forms which came to the fore during the events of May seeped into the cinema of the 1970s and to what extent the films of this neglected decade have had influence in their turn on later developments in the French cinema.

REFERENCES

Althusser, Louis (1976) 'Idéologie et appareils idéologiques d'état', *La Pensée*, 151, juin 1970: reprinted in *Positions*, Paris: Editions sociales, pp. 81–137.

Atack, Margaret (1999) *May 68 in French Fiction and Film*, Oxford: Oxford University Press.

Cinéma d'aujourd'hui (1976) 'Cinéma militant', special issue, 5/6, mars–avril.

Cohn-Bendit, Daniel (1975) *Le Grand Bazar*, Paris: Denoël/Gonthier.

Hamon, Hervé (1989) 'May '68 – a generation', in D. Hanley and A.P. Kerr (eds), *May '68: Coming of Age*, London: Macmillan,

Kessel, Patrick (1972) *Le Mouvement maoiste en France*, vol. 1, Paris: 10/18.

Kessel, Patrick (1978) *Le Mouvement maoiste en France*, vol. 2, Paris: 10/18.

Maarek, Philippe (1979) *De mai 68 … aux films X: cinéma politique et société*, Paris: Editions Dujarric.

Sartre, Jean-Paul (1974) Interview with Pierre Victor, in Philippe Gavi, Jean-Paul Sartre and Pierre Victor, *On a raison de se révolter*, Paris: Gallimard, 148–60.

Singer, Daniel (1970) *Prelude to Revolution*, London: Cape.

1
May in the cinema

Representations on the screen of the May events themselves were a much rarer occurrence than might have been expected; although passing mentions were frequent as explanations for the behaviour of characters or the origin of certain situations, rare are the films to which May 1968 was explicitly central. In the early years of the 1970s, although a preoccupation for many, they were a subject only for films on the borders of the mainstream and the underground (Godard's *Un film comme les autres* or Hanoun's *L'Eté*, both 1968). It was not until 1974 that the abundant footage of the events was edited into a documentary and distributed, to a rather muted welcome, and prior to 1974 the scarce direct references which existed tended to be disguised, for example in Alain Tanner's *Charles mort ou vif*, discussed in Chapter 8, which transplanted them, unhistorically, to Switzerland. In the latter part of the decade, as the memory receded into imagery, representations and even reassessments began to appear. Philippe Defrance's *Le Fou de mai*, probably the first film to offer a serious exploration of the legacy of those days ten years on, will be discussed in detail; although the audience for this careful semi-documentary was limited, its assessment of the significance of May is interesting and thoughtful and it has often been overlooked. Better-known was Romain Goupil's bitterly nostalgic *Mourir à trente ans*, released in 1980. By this point, however, the memory of 1968 had been assimilated into the imagery of the previous decade, and could be spoofed good-naturedly along with other historical incidents by even the most 'establishment' of film-makers, such as Yves Robert who makes Jean Rochefort an unlikely revolutionary student in *Courage, fuyons!* (1979). For Diane Kurys (*Cocktail Molotov*, 1979) the decisive event in the lives of her adolescent protagonists is *missing* 1968.

There was however one early exception to the absence of direct reference to 1968 in fiction films. Jean-Pierre Mocky's anarchic political thriller, *Solo*, released in 1970, acquired a cult reputation which its content certainly did not really merit by virtue of its unique effrontery in converting the May events into syntactic shorthand in a romantic-parodic adventure so soon after they had taken place. Mocky, who had been making faintly subversive comedies since 1959, also made another film, *L'Albatros*, in 1972, which was based on his idea of 1968, although its references were less direct and explicit. *Solo* was taken very seriously, both by its director and by the film critics, perhaps more seriously than with hindsight one might expect, but its ambitions were of a quite new kind. Although a small-scale film without major stars – indeed Mocky, a sometime successful actor, plays the main role himself – its vocation was clearly *popular*. Unlike the *série-Z* (see the next chapter) it had no factual foundation, was entirely governed by irony and did not pretend to reveal political machinations or to seriously treat major issues. But it was undoubtedly a 'commercial' thriller, and, unlike the more serious films, it took its inspiration directly from May '68, rather than merely responding to an increasingly politicised public. This seems to have led to an assumption of political importance that Mocky was more than willing to reinforce in interviews. Thus when *Cinéma 70* mentions *Solo*'s 'natural wish to be a film *born* of May '68 … to "continue the fight" in spirit and form' (Mocky 1970b: 112),[1] Mocky claimed it almost as a revolutionary act: 'We must try to "continue the fight" as the young people in *Solo* do; in fact it's a film of resistance, the young people's maquis against the oppressors in power, but it's not an anarchist film as has been claimed. No one ever thought of the Resistance as anarchists!'[2]

Solo does not portray the events in the Paris streets directly, but rather presents an imaginary picture of the groups behind them. The film starts with a machine-gun attack on a rather pathetic orgy, which an enquiry, quickly and correctly, attributes to the readership of an anarchist student magazine and specifically one member, Virgile Cabral. The film is concerned with

[1] 'naturelle volonté d'être un film *issu* de mai 68 … de "continuer le combat", dans l'esprit et dans la forme'.

[2] 'Il faut essayer de "continuer le combat" à l'image des jeunes de *Solo*; c'est en fait un film de résistance, le maquis des jeunes contre les oppresseurs au pouvoir, mais ce n'est pas un film anarchiste, comme on l'a déjà prétendu. On n'a jamais considéré les résistants comme des anars!'

Virgile's efforts to escape the police and to carry out another planned attack, aided (although he is unaware of the fact) by his elder brother Vincent, a musician and part-time jewel thief.

The centre of the film is Vincent not Virgile, and Mocky portrays him as at once romantic hero and identification figure. Vincent's practical common sense is opposed to the ideological idealism of Virgile and his comrades; this 'unengaged' protagonist allows Mocky's irony free rein on the police and the anarchist group alike, although between the two there is no doubt where his sympathies largely lie. Since Vincent is at first only interested in finding his brother, the audience, espousing his search, can take a sympathetic interest in Virgile without necessarily endorsing his ideas or approving him as a 'true and accurate caricature'. However, his 'crime' is treated as burlesque and the victims as mostly ridiculous, so that it can be discounted as the film progresses and Vincent becomes more involved with the student group, begins to approve its other aims, and takes the audience with him. Not that Mocky is merciful towards his young resistants, Brigades Rouges without a party line, totally humourless and far from analytical; the worldly-wise 'late revolutionary' Vincent cannot but gain by the contrast.

Despite his claims, Mocky's image of May is in many ways a caricature. The students as much as the 'gratin' are puppet figures, on whom Mocky fixes a stereotyped and highly unlikely discourse. For example they are prepared to kill each other for suspected treachery, and this is accepted by the audience as part of the characterisation. 'Romantic revolutionaries, that's what you are', Vincent tells Marc, the false 'traitor' who is as firmly faithful to the cause as Virgile, but they are not so romantic that the audience cares about them; Marc's assassination seems no more significant than the death of a puppet. Vincent is the only three-dimensional character in the film (and *his* death is tragic); but lost among such cardboard figures even he acquires density mainly as a puppet-master,[3] since human sympathy for Virgile's *groupuscule* is not quite credible.

However, if the students do not exist as characters they do exist as embodied discourse and as such, in 1970, they are

[3] Mocky could have created a very interesting formal effect by inscribing clearly into the text of the film his own identity as author. However, he does not do so.

significant. Their existence and their function in the film are in their words and actions, caricatured because they are shorn of any contradictory elements or human failings,[4] much over-simplified but recognisable and interesting as a reflection of how the actors of 1968 could be perceived to a sarcastic and unsophisticated, but nonetheless nominally sympathetic, outsider. Their aim is to 'change society' and everything they do or say is directed to that *per se* desirable goal, but if we seek further precision we come up against the demand to 'get rid of everyone with money(!)'; and that, apparently, is what they are literally in the business of doing. Vincent needs little persuasion to become an accomplice and helper although he is at first inclined to defend his own solution: 'You want to change society, I exploit it', he declares. His help never goes as far as *commitment*; it is an offer tacitly accepted and Vincent – like Mocky, presumably – is not to be taken for granted as a supporter. The film largely bears out Mocky's reputation as an anarchist, but the expression of his anarchism is nearer to right-wing than to left-wing ideals. Mocky, however, would clearly have denied any such suggestion, and indeed where the film was discussed by critics at all its ambivalence seems to be shrugged off very easily.

May is a major reference point both explicitly (various weapons are hanging in Virgile's room, marked 'Souvenirs du mois de mai', and his neighbours tell Vincent that it is since May that his brother's behaviour has changed: 'Before the events, yes, he worked pretty hard, now he comes and goes …') and implicitly (the policemen greet the news that they will have to search the Latin Quarter for the escapees, at the end of the film, with a resigned but menacing reflection that it won't be the first time). What use, then, does Mocky make of the events? He firmly maintained that the film was his personal response to them: 'I could be reproached with not having made, for example, a film on the month of May like so many others [*sic*]. I started from a principle, the principle of my whole career: I have always wanted to keep a very objective position with regard to politics', he told *Revue du cinéma*[5] (1970a: 81) and, in the same interview, 'I didn't

---

[4] Although this is true of Virgile and his accomplices, the compilers of the anarchist magazine (who have a much lesser role in the action) are allowed some human credibility: they even indulge in irony – otherwise Vincent/Mocky's monopoly – at the expense of the policemen.

want to make either a naturalist film, or a political one. So, to avoid the two traps, I made a romantic film, an adventure story' (1970a: 84).[6]

The whole of this six-page interview is an elucidation of Mocky's ambivalent relation to the events. It would appear from it (and from other interviews given, for example, to *Cinéma 70*), that he felt himself at once attracted to and excluded from May, and although he claims that he only played the role himself to keep the budget low, there is undoubtedly much that is personal in Vincent. Sometimes it is uncertain whether he is talking about the character or himself:

> Vincent, when he was 17, felt the same sense of revolt against the imbecility of today's society, in France or elsewhere. This society with no more place for love, for justice, for liberty … The student that I was twenty years ago would have liked to build barricades. But I was alone. I mean there weren't many of us. There wasn't this move-ment that there was in May. As a consequence, Vincent has been frustrated. (Mocky 1970a: 84)

The film represents, then, Mocky's very strong desire for involvement in the festival of a younger generation; at the same time, however, he refuses to engage in any form of structured politics. His view of 1968 is exaggeratedly romantic, even by the standards of the period. It is by no means exempt from self-aggrandisement, but the self-aggrandisement is projected onto the idealised figure that is Vincent, on the one hand, and on the other on to the possibilities which Mocky perceives in 1968: 'It's possible that if Vincent had experienced the events, he would have founded a total revolutionary movement. But, in the time-span of the film – one day, he doesn't have time … Vincent glimpses Virgile, just through a window. He doesn't manage to meet up with him until the end of the film, just before he dies' (1970a: 83).[7]

---

[5] 'on peut me reprocher de ne pas avoir fait, par exemple, un film sur le mois de mai, comme il y en a eu beaucoup. Moi je suis parti d'un principe, qui est le principe de ma carrière: j'ai toujours voulu garder, sur la politique, une position très objective'. Presumably, the 'many films' on May referred to are the short political documentaries, such as the 'Reprise de travail aux usines Wonder', shot during the events and circulated by underground channels in their immediate aftermath.

[6] 'je n'ai voulu en faire ni un film vériste, ni un film politique. Alors, pour éviter ces deux pièges, j'en ai fait un film romanesque, un film d'aventures'.

[7] 'Il est possible que Vincent, s'il avait vécu les événements, aurait fondé, lui, un mouvement révolutionnaire total. Mais, dans la durée du film – une journée, il n'a

In effect, *Solo* represents an extended day-dream regarding May '68, and as the title suggests it is a distinctly uncollective daydream. As far as the ideals of the protagonists are concerned, 'love, justice and liberty' are less in evidence than ruthlessness and a fair amount of swashbuckling action. At the end of the film Virgile escapes (although Vincent is killed), and Mocky emphasises that 'they will go on since they haven't been arrested'. Virgile, Vincent's brother/double, the most uncompromising and the least caricatured of the 'revolutionaries', escapes caricature largely because he speaks little, contenting himself with action while his colleagues explain their position. Mocky idealises Virgile as much as he does Vincent: 'The "desperado" type ... whose only family was his brother far away, who didn't take care of him. Virgile is the classic anarchist student' (Mocky 1970a: 83).[8] According to what canons Mocky defines the 'classic' anarchist student is not clear, but paradoxically given the tone of the film, the strongest impression made by Mocky's interview is a desperate romantic seriousness, more akin to the tone of the student group in the film than the worldweary quips of Vincent. It does not seem to occur to him that the students themselves may come across as caricatures. Asked how he reacts to the criticism that his film is anarchist and negative, he takes this immediately as a criticism of the students' actions, not of how they are presented:

> It's obvious that *Solo* could be treated as anarchist because if there hadn't been this movement in May, these young people would frankly be isolated anarchists. But in my film they are under the influence of the events. For them the barricades represented something. They would have liked to continue by themselves. In fact, Virgile and his friends aren't exactly isolated: they are isolated but they come from a big movement. (1970a: 87)[9]

---

pas le temps ... Vincent entrevoit Virgile, juste par une vitre. Il n'arrive à le rejoindre qu'à la fin du film, juste avant de mourir'.

[8] 'Le gars "desperado" ... qui n'avait, pour toute famille, que son frère qui était loin, et qui ne s'occupait pas de lui. Virgile, c'est l'étudiant anarchiste classique.'

[9] 'Il est évident que *Solo* pourrait être traité d'anarchiste parce que s'il n'y avait pas eu ce mouvement du mois de mai, ces jeunes seraient carrément des anarchistes isolés. Or, dans mon film, ces jeunes sont quand même sous l'influence des événements. Pour eux, les barricades représentaient quelque chose. Ils auraient voulu continuer tout seuls. En fait, Virgile et ses camarades ne sont pas exactement des isolés: ce sont des isolés sortis d'un gros mouvement.'

It seems that Mocky wished with all his heart for *Solo* to be considered as revolutionary, despite its simplistic politics. There is no point in looking for political analysis in the film, that is not its aim; anarchism is reduced to violence against society, with which we are asked to identify through the mechanisms of the thriller at their most frenetic. Mocky's films prior to 1968, with their reputation for black humour, are themselves, in a sense, such acts of violence; it is perhaps unfortunate that humour (as Tanner commented after his first two films) is a two-edged weapon, and the habit of caricature which has slipped into the film possibly betrayed Mocky's own intentions. *Avant-scène* published the screenplay of *Solo* (which marked a turning-point in Mocky's career; he commented in 1977 that: 'after 68, the daily and weekly papers started to devote several columns to me whereas before they never gave me more than a few lines. It was *Solo* which unblocked the situation. With *Solo* it was officially recognised that I was on to something real' (Mocky 1977: 17)[10]). Michel Mardore, in the introduction to *Avant-scène*'s reproduction, commented: 'this isn't an opportunist film on the aftermath of 68 and the anarchist bombs. It's a cry of rage which brings to the light of day ten years of unformed anger against people's pettiness, the *ridiculousness* of their "morality", the hypocrisy of their actions' (Mardore 1970: 9).[11] It is in this light, at least, that Mocky seems to have intended the film.

The only political thriller to refer specifically to the events of 1968, *Solo* presents them – or rather, a discourse recognisably to be associated with them – as a form of individualist, romantic wish-fulfilment, projected onto an isolated, and disaffected, individual. In fact, like Vincent, Mocky refused to accept real involvement, although it does not seem that age was such a barrier as he claims. Even while claiming the film to be revolutionary (and making the nostalgic most in interviews of the mild censorship problems it encountered), he denied that it was political – a

[10] 'après 68, les quotidiens et les hebdomadaires se sont mis à parler de moi sur plusieurs colonnes alors qu'auparavant ils ne me consacraient que quelques lignes. C'est *Solo* qui a débloqué la situation. Avec *Solo*, on a reconnu officiellement que j'étais accroché à quelque chose de réel'.

[11] 'ce n'est pas un film opportuniste sur les suites de mai 68 et les attentats anarchistes. C'est un cri de rage qui expose au grand jour dix ans de colère larvée contre la méchanceté des gens, la *dérision* de leur "morale", l'hypocrisie de leurs actes'.

rather dangerous position. What saves the film is its persistent irony: it is not really 'committed', but the action of Vincent and his friends is as conceivable a form of revolution as, say, that of Claude Faraldo's Themroc, and the society it is acting against is recognisable, although the basis of Virgile's rebellion is neither so clearly established, nor is his environment so demonstrably inhuman, as that of Faraldo's protagonist. Certainly, *Solo* is a long way from the legalism of the 'Série-Z', and it was perhaps this which raised the interest of critics and audiences. It is a very flawed experiment, and one without inheritance, but a genuine and unique cinematic response to May, and one of the very few films to refer to the events so directly at this early stage.

Of course, the parallel circuit began editing and distributing films representing and interpreting the events from a very early date, under the aegis of the Etats-Généraux du Cinéma, the organisation which was created as a result of the talks held by cinema professionals during May itself. Some of these gained a wide reputation, *La Reprise du travail aux usines Wonder* being undoubtedly the best known, and they were certainly not unseen at the time, although they were very elusive for a long while afterwards.[12] Most were short, however, and their distribution like their production depended on groups of committed activists. From the start, it would appear, there had always been a half-formulated intention to collect and amalgamate them eventually into a definitive account of May 1968, but the volatile nature of the groups worked against that, and when in 1974 a film did indeed emerge, it was made by an English journalist, Gudie Lawaetz, and it was by no means the exercise that the original makers of the footage had intended, even though much of their material was used (Huleu 1975). It was perhaps inevitable that *Mai 68* would disappoint; it was, as Serge Daney observed (Daney 1975: 6), too long after the events to capture the passion of involvement, and too soon to be objective. Of the two, its aim seems to have been objectivity, but in 1974 (and indeed, as later films were to show, until the end of the decade) an objective view of 1968 was simply non-existent in France. The result, for those involved, was simply 'a sort of doxa, a certain number of average confused ideas,

---

[12] *La Reprise du travail* has recently (2003) been edited on DVD in France, along with Marin Karmitz' post-68 films *Camarades* and *Coup pour coup*, of which more later.

minimal understanding well presented', and it led to resentment at the translation of 1968 into a commercial cinematic spectacle: 'it is vital [for the cinema industry] that we know that May '68 is digestible, that images of 1968 are also visible in cinemas and ... that it's there and only there that they are visible *today*' (Toubiana 1975: 11).[13] The film was thus interpreted as a means of recuperation. This attitude, which probably partly explains the reluctance to include images of '68 in even politically committed fiction films, meant that *Mai 68* was not particularly successful, and the footage it used was taken out of other circulation. William Klein, who refused to contribute the film he had shot to an enterprise he considered 'a thing distributed by soup-merchants' (Klein 1978: 41),[14] produced in 1978 a film using different material, but its appearance was much less publicised. (This film, *Grands soirs et petits matins*, is discussed in Chapter 8.[15])

The conclusion to Lawaetz' film is ambiguous: 'from the post-May period ... post-Gaullism was born' can be construed negatively but at least suggests that there was a change of some description. The only other film incorporating direct footage of May 1968 to cross the divide from the militant to the mainstream circuit during the 70s took as its programme the assumption that all the radical efforts of the preceding decade had more or less failed, with May 1968 as the one eminent case in point. Chris Marker's *Le Fond de l'air est rouge* appeared in 1977, a year before 'official' commemoration in 1978 failed once again to produce a high-profile feature film which successfully summed up the era. Marker was one of the main forces behind the best-known of the militant cinema collectives, SLON/ISKRA (it changed its name in 1974), responsible for earlier 'cross-over' projects such as *Le Bonheur/ Le Train en marche* (1973: a reissue of a Soviet silent comedy of 1934 with an accompanying 'introduction' interviewing the film-maker) and, in 1967, *Loin du Viêt-nam*.

---

[13] 'une sorte de doxa, un certain nombre d'idées moyennes et confuses, un savoir minimum mais bien réparti' ... 'il est vital [pour l'appareil cinéma] que l'on sache que mai 68 est digérable, que les images de 1968 sont aussi visibles dans une salle de cinéma, et ... que c'est là et uniquement là qu'elles sont visibles *aujourd'hui*'.

[14] 'un truc distribué par des marchands de soupe'.

[15] A collection of short militant films was however distributed to a few cinemas in 1978: this programme, entitled *Mai 68 par lui-même*, made no pretence of being an integrated product.

Le Fond de l'air est rouge is four hours long, divided into two parts. Its main achievement is probably to present 1968 in a global context; the events form the climax of the first part of the film, but Marker continually insists on actions occurring elsewhere. Developments in Vietnam, Cuba, Ireland, America and Germany precede the representation of the French demonstrations, which are thus de-dramatised; the film points out besides that the most dramatic demonstrations of the period, such as those in Japan, were the least constructive, and student activity is soon left behind to concentrate on the long-lasting workers' movement and the ambivalence of the CGT and the Communist party. The film's second part begins with the Soviet invasion of Prague, and is a chronicle of fragmentation and triumphant authoritarianism. The discredit of the two major Communist regimes and the fall of Allende's Chile are interspersed with reminders of the power of right-wing dictators such as the Shah of Iran, regimes of the right in the USA and France, and private enterprise (Minamata). Protest is shown as disorganised and fragmented into single issues, and easily dispersed or ignored despite its continued existence. *Le Fond de l'air est rouge* is concerned with the persistent recurrence of demonstrations in many different circumstances: it presents activism as a tradition (flashbacks in the film return to the Soviet revolution and to the 1930s) which needs to survive setbacks and to find new ideals, but the impression it leaves is that the tide of failures and disillusions is increasingly hard to resist

However, the first film to seriously explore the legacy of May '68 was made a year earlier, in 1976, but it did not achieve distribution at the time of its making. Philippe Defrance's *Le Fou de mai* did not appear on French cinema screens until 1980, when the political culture had already profoundly changed. Its structure is self-reflexive, with the protagonist, Pierre, setting out to write a book on the fate of various aspects of the '68 movement eight years later. The subject of Pierre's book is the subject of the film, and the process of creation of the one provides the major narrative thread of the other. Since the book is still unfinished in the last scenes of the film, there is finally only the cinematic result of Pierre's work; the film *is* the book.

The documentation which Pierre gathers for incorporation into the finished work provides one important part of the content of the film. Pierre and his assistant (Defrance himself, who also played Michel Recanati in Romain Goupil's 1980 *compte-rendu*, *Mourir à trente ans*) carry out a number of interviews; that is to say, Defrance and his friend Jean-Pierre Moulin, who plays Pierre, carry them out, for the interviewees are quite genuine.

The interviews provide the 'official' or documentary side of the film, that which is worthy of inclusion in the factual book that is supposedly being prepared. The fictional content of the film, which revolves around Pierre himself, his family and friends, provides another angle on the same question – what has become of the ideas of May? Pierre's present situation, his attitude to his friends and his relationship with his wife, can all be assumed to have been influenced by his involvement in the events eight years before; the process of recalling those events, and therefore of bringing the past back into the present and comparing them, has a devastating effect. The enquiry conducted by Defrance, then, takes place on two fronts which can loosely be characterised, to reactivate the duality so important to the events themselves, as the political and the personal.

The starting point for Pierre's enquiry is the renewed consciousness of the conjunction of these two spheres; the personal emotion which he feels on watching footage of the May demonstrations. It is thus film which operates the conjunction; and although we are led to understand that he is watching these films because he had already decided to undertake his research, their immediacy provokes a qualitative shift in the nature of memory and of his relationship to his personal history. 'I was surprised by my emotion', he says, almost to camera. The contradiction between detached and passionate history, objectivity and subjectivity, provides one of the first dilemmas of the film: 'If you say, "I was there, I was on such and such a committee" you sound like a war veteran. If you stand back to take stock, it's left-wing intellectual recuperation.'[16]

As Pierre's research, and the film, progresses, this problem becomes incorporated with another: that between organisation and spontaneity. In the first sequences, he claims to be researching: 'how the ideas and the liberating demands of 68 have survived: "take your desires for reality", "power to the imagination", "be

---

[16] 'J'ai été surpris de mon émotion' ... 'Si tu dis, "j'y ai été, j'ai fait telle comité", ça fait ancien combattant. Si tu prends du recul pour faire un bilan, c'est de la récupération intellectuelle de gauche.'

realistic, ask for the impossible"'.[17] His choice of slogans, from the
street graffiti, are among the most famous and the least 'political'
in the sense of referring to organised political structures. Pierre's
aim seems to be to highlight spontaneity and on several
occasions he insists that an essential key to understanding May is
to remember that it took place outside official organisations. The
theme is taken up by his first interviewee, a journalist on *Libération*:
'The things that have happened since May '68 have happened
outside the organisations, be it the women's movement, homo-
sexuals, prisoners, the secondary school students, drug-addicts
now, all that has happened outside the organisations.'[18] And yet,
the interviews which are incorporated in the film reflect a very
different set of priorities. The words quoted above are pronounced
by the representative of a newspaper which, if it still considers
that 'it's for these people that *Libération* is now the mouthpiece',
is nonetheless becoming an 'institution' of a sort. Subsequent
interviews take place in the offices of the PSU (Parti socialiste
unifié) and of the PCF. The fourth choice, an ex-militant worker at
Renault-Billancourt, is closer to the grassroots, but the subject of
the interview is exclusively the organisational losses or gains in
the factory. The last interviewee in the film, Edgar Morin, the
intellectual–analyst of 1968 *par excellence*, also concentrates on
the reasons for the events at the time, and on the change (or lack
of it) in institutional discourse. Thus, despite Pierre's insistence
that it is the *personal* which has been most affected by 1968 – or
rather, that the interface between personal and political is the
area of most interest – this is not what he studies; nor do
representatives of this sort of trend appear in the film, at least in
their own persons. Pierre claims to have interviewed some
militants from the MLF (Mouvement de libération de la femme),
but the film does not. Defrance, in his interview with *Avant-scène*,
stood by his choice of interviewees, although admitting that 'if I
had really undertaken the book that Pierre wants to write, I'd have
interviewed many other people' (Defrance 1980b: 5),[19] but the

---

[17] 'comment ont survécu les idées, les revendications libertaires de 68: "prenez
vos désirs pour de la réalité", "imagination au pouvoir", "soyez réalistes, demandez
l'impossible"'.

[18] 'Les choses qui se sont passées depuis mai 68, elles se sont passées en dehors
des organisations, que ça soit la révolte des femmes, que ça soit les homosexuels,
que ça soit les taulards, que ça soit les lycéens, que ça soit les drogués maintenant,
tout cela s'est passé en dehors des organisations.'

contrast between Pierre's vision of 1968 and his choice of representatives is intriguing; all the more since Defrance himself in his role of Pierre's assistant Martin is made to advocate dividing their enquiry into two parts in order to concentrate at least up to a point on the more 'marginal' developments. Martin is presented as being 'objective' – in that he was out of the country when the events took place – and therefore perhaps the 'voice of reason' to counterbalance Pierre: but despite the good intentions of both, only the institutional issues are debated in documentary mode.

Marginal movements are thus mentioned, exalted as important, proposed as a major element of the book but not dealt with in the film. The domain of the truly personal, on the contrary, is never mooted for possible inclusion in the book. Indeed Martin sees Pierre's emotional involvement in his subject as a hindrance: 'I think you're mixing everything up. Politics isn't life.' This establishes at once an insurmountable difference in the understanding of the nature of politics between those who experienced the events and those who did not. For Pierre, politics and life *are* inseparable, and this is a direct result of his deep involvement with a movement which insisted on their connection. If Pierre's reappraisal of 1968 leads to a reappraisal of his own life, that is in itself a survival of the mentality of 1968 in one former participant. Neither Martin nor Pierre seem to be aware of the significance of Pierre's involvement with his subject; both see it merely as a problem which must be surmounted if the book is to be finished, but Defrance makes it an integral part of his subject. Whereas the projected book will concentrate on institutional change and on marginal movements which could be seen as mini-institutions (the Mouvement de libération des femmes or the ecology movement), the film, while in its documentary part concentrating on the institutional – a most unimpressive record – devotes its fiction to a study of the effect which 1968 had on mentality.[20]

[19] 'si j'avais réellement entrepris le livre que Pierre souhaite écrire, j'aurais interviewé beaucoup d'autres gens'.

[20] 'à mon sens, la politique ne pourra changer, on ne pourra changer la politique, que si les locuteurs ne se réfugient pas derrière une parole officielle, une parole de bois, mais se positionnent, s'assument, en tant que sujets affectifs, aimant, souffrant, fragiles, angoissés, etc.' ['to my mind, politics cannot change, we cannot change politics, unless those involved don't hide behind official jargon, but take up positions, and accept themselves as emotional subjects, who love, who suffer, who

Pierre is the most extreme example of this, but all the protagonists have been in some way affected by the events, even if indirectly and even if they are unaware of it, and Defrance is equally interested in the effect which the experience missed has had on Martin. Clearly fascinated, and, despite his occasional incomprehension (or provocation) very respectful of Pierre and his uncompromising attitudes ('he would never have worked in the private sector'), Martin – who is a teacher in a private school – questions the validity of doing so with reference to an idealism which he does not quite share. Pierre's son claims that 1968 has made little difference to his life, but he studies under-development in Africa as part of his school syllabus, and he and his sister freely discuss their parents' relationship and even ask about their sex-life. Another form of survival is exemplified by a young couple whom Pierre meets almost by accident when at the lowest point of discouragement with his project; the man confirms the general diagnosis that in the world of work, within the system, little has changed since 1968, but he also indicates his intention to move outside the system as soon as he can. He has a renovated boat on which the family hopes to live. 'What will you live on?' enquires Pierre, unconvinced, but the young man is not deterred: 'You don't need much … there's still a few fish under the oil-slicks.'

It is in the relationship between Pierre and his wife Anne, however, that the most complex interaction occurs between 1968, the memory of 1968, and the conduct of the most personal aspects of their lives. On the one hand the effect is divisive. This had been so originally (Martin recalls that just after 1968, Pierre 'was completely disorientated, he said he wanted to quit everything and go and live no-matter-where') and becomes so again. When he brings the past into contact with his present, Pierre experiences an immense frustration, rather aimless but with a disastrous effect on his temper. Anne appears to have remained detached from the events (she is not French, and therefore by implication 'semi-detached' from '68), and she does not become involved in Pierre's re-living of the past in any obvious way. Pierre's frustration implies a temporary rejection of her, which she accepts without apparent problems.

---

are fragile and anxious, etc.]. Defrance1980b: 6. Defrance took part in the events as a (theatrical) actor, and has clearly assimilated this attitude deeply.

However, it is she who feels able to call their couple into question more seriously, and her manner of doing so indicates that the process of self-reappraisal has not after all been unique to Pierre. In her case it is even much more positive. While Pierre's request for a period of separation is based largely on dissatisfaction and frustration, with his achievements over the previous eight years and with the possible results of his research (uniformly depressing in the cases included in the film), Anne has definite aims, and her dissatisfaction leads her to move towards action: 'I realise today that I've spent 15 years in your shadow: your children, your projects, your books. Certainly I was happy, but today I want something else.' The cause of this reassessment is not 1968, but it is certainly linked to the effect that the memory has had on her husband. He attempts to deny her involvement in a crisis which 'was mine, you weren't in question'; her response is 'I'm putting myself into question'.

At this point *Le Fou de mai* betrays affinities with a number of other works which, in the latter part of the 1970s, explored the concept of the couple. The impetus for this came, almost certainly, from the increasing influence of the women's movement, the ideas of which are frequently cited in the films as the starting-point for the series of events which follows. The 1970s saw a considerable rise in the number of women making films which reached the screens, and many of these films dealt with gender relations, often – but not always – in the context of the couple. Utopian visions were elaborated of possible new formations of the nuclear relationship, for example Coline Serreau's first feature film, *Pourquoi pas?* (1977). Serreau started her career with a documentary, *Mais qu'est-ce qu'elles veulent?* (also 1977), which proposed a cinematic *prise de parole* to a number of women.

It was not only women, however, who called the concept of the couple into question. A number of such films, at first glance a surprising number, were made by men, in the very large majority men whose intellectual commitment to change in the late 1960s had been considerable. By the middle of the following decade, we may observe a growing tendency for the difficulties of sustaining idealism through the disillusions of the 1970s to be expressed through the private sphere. The ex-militant, often in co-operation with a woman, uses his confrontation with the new sexual and economic perspective of the women's movement as a way of examining the failures of his own concepts of renewal. *Le Fou de mai* is a particularly clear example of this displacement of the public onto the private, and of the transformation of the self-imagined subject into the object of change. These films offer a conjunction between a feminist discourse – the unsatisfactory position of the woman in a traditional couple must and can be changed – and a narrative structure, typical of revolutionary fiction, based around the *prise de conscience* (sometimes slow and partial, it must be admitted) of a central character initially – even if unconsciously and unwillingly – in the position of 'the oppressor'.[21] Pierre, in spite of his revolutionary past, cannot at first comprehend Anne's decision, and can only say in astonishment: 'And the children?'. Later, however, he not only gains better understanding of the situation but himself finds it liberating. The couple retains an occasional relationship; again, Pierre at first finds this hard to accept while Anne welcomes the change ('I feel as if I've got a mistress' … 'I am your mistress'), but he comes to respect her need for freedom. Outside his conventional family situation, Pierre returns more confidently to his book, which by the end of the film is nearing completion. One of the last interviews included in the book (but not in the film) is with a group of feminists, which suggests that he is aware that his wife's demands have a connection with 1968 and what resulted from it.

The variety of personal responses to 1968 portrayed in *Le Fou de mai* has some affinity with the catalogue of post-'68 discourses which Alain Tanner made into the structure for *his* 1976 film *Jonas qui aura 25 ans dans l'an 2000* (see Chapter 8); there is the desire for a simpler lifestyle outside the system (the young couple), the disillusioned activist (Pierre), and the possible development of education, so important to Tanner's film, is at least indicated in the homework and the behaviour of Pierre's children. Defrance declared his admiration for Tanner (Defrance 1980b: 6; Douin 1976: 62). However, Defrance's film puts itself forward, at least in part, as documentary; the notations of personal behaviour are interspersed with political interviews, and the narrative is carried forward by the progress of a research assignment. Despite *Revue de cinéma*'s conclusion, attributed to the film, that 'History is less

---

[21] Other examples of this theme are *Anatomie d'un rapport* (Luc Moullet, 1975), *Mais où et donc ornicar?* (Bertrand van Effenterre, 1978) and *Pour Clémence* (Charles Belmont, 1976).

a theory of key dates than a collection of everyday actions',[22] we notice the latter in the film as if by accident. Despite its importance to Defrance, Pierre never changes the direction of his research to incorporate it, and yet his book satisfies both him – at least relatively – and his publisher. Also, in Tanner's film looking back on the past is unequivocally negative, and the future of post-'68 discourses resides precisely in their freeing themselves from the memory of previous disappointments. The only positive progress which takes place in *Le Fou de mai* is a result of reliving the past, comparing it to the present and thereby generating dissatisfaction, in Pierre and, through the more-or-less revisionist interviews, in the audience. Defrance in 1976 saw 1968 as a positive force, albeit an almost spent one, and he gives little indication that there is any source of revolutionary energy available other than by a return to that source. In this respect he is decidedly pessimistic, and by 1980 he has become more so: 'May '68 is part of history, it's no longer a reference-point' (1980b: 5).[23]

Le Fou de mai appeared four years after it was made. *Jeune cinéma*[24] recorded that 'this film about May '68, directed at those who would be classed left-wing, aroused an enormous number of allergies, as if the questions that it was asking at the time about the legacy of May and the viability of the Union de la Gauche could not be asked' (Defrance 1980a: 27) Certainly the picture which emerges from the sequence of official interviews is not an encouraging one. For the major parties the memory of 1968 is overshadowed by the perspective of approaching elections, and the implicit criticism levelled at this attitude by a protagonist who at least dreams of being uncompromising was no doubt hard to accept; the evidence of failure in all obvious fields (the adolescent denies 1968's significance, the Renault worker reports a deterioration in conditions after May) would not add to the credibility of those politicians (notably the PSU) who were still acting with reference to the events. In 1980 however, although election fever was even more in evidence, the issues seem to have been

---

[22] 'L'Histoire était moins la théorie des grandes dates que la collection des gestes au quotidien'.

[23] 'mai 68 fait partie de l'histoire, ce n'est plus une référence'.

[24] 'ce film sur mai 68, s'adressant à des gens qu'on peut classer de gauche, a suscité énormément d'allergies, comme si les questions qu'il posait à l'époque sur l'héritage de mai, sur la viabilité de l'union de la gauche, ne pouvaient pas être posées'.

considered 'safe', and 1968 was now far enough away for the accusation of intellectual recuperation (levelled at the film almost as a matter of course) to have lost some of its force. In any case, the turn of the decade saw the appearance of two other films which evoked May: Diane Kurys' *Cocktail Molotov* in 1979, and, in 1980, *Mourir à trente ans*, made by Romain Goupil.

In *Cocktail Molotov* the events of May are little more than a backdrop for the escapades of the young protagonists, whose conquest of independence and maturity is explicitly *divorced* from their influence, since they are continually in another place. *Mourir à trente ans* is even more pessimistic in outlook than *Le Fou de mai*. Goupil set out to make a film-biography both of the May events and of the *lycéen* leader Michel Recanati, a personal friend. The thesis which emerges from the film, behind the enthusiasm and energy which characterised May, is that of an introverted character who plunged into political activities in order to compensate for an inability to establish personal relationships. Goupil, by emphasising the trauma caused to Michel by the discovery that the man he believed to be his father is not so in fact, seems to reverse the famous theory of the May events as a *psychodrame* aimed at the overthrow of the authority/father-figure. It is through the need for a directing father-figure that this particular revolutionary had become involved in revolution; dogma took the vacant place, and the apparent failure of the Marxist-Leninist ideal therefore leaves Recanati lost and leads to his suicide.

The importance given to the tragic personal story of Recanati does not entirely overshadow the positive, exhilarating atmosphere of 1968 remembered; nonetheless *Mourir à trente ans* leaves no doubt that the past is buried. The elation experienced remains only a memory, and the projection of memory onto present experience leads at best to a weary nostalgia which engenders no action and at worst, as with Michel, to despair. *Mourir à trente ans* situates 1968 firmly in history, and most especially in personal history: politically, there is every indication that similar conditions will never again arise, while personally it is painful or even dangerous to evoke them, however positive they may have been at the time.

Mourir à trente ans constitutes the last attempt of the cinema to come to terms directly with 1968, at least until the events were resurrected to provide a suitable backdrop to the comedy of *Milou en mai* (Louis Malle, 1989), where their function seems to be to

provide a certain 'retro' charm similar to the many evocations of
the Resistance and the Liberation which blossomed in the early
1970s. By the end of the decade the idea of 1968 as a dynamic
source of, and force for, change seems largely overshadowed by
its capacity to engender nervous trauma in its disappointed
participants.

But if the cinema of the 1970s was little inclined to reach an
accommodation with recent events through their direct representation, the language, the ideas and the assumptions which
constituted the background, the strength and the enduring legacy
of May found their way into the cinema in many less direct ways.
Cinema's engagement with 1968 was perhaps most in evidence in
the *auteur* sector of the French industry, although of the
established stars of the Nouvelle Vague and its satellites only
Godard really registered a change in his trajectory. But even in the
world of mainstream genre production some new factors did
make their appearance. Chief among these was the political
thriller, or *série-Z*.

REFERENCES

Daney, Serge (1975) 'Problèmes théoriques du cinéma militant',
    Cahiers du cinéma 256, février–mars: 5–6.
Defrance, Philippe (1980a) Interview, *Jeune cinéma* 126, avril–mai:
    26–30.
Defrance, Philippe (1980b) Interview, *Avant-scène* 247, mai: 5–6.
Douin, Jean-Luc (1976), 'Philippe Defrance: le fou de mai', *Télérama*
    1387, 11 août: 62–3.
Huleu, J.-R. (1975) 'Images à défendre', *Cahiers du cinéma* 256,
    février–mars: 13–19.
Klein, William (1978) Interview, *Impact/Revue du cinéma direct* 8/9,
    mai: 40–1.
Mardore, Michel (1970) '*Solo*', *Avant-scène* 103, mai.
Mocky, Jean-Pierre (1970a) Interview with André Cornand, *Revue du
    cinéma/Image et son* 235, janvier: 80–7.
Mocky, Jean-Pierre (1970b) Interview with Max Tessier, *Cinéma 70*
    145, avril: 110–13.
Mocky, Jean-Pierre (1977) 'Le Combat solitaire de J.-P. Mocky',
    interview with Claude Benoit, *Jeune cinéma* 102, avril–mai: 17–21.
Toubiana, Serge (1975) 'Le Pouvoir parlé (2): Images à vendre',
    Cahiers du cinéma 256, février–mars: 7–12.

2

The *série-Z*, politics and the thriller genre

The most frequently noticed effect of the new post-1968 climate on the French cinema was a change in the nature of the thriller. In 1968 itself (and therefore unaffected in its conception by the actual events of that year) Constantin Costa-Gavras' *Z* reached the screens and found an eager audience for whom it summed up the new requirements of the time. By the end of 1969, *Z* had achieved an audience of 700,000 in Paris, which made it one of the biggest successes of the year and indeed of the whole decade. It proved to be the forerunner of a number of films which adopted the narrative and visual conventions of the *policier* in order to examine suspect political scandals or social abuses. This typical 1970s genre was soon christened by its detractors the *série-Z*, by analogy with *série-B*, 'B-movies'. The obviously unflattering connotations of the term reflect the fact that, at the same time as a number of imitators, *Z* sparked a lively polemic among the critical press, which continued to rage around the subsequent exponents of the genre.[1] The polemic hinged on the political aspect of the films and their relevance to contemporary concerns; their merits or demerits as traditional thrillers (an ever-popular genre in the French cinema) tended to be lost in arguments over the extent to which their emphasis on narrative flow served or betrayed their content. It should at least be indicated that at this period the term '*série-Z*' was not regularly used to refer to the lowest depths of trash cinema, as it is today.

Apart from Costa-Gavras himself, the name was applied most frequently to the films of Yves Boisset and André Cayatte. The latter is perhaps the only French film-maker who might claim to have ventured into this territory prior to 1968. Cayatte's long

[1] The term *série-Z* is still in use in France, but now with much more straightforward implications: trashy, no-budget exploitation movies and straight-to-video offerings. There is, of course, no longer any connection with Costa-Gavras' film.

cinematic career (he made his first film in 1942) proves that he did
not require the inspiration of Z to determine his path, although
there are indications that the events of 1968 and the subsequent
upsurge in political consciousness among the public confirmed
him in it. However, the quality of Cayatte's films was variable and
his critical reputation was low. In fact, the forerunners to the
genre were more likely to be found outside the French cinema,
and especially in Italy, where Francesco Rosi particularly had
developed the fictional treatment of real news-stories from the
early 1960s (*Salvatore Giuliano*, 1962). Costa-Gavras appeared in
1968 as the initiator of a genre, and Yves Boisset, in *L'Attentat* four
years later, as his successor. Both Costa-Gavras and Boisset
immediately attracted considerably greater critical attention than
Cayatte had ever achieved.

Costa-Gavras' first two films were relatively straightforward
and moderately successful thrillers, although he later claimed
that his interest in presenting left-wing politics sprang from the
authorities' refusal to allow him to make the killer in *Comparti-
ment tueurs* (1966) a full-time policeman (Costa-Gavras 1969).
After Z (1969) came *L'Aveu* (1970), *Etat de siège* (1973) and *Section
spéciale* (1975), all founded on documented historical events:
respectively, the assassination of Lambrakis, the trial of Artur
London, the abduction of a CIA agent by revolutionary forces in
Uruguay, and the Riom trials during the Occupation. Costa-
Gavras' politics are international; indeed, only the 'historical'
Section spéciale relates to France, a fact which was not neglected
when his impact on the politicisation of *French* cinema was
considered. Christian Zimmer remarked that 'the public's lack of
information about the Lambrakis affair, more generally the
political situation in Greece, and therefore its relative indifference
to Hellenic problems' (Zimmer 1974: 42)[2] led Z to be read by many
as little more than a good thriller. This is probably less true of
L'Aveu, or even of *Etat de siège*: nonetheless the structures of
French society are never the direct focus of these films' critique,
even if their image of political manipulation clearly has relevance
wider than the specific anecdote they purport to analyse. *Section
spéciale* has the remoteness which comes with history; by 1975

---

[2] 'le manque d'information du public au sujet de l'affaire Lambrakis, plus
généralement de la situation politique en Grèce, et, partant, sa relative indifférence
envers les problèmes du peuple hellène'.

the shock of *Le Chagrin et la pitié* (1971) was past and revelations about collaboration were already beginning to be absorbed by the 'cynicism of the dominant class and the disillusionment of the exploited classes' (*Cahiers du cinéma* 1974: 5)[3] to quote *Cahiers'* explanation for the popularity of re-evocations of the Occupation in the mid-1970s. The films which Costa-Gavras made in America in the early 1980s are much more closely connected to the society that produced them than are his 1970s French works, and his last film in the decade, *Clair de femme* (1979), is neither openly political nor a thriller.

Yves Boisset was more prolific during the 1970s than either Costa-Gavras or Cayatte, with twelve titles to his credit (see filmography). Not all of them attempted a socio-political dimension; his contribution to the *série-Z* rests most notably on *L'Attentat* (1972), *R.A.S.* (1973), *Dupont Lajoie* (1974) and *Le Juge Fayard* (1976).

Apart from these three representative names of the genre, the political entered the arena of the commercial cinema in France very visibly in the work of Bertrand Tavernier. Tavernier made two films with a contemporary setting in the course of the 1970s, *L'Horloger de Saint-Paul* (1974) and *Des enfants gâtés* (1977). These films perhaps occupy a middle ground between the frankly commercial political thrillers and the more individual auteur dramas with their roots in the Nouvelle Vague, which will be discussed in the following chapters on the New Naturalism and its affiliates. Both are personal stories concerning the reactions of a peaceable middle-aged male protagonist to the irruption of social unrest in his life. Both the central characters (played by Philippe Noiret in *L'Horloger* and Michel Piccoli in *Des enfants gâtés*) have their complacency shaken and their assumptions about society broken. Noiret ends the film in unconditional sympathy with his taciturn son accused of the murder of a brutal foreman; Piccoli (playing a film-maker who seems to be Tavernier's alter ego) becomes wholeheartedly involved with a fight by tenants against unscrupulous landlords. Tavernier's model (also to some extent used in his historical films such as *Le Juge et l'assassin*, 1976) of the apolitical fifty-year-old drawn into struggle largely for personal reasons is adopted by Costa-Gavras in *Missing* in the 1980s, although the political situation here is much more dramatic. The choice of

[3] 'cynisme de la classe dominante, désenchantement des classes exploitées'.

protagonist might seem to be symptomatic of the sex, age and class of audience to which the films were directly addressed, but in fact a simple equation of protagonist and target audience seems rather unlikely. The radicalising of the most established social paradigm, the 'father-figure' par excellence, might be seen to be, in fact, the most unequivocal image possible of the *necessity* of social change, and as such the pattern was adopted, in a much more stylistically and thematically adventurous context, in the 1968 début of the Swiss Alain Tanner, *Charles mort ou vif*, of which more later.

Tavernier's contemporary films are about social rather than international politics, but they made a considerable impact, and his association with 1968 in the minds of popular audiences continued into the 1980s, even though his 1970s films were not particularly radical. In fact Tavernier's distinguished career, which continues to the present day, has been founded on a perception that, while looking for a general audience, he is a committed activist, and his occasional high-profile documentaries since the 1990s have contributed to maintaining this reputation. He has, in fact, continued to ask awkward questions about the dominant representations of French history (*La Guerre sans nom*, 1992), society (*De l'autre côté du périph'*, 1998) and institutions (*L627*, 1992, *Ça commence aujourd'hui*, 1999), and his popularity increased when he found his brand of easily assimilable social realism in tune with the 1990s ethos. At the same time, of course, he has produced films of pure entertainment such as *La Fille de d'Artagnan* (1994) and versions of popular formulae (*L'Appât*, 1995, less a serious examination of the difficulties of youth than a thriller in the mould of *Natural Born Killers*).

Our discussion of the 1970s political thriller will concentrate principally on three films: *Z* itself, Boisset's *L'Attentat* and René Gainville's *Le Complot* (1973), which adopted the strategies of Costa-Gavras and Boisset in the service of a right-wing theme. As an introduction we will look briefly at the general characteristics of the thrillers of the decade, of which there were many: particular actors found themselves associated closely with the genre, while the themes of the *série-Z* crept, in adulterated form, into more traditional narratives and the tropes of the straight-forward *policier* were of course fundamental to its political version. Finally we will consider the debate which was provoked by the intrusion of radical politics into a popular genre, and the disquiet that this caused among the defenders of both genres of film.

The political thrillers generally extracted as much capital as possible from the prestige of their stars, and it is noticeable that certain faces recur in them: some were the well-known actors of the general thriller genre, but particular stars carried with them a baggage of connotations – including vague political connotations – which they had gathered from their previous work, and that baggage was used to effect, and sometimes subverted, in this decade which had become highly sensitised to it. Three of Costa-Gavras' four films were made with Yves Montand. The star of what is perhaps the only pre-1968 commercial French political fiction, Resnais' *La Guerre est finie* (1966), Montand was also known as a singer connected to the PCF. (It was partly the reaction of the Party to the events of 1968 which led to Montand's break with it (Semprun 1983: 163).) He also, of course, took part in Godard's return to 'commercial' cinema after the latter's well-publicised but cinematically invisible Dziga-Vertov period; in that film, *Tout va bien*, the ambiguities of politically committed stardom incarnated by Montand and his co-star Jane Fonda were highlighted and to a limited extent critically explored. For Costa-Gavras he contributed a sense of *gravitas* and political credibility both to the films and to the characters whom he portrayed, the known opinions of the actor being an assurance that a sense of personal identification between actor and character would not be too obscene a mismatch.

Other actors known to be of the left appeared in the New French Thriller of the 1970, such as Michel Piccoli – whose immense reputation had been garnered largely in the theatre and in the more surreal and anarchic ventures of the art cinema, especially with Luís Buñuel or Marco Ferreri – or the Italian Gian-Maria Volonté, whose hard-man image had been politicised by his frequent work for Rosi. The presence of actors such as these tended in itself to colour the films in which they appeared with a topical aura of commitment, so that the appearance of Montand and Piccoli together in Claude Sautet's *Vincent, François, Paul et les autres* (1974) prompted audiences and critics to look for socio-political connotations in a film which was largely about the personal and creative crises of middle-aged, middle-class men. The reputations of the actors thus affected the reception of the films in which they appeared, while their willingness to take on openly political roles conversely reinforced their reputations. These men were recognised stars, but there were also supporting actors who while accepting roles in very varied films became so associated with political radicalism that they were regularly type-cast, thus confirming the existence of the political radical as a new social stereotype while, through their own well-publicised and genuine commitment, boosting the credentials of otherwise quite apolitical films. Examples are Rufus, who appears in Yves Boisset's early thriller *Un condé* (1970), scarcely a piece of political analysis despite its unflattering image of the French police force, and Jacques Denis, who worked frequently with Alain Tanner and is selected as the face of the protagonist's political conscience in *L'Horloger de Saint-Paul*.

But while the actors mentioned above are to be expected in political work and accredit it by their presence, the dominant faces in the New Thriller are those who also dominate the Old, the male stars of the French popular cinema of the period. Michel Bouquet's ambivalent baby-face appears in both *Un Condé* and *L'Attentat*, as well as Cayatte's *Il n'y a pas de fumée sans feu* (1973) and *La Raison d'Etat* (1978). He also appears in the leading role of the right-wing *Le Complot*, creating a link between this film and the *série-Z* to which it was a reaction. Philippe Noiret is Tavernier's preferred actor, starring in the first three of his films; he is also an extremely sinister TV producer in *L'Attentat*. Jean-Louis Trintignant who takes a central role in *L'Attentat* and in *Z* was undertaking similar employment for Labro or René Clément, along with garnering a reputation in the established realms of the art cinema (Chabrol, Rohmer, Bernardo Bertolucci, but also Alain Robbe-Grillet; he was also, incidentally, preparing to make two unhinged and anarchic thrillers himself). Costa-Gavras and Boisset both employ Trintignant to unmask the truth concerning the fate of the assassinated political 'hero' (Montand or Volonté). As the little man, literally and figuratively, bound up in great events, Trintignant's role in these films was to function as an entry-point for the audience as well as to bear the charge of suspense which makes a thriller a thriller; everything hinges upon his persistence and his ultimate success (*Z*, although it is a transient success) or failure (*L'Attentat*). The uncompromising 'petit juge' of *Z* became an archetype for the dogged search for unpalatable political truth, which gives another charge of irony to Trintignant's role in 1994 in Jacques Audiard's bitter comedy about the impossibility of unmasking political truth, *Un héros très discret*. Jean Rochefort, the archetypal 'gentleman' of the most established and academic French comedy of the decade, finds his way into *L'Horloger de Saint-Paul* after appearing in *Le Complot*. The most persistent face of the *série-Z*, however, was Jean Bouise, who appeared in *L'Attentat*, *Dupont Lajoie*, *Le Juge Fayard*, *Z*, *L'Aveu* and *Section spéciale*!

All these actors, apart from Rufus and Denis, had reached forty by 1970. They had a solid career, assured recognition among the public, and a certain established 'character' which reassured their more traditional audiences. They are not necessarily type-cast (Tavernier's Noiret is superficially very different from Boisset's Noiret), but any role which they play will take on some of the features of the actor. With the exception of Trintignant, they bore with them a history of involvement in a cinematic establishment which, in the post-'68 era and in films which twist their established formulae, could itself become a shorthand for the social and political establishment. Thus Bouquet or Jean Rochefort, while not necessarily themselves right-wing, came to suggest the right almost as certainly as Montand did the left: even in comedies, Rochefort tended to find himself cast as the upholder of the social order, for example in the blockbuster hit of 1972, *Le Grand Blond avec une chaussure noire*. When Tavernier subsequently chose him to play the police inspector, memories of that earlier, and hugely popular, incarnation assured that, up to a point, he 'was' the epitome of a certain face of the French police force. To find these actors cast in contradiction to their own stereotype, on the other hand, though rare creates an instant spark of ambiguity.[4]

There is no such consistency as regards the actresses. The political thriller follows the convention of the traditional French thriller in giving little importance to women, and indeed in many cases it exaggerates the tendency. The many debates on the characteristics – technical, narrative or functional – which these films owe to the conventions of the genre, and on their political implications, all largely ignored this element, which nonetheless bound the audience firmly into the safe cocoon of convention

---

[4] Piccoli, of course, plays exploitative bosses and corrupt ministers with glee, but we are *always* aware of the irony of his characterisation.

before opening the doors to political controversy. Strong or unconventional women are more likely to be found in thrillers where the social conventions of police and gangsterdom are otherwise unchallenged, although Alain Corneau's use of Simone Signoret in *Police Python 357* (1976) provides a partial exception.

In the films principally to be considered here, we can observe a similar pattern: one significant female star, a different one each time, is assigned the role of support and help to the male protagonist: Irène Papas as Montand's wife in *Z* has very little indeed to do, Jean Seberg in *L'Attentat* and Simone Signoret in *L'Aveu* are a little better served, while *Le Complot* uses Marina Vlady in exactly the same way as its left-wing counterparts. In *Z* there is also a thoroughly dangerous role assigned to a woman, the sister of the witness Nick, played by Magali Noël. Five female characters between four films is not a great score, and in other examples of the genre there is not even one significant female star. The functions assigned to the woman are strictly limited: positive but passive supporter of the man, or treacherous betrayer. Papas is an extreme case among all the thrillers of the period of the entirely passive woman, existing merely to mourn and to be protected. Jean Seberg in *L'Attentat* is more actively involved, the most positive female character in all the films under discussion – except Tavernier's *Des enfants gâtés*, which is really a civic film rather than a thriller – but she is still no more than a foil and support for Trintignant. The assassination of Ben Barka/Saddiel, which constitutes the serious theme of the film, cannot accommodate a woman as investigator, so despite relative independence of action (and, unusually, a firmer character than her man) she is still marginal to the main point of the film, permanently worried and unaware of what is really at stake. Vlady, in the right-wing *Complot*, combines a supportive role with a faintly negative implication of passivity as a deterrent to decisive male action. Magali Noël's role in *Z* is not only marginal to the action, but negative and treacherous to the point of caricature. Simone Signoret in *L'Aveu* has a more complex because ambiguous role: at first support to her husband, she later 'betrays' him although for relatively noble motives, before achieving redemption. The dichotomy of support/betrayal recalls the good woman/femme fatale pairing, but nowhere in these films is there room for any woman, positive or negative, to be assigned a *sexual* role. Even Seberg/

Trintignant, although almost credible as a pair of lovers, essentially act as partners. Neither does any woman with a positive role ever have a functional *political* identity. The Seberg character has political beliefs which are shown as acting in her everyday life, but they are of no relevance to her action in the thriller and therefore seem likely to have been inserted only to make her attractive to the audience. On the other hand, women's political beliefs are the given motive for betrayal, whether they are caricatured as in the case of Noël, or portrayed more thoughtfully as well-meaning, but dogmatic and misguided, for example Signoret in *L'Aveu*. Politics, in these films, is clearly a field which it is safest to leave to men.

The *série-Z* did not, of course, invent these stereotypes, but it exploited them particularly unreflectively and, in particular, it excluded women from positive and active participation in just those areas where the thriller was transgressing its tight genre boundaries and aspiring to some social relevance. This was really the only genre – apart from the explosive development of pornography – in which the movement for the renewal of cinema touched the truly commercial product. The almost exaggerated respect for gender hierarchy which almost all the New Thrillers show is highly significant in this period of questioning and redefining of all institutions of social authority. It acts as a powerful reassurance that in these films 'politics' does not imply any fundamental change in lives or values, no matter how left-wing the views espoused by the central characters may nominally be. The screen is dominated by men in their forties and fifties, literally 'father-figures', and not only women but also the young are marginalised while the significant conflicts are carried on between the 'qualified' few. Within the films opposing forces meet in the common ground of age and gender stereotypes: it is only that the negative stereotypes are reserved for those who are, temporarily or permanently, in alliance with the 'wrong' side. This is not to say that the films assume that these stereotypes will necessarily be accepted as reality: in *Z* they are so schematic that they arguably contribute to *de*-realising the film and holding its semi-documentary identity firmly in the bounds of the thriller genre. They are more likely to be received as the representations that they are, and accepted as reassuring on those terms: as much as to say that left-wing political activists, when they make thrillers, represent themselves very much as conservatives, or for that matter right-wing political activists represent themselves. The fundamental, mythic categories of 'Good' and 'Bad', of 'Male' and 'Female', 'Hero' and 'Traitor', are recognisable across ideologies.

The scenario of Z was written in the autumn of 1967, and by May 1968 it was already in full existence on paper. It was not, however, yet shot. Despite the innumerable criticisms which were subsequently levelled at Z on the grounds of insufficient politi-cisation, and despite the kind of reassuring effects mentioned above, in the early months of 1968 it was considered too political to be commercial; Jacques Perrin, actor and producer, has recalled that some potential distributors reacted with alarm: 'You've got a great set-up, a wonderful cast: you must find another subject' (Costa-Gavras et al. 1969: 6).[5] It seems however to have been sheer coincidence that the film eventually found backers in May 1968, during the Cannes festival. As a result, it was shot after May, but the scriptwriter Semprun insists that 'we changed nothing in the script. Not a comma was added or removed, to try to catch on to the current events of the student revolt' (Semprun 1983: 164).[6] Costa-Gavras himself extends this: 'there's mention of "extremists" somewhere or when the general says: "Half-Jews are the worst". People said to us: you're making allusions which are too close, you're talking about Cohn-Bendit, etc … Finally, we didn't cut anything.'(Costa-Gavras et al. 1969: 7).[7]

Indeed there is very little sign that Z bears directly on the events or the themes of 1968. It in no way foreshadows what happened, and is only prophetic in the sense that it is occupied with politics, whereas the received wisdom prior to May was that politics was box-office poison. The basic material of Z as of most of its many emulators is the unravelling of plots and extra-parliamentary scandals such as the 'Affaire Lambrakis', rather than an analysis of the underlying political forces in social organi-sation: it is a long way from the universal contestation of 1968. A much clearer relevance to May as it was lived could be found in

[5] 'Vous avez une affaire formidable, une belle affiche; il faut trouver un autre sujet'.

[6] 'nous n'avons rien changé au scénario. Pas une virgule n'a été ajoutée ou enlevée, pour essayer de coller à l'actualité de la révolte étudiante'.

[7] 'il est question quelque part d'"enragés" ou encore lorsque le général dit: "Les demi-juifs, ce sont les pires". On nous a dit: Vous faites des allusions trop précises, vous parlez de Cohn-Bendit etc. … En définitive, nous n'avons rien supprimé.'

Resnais' *La Guerre est finie*, as far back as 1965. Also scripted by Semprun and acted by Montand, this exploration of the dying ripples of Spanish republicanism includes the rising generation of student radicals as an important factor in the plot, who are allowed a debate with the ex-republican fighters in which the old and the new radicalism confront each other with questions and redefinitions. Since Montand's portrayal of Lambrakis has considerable similarities to the Diego of the earlier film, which Costa-Gavras had seen and admired, it is possible that the director intended the audience to read the one with reference and comparison to the other. However, here there is no alternative form of activism, and no conflict of generations.

Costa-Gavras noted, at the time of *Z*, the existence of other events to which the film might be seen to refer: there had been no lack of political assassinations in the recent past – along with Kennedy and Martin Luther King he did indeed evoke the Ben Barka affair (Costa-Gavras *et al.* 1969: 8), but only to dismiss it immediately: 'As for the Ben Barka affair, no chance of making a film of that in France: even if all the "obscurites" weren't unveiled, the film would be stopped at the beginning of the shoot, if not at the script stage' (Costa-Gavras *et al.* 1969: 8).[8] However, in 1972, *L'Attentat* was made, and while Boisset had his share of problems,[9] it was not stopped either at the script stage, nor at the beginning of shooting, nor even at distribution. *L'Attentat*'s very existence however is probably due to Costa-Gavras and *Z*; a film about Ben Barka can by 1972 appear as part of a genre, thus diluting its shock value.

Z in fact met its ideal audience in the aftermath of May: it seemed sensitive to the change in public demand, it was intelligent

---

[8] 'Quant à l'affaire Ben Barka, impossible d'en faire un film en France: même si on ne dévoile pas toutes les "obscurités", le film serait stoppé dès le début du tournage, si ce n'est au stade du scénario'.

[9] 'Quand j'ai fait *L'Attentat*, on avait prévenu les gens qui étaient supposés investir de l'argent dans le film, qu'il valait mieux pas. Ils avaient reçu de coups de téléphone d'amis, de relations haut placées, qui leur disaient: "Tu ne devrais pas mettre de l'argent là-dedans; tu vas avoir des ennuis; d'après ce que je sais, ils ne vont pas te rater ... et ainsi de suite'. [When I made *L'Attentat*, the people who were supposed to invest money in the film were warned that it would be better not to. They got telephone calls from friends and relatives in high places, saying: 'You shouldn't put money into that; you'll have problems; from what I've heard, they'll be sure to get you for it ... and so on'] (Boisset 1977: 11).

and committed but not revolutionary either in content or, even less, in style. It owed a direct and practical debt to the events, which created the conditions which allowed it to find producers, distributors and the mass audience for which its form destined it but which its topicality and harshness, not to mention its potential to cause diplomatic ructions with Greece, might have discouraged previously. Costa-Gavras, however, was not particularly interested in 1968 nor the French debates which had preceded and followed it; Z reflected his own Greek experience, and he refused the label 'political film', because, he said, it implied party politics. 'When people hear mention of politics, they immediately think of a few names, *Lecanuet, Sanguinetti, Mollet, Mitterrand* to name but a few' (Costa-Gavras *et al.* 1969: 64).[10] This may have been true for the majority at the time the film was conceived, but it was outdated by 1969, something which Costa-Gavras does not seem to have sensed. His next film, *L'Aveu* (1970), also belongs largely to the political culture of the previous generation, which had put its hopes in Communism throughout the 1930s and 1940s and then lived through the shock of revelations of the horrors of Stalinism. For those involved in the film, the only relevant reactions were those of their own generation and culture, particularly the PCF with which they entertained relations of nostalgic enmity. The theorists of 1968 were of no interest to Costa-Gavras, Semprun or Montand, and their criticisms were resented, ignored or ridiculed.

Both *Z* and *L'Attentat* loosely cover with fictional names the real political events to which they refer, but no one was duped nor were they intended to be, and the films and the original cases were usually discussed together. The famous disclaimer which opened *Z*, 'Any resemblance to real events is not a coincidence. It is INTENTIONAL' applied with, if anything, more force to *L'Attentat*, in that the average French audience might be expected to be more conversant with the Ben Barka affair than with the recent history of Greece, but it could reasonably be adopted as a motto for the whole of the *série-Z*. Latterly, such references were assumed, and the close correlation which such films were considered likely to have with the facts became one of their dangers. If Boisset

---

[10] 'Quand les gens entendent parler de politique, ils pensent tout de suite à quelques noms, *Lecanuet, Sanguinetti, Mollet, Mitterrand*, pour ne citer qu'eux', emphasis Costa-Gavras.

dispensed with the primary reminder in *L'Attentat*, it was because he considered himself entitled to assume familiarity, although that assumption was challenged by several critics even in 1972. In any case, it is quite possible to read *L'Attentat* as simply an exercise in suspense. Boisset's preference was that its particular application should not exclude a more general one: 'the theoretical, but rigorous, demonstration of the workings of a global strategy for eliminating awkward customers', as one critic put it.[11] Again a phrase conceived for one film proves applicable to others (*L'Aveu*, as well as *Z*, could be included), and it implies a degree of political analysis which for many of the post-68 theorists was rather debatable, or at least counter-productive. The *série-Z*, claimed the radicals, tended to conclude with support for a liberal version of the current system and to dissuade the non-political class from engaging directly with politics – factors which probably contributed in no small measure to the films' success.

The relation between politics and thriller in *Z* and *L'Attentat* is constructed around two major figures: the political hero, Montand-Z-Lambrakis or Volonté-Saddiel-Ben Barka, and the apolitical investigator, Trintignant in both films. It is the 'political heroes' who lock the films onto an anterior political reality, and for the informed audience taking their seats they are the subjects. Even if the central characters are less present in the film text than in, for example, Rosi's *Il caso Mattei* (1972) where Volonté's reconstruction of the assassinated industrialist carries the film much as does Welles' *Citizen Kane*, the camera nonetheless establishes them as stars. The thin veil of fiction covering the facts of history perhaps requires this (although Rosi used no veil): in Oliver Stone's *JFK* (1991), a direct descendant of *Z,* the historical fact is announced from the start, Kennedy's status is taken for granted, and the presence of a major star in the role would in fact cause a problem since it would inevitably clash with a known, and undisguised, reality.

Z announced itself as the autopsy of a political murder, while *L'Attentat* was thus described after its appearance, and their founding cases were known; the majority of the audience, therefore, already knows that the political figurehead is doomed, and that this is the *raison d'être* of the film. Lambrakis and Ben Barka

<hr>

[11] 'la démonstration théorique, mais rigoureuse, du fonctionnement d'une stratégie planétaire d'élimination de certains gêneurs'. Etienne Fuzellier, *L'Education*, cited in *Revue de cinéma/Image et son* 1973: 40.

are taken as the subject-matter of the film because of the manner of their deaths, and what they stood for while alive comes second if considered at all. Z/Lambrakis and Saddiel/Ben Barka thus occupy a position at once central and marginal in the films; central in that they are the primary object, the cause of the action, but marginal in that even when they are apparently present and active, their activity is subordinate to their imminent inactivity. They are not political actors, merely dead men on leave. Of course, either film could have made that inevitable end into a source of energy informing the activity of the 'hero' – a pattern in which Rosi arguably succeeded with Mattei, where knowledge of the result of the actions which are reconstructed give them an extra subversive charge. But neither *Z* nor *L'Attentat* are concerned with the career of the target, and their aim is to elucidate not the why but the how, the mechanism which can eliminate a politically awkward individual. This characteristic applies equally to *L'Aveu*; Artur London is eliminated by admissions of things he did *not* do, we do not see what he *did* do which could encourage the authorities to eliminate him. The central political figure functions in these films as a pure object – of the film-text itself, but also of the gaze and the constructing discourse of the other protagonists. He does not have a voice of his own. Z's political utterances are reduced to a minimum, and his death occurs less than halfway through the film. Saddiel is allowed a little more self-expression, especially in his confrontation with his arch-opponent Kassar/Oufkir (Piccoli), and he remains alive throughout most of the film. Nonetheless actual political utterances are minimal, and anything these men say is in any case overshadowed by the knowledge that it is inoperable, since their death or definitive removal from influence is not only inevitable but imminent.

Their role is, therefore, symbolic and open. They are victims and martyrs, but it is uncertain what cause they are martyrs to. Since we are deprived of any considerable sample of their beliefs, we know only that they are in some way opposed to the present régime which is defined as oppressive; they are, therefore, against the oppressors, therefore on the side of the oppressed, therefore indubitably positive. The audience is thus offered a perfect hero-figure – a champion of the oppressed, himself oppressed to the point of murder – without being required to swallow a possibly controversial or complicated political position. Since we cannot begin to debate issues which are not exposed to debate, we merely put the hero on his pedestal, where his imminent de-activation prevents us even considering him as a serious threat to social stability. As we shall see, the films do not even really advocate an *active* position of protest in response to the scandal of the hero's downfall. In *Z* particularly political action by the non-political class is inevitably accompanied by manipulation, and is largely the province of criminal accomplices of the generals; the film is marked by a rather uncomfortable distrust of ordinary people. Interference in the malfunctioning current system is left to the qualified, in particular to the members of certain professions – the law and the press – which are assigned that role. There is no place available for the majority of members of a notional mass audience, except as the passive recipients of the beneficent or malevolent attentions of well or ill-intentioned leaders.

Artur London, in *L'Aveu*, is much more developed than the assassinated heroes of *Z* or *L'Attentat*, and becomes an identi-fication figure as they do not, but here too the opinions which led him to the predicament he is in are kept from expression, even if in a somewhat different way. In the immediate sufferings of his imprisonment and torture, we are not led to concern ourselves much with his past, which indeed is only evoked in order that lies shall be told about it. Rather than an irreproachable hero, he becomes an Everyman figure characterised by confusion and baffled good intentions. The film-makers did make some attempt to create a critical distance between the audience and the protagonist, with the result that during scenes of physical and mental torture we are relegated to a position of voyeur. Jean-Louis Comolli in *Cahiers* fiercely criticised the 'revulsion-pleasure' towards the process of torture to which the spectator is forced, seeing this not only as an ethically dubious method of engaging the audience, but also as a way to overshadow London's potential significance as a political force by an overwhelming fascination with his suffering (Comolli 1970: 49–50). The tension and the power of *L'Aveu* is scarcely reduced by having little or no political reference at all, and there is considerable force in Comolli's argu-ment that its strategies are at best ambiguous, at worst distasteful.

Among the mechanisms which are used to establish the political hero of the Z-films as uncontroversially positive and therefore depoliticised, the personae of Montand and Volonté also play a role. Both are almost automatically identified with the left, both are in their late forties and project a strong impression of integrity, but they are not interchangeable; Montand – tall, awkward, with almost constantly furrowed brow – conveys vulnerability while Volonté, whose 'honesty' is projected principally through a steady gaze and constant air of dignity, is decidedly more aggressive. Those different images were already a feature of their established genre reputations; Volonté had played several memorable tough-guys with no particular political or moral conscience, while Montand had rarely, perhaps never, played an unambiguous villain. When entrusted with a positive, but largely uncharacterised, hero-figure, this gave Volonté more potential ambiguity than Montand, something which coincides with the greater opportunities for expression afforded to Saddiel/Ben Barka. He is potentially an active force, his political effectiveness is credible, and he is also not as legalistic as Z and his supporters, allowing him both more potential scope for action and a possible capacity to raise doubt – and thus curiosity – in the minds of the audience. The potential, however, is hardly exploited.

The political protagonist of these thrillers is thus often distant and somewhat undefined; the thriller protagonist (Trintignant in both *L'Attentat* and *Z*) is much more central and active in the narrative, although marginal to the historical event. The *juge d'instruction* in *Z* and Darien in *L'Attentat* are based on real individuals, but unlike the political heroes their names are unlikely to be known to the audience so that they can be absorbed completely into the fiction. Their involvement in the political action of the 'affair' is at one remove; they have little or no official power, and, what's more, their attitude with regard to the political conflict underlying the assassinations is not straightforward. This latter point means that their role may produce questions, explanations and eventual understanding, something the simplified politics of the people's Hero opposed to a powerful Villain cannot provide.

The principal motor of suspense in *Z* is the uncovering of the plot which commanded a murder already past, and the hope of seeing justice done: Trintignant's role is that of investigator. In *L'Attentat* it is the assassination itself which is at stake, and Trintignant is the informed person whose actions may uncover the plot or foil it before it is carried out. Given the semi-documentary character of the films, this gives *Z* the clear advantage as a thriller. The process of the enquiry can generate some real doubt in the mind of the audience, while Saddiel's disappearance is inevitable. Boisset is therefore obliged to introduce a secondary, personal narrative the outcome of which may at least leave room for doubt, and thus the force of *L'Attentat* as a revisitation of history or an investigation into the anatomy of political murder is attenuated. Darien's problems are personal and presented as a personal drama, without reference to social forces.

In both films however the Trintignant character does invite a degree of audience identification, something the hero–martyr clearly cannot do. He is outside the higher levels of political influence and therefore closer to audience experience; at the start of the film he is neutral or even ambiguously tied to both sides, and in the course of the action he is seen to be won over to the side of the 'hero', not because of any political *parti-pris* (the Hero's opinions are immaterial), but simply in the interests of justice.

In *Z* the neutral investigative role is divided between Trintignant and Jacques Perrin, who plays a newspaper photographer whose cynical search for a scoop gradually transforms into a commitment to see injustice uncovered: in *L'Attentat*, it is largely Darien/Trintignant – with a little help from Edith (Jean Seberg) – who carries the thread of the plot. Although the actual characters that he plays could not be more different, Trintignant's tense acting, and his small stature which makes him literally as well as metaphorically the 'little man', make him perfectly suited to the role of a perplexed individual trying to negotiate his way through a labyrinth of greater forces, and it was a role which he regularly took on in other contexts, from Robbe-Grillet's dream-like fantasies to playful thrillers such as René Clément's *La Course du lièvre à travers les champs* (1972), not to mention *The Conformist* (1970). Almost every commentator of *Z* refers to his character as 'the little judge' and under that title he even made headlines at the time of the overthrow of the colonels: 'The little judge of *Z* becomes president of the Greek republic' (quoted in Poulle 1985: 26)[12]

Costa-Gavras' judge is defined merely by his function, and we know nothing of his private life or even of his opinions. Darien is practically defined by his lack of official function and his fascination

---

[12] 'Le petit juge de *Z* devient président de la République grecque'.

with the political milieu; he is an everyman who, as the secret services say dismissively, 'gets everywhere'. He is despised and considered corruptible, and his first appearance confirms this impression. He takes part in an anti-American demonstration (a 'safe' theme in Gaullist France in 1972, and one which *Z* also plays on), stays on when his more cautious partner decides to leave, but does not participate in the 'trouble' which almost immediately ensues, and so when he is arrested, we already *know* that the arrest must be pre-planned, that he is not a spontaneous demonstrator, that he must have a record of some description. In the police station it is revealed that some previous involvement in political activism had proved more than he could handle, and that as a result he has collaborated with the police from 1960. This whole introduction confirms the message, previously evoked, that for the 'little man', involvement in direct-action politics is suspect and probably dangerous.

In both films then, first impressions of the Trintignant character are, if anything, 'negative', assuming that this is defined as being in alliance with established power and a potential threat to the 'hero'. However, while the 'little judge' is a relatively stable figure, who has his own, limited, authority and appears calm and self-confident, Darien is dangerous because he is an apparent rebel who cannot support his stance with any personal courage. The significance of this is wider than simply the establishment of character. Although Darien never becomes a really positive figure, his wavering conscience allows the audience to identify with him: he is a little man involved, through a series of errors on his own part, in events much bigger than himself. Throughout the film he is entirely manipulated. This structure is an absolute *dis*courage-ment to any little man's involvement in politics and, indeed, Darien is so central to the film that one is practically led to the conclusion that Saddiel's (read: Ben Barka's) assassination was *caused* by Darien's political irresponsibility. Such an exaggerated accusation somewhat defuses the 'rigorous theoretical demon-stration' of the mechanics of elimination of the opposition, and, incidentally, presents direct action, street politics and protest as not only personally dangerous but globally counter-productive. Darien's role occludes the complex issues of power-play and international relations which are implied, but not explored.

In *Z* the status quo is relatively desirable: revolution, in the sense of total change of the structures of society, is a fascist impulse. The clandestine groups and active demonstrations which take place are all staged by the right-wing parties, with the tacit support of the police and of the military who are part of the current power-structure, but against the established democratic system which nominally exists. The final story-card informs us that despite the defeat that we have witnessed, this right-wing revolution was ultimately successful; defeated by legal means (the process which constitutes the main body of the film), the military take power illegally and neutralise their opponents. These methods, however effective, are also consistently and unambiguously condemned. In a film where politics are largely reduced to easily recognisable shorthand (the left are pacifist and reject American intervention), it is from the right that we hear the most formulated political programme. In a flashback to a meeting, the speaker uses recognisable (Pétainist) rhetoric, and there are calls to action: 'We must rally young people', 'Abroad they're saying, make war not love'. The equivalent meeting of the left, which Z is to address, is in comparison merely anecdotal. As demonstrators and police gather outside the building, the suspense generated by the police chief's proposal to unplug the loudspeakers means that we no longer bother to listen to the speech he wants to silence. The only phrase not interfered with by dramatic outside action is the opening: 'Someone hit me. Why?' It holds the promise of analysis, never fulfilled: all we hear is the fact, the immediate injustice.

Throughout Costa-Gavras' films legality, or more precisely the procedure of the law, is a constant narrative thread. Even when these procedures are subverted – that is, presented as serving the cause of injustice, as in *L'Aveu* or *Section Spéciale* – the actual mechanism of the law is never questioned; except, perhaps, much later in *Missing*. The opposing forces in *Z* are not really defined in political terms, despite the Fascist rhetoric: what counts is their methods. Z's liberal (rather than socialist) credentials are assured by the number of representatives of his party who seem to be lawyers; be they proponents of aggressive (Charles Denner) or of strictly legalist (Jean Bouise) approaches to the obstruction of their investigations, they are still part of the judiciary. However politically ambiguous Trintignant's Judge may be, he is led to support Z's cause *merely* through his respect for the law, and throughout the second part of the film, in which he becomes the only hope *in extremis* of preventing the triumph of fascism, he is defending not a political line but legality against the illegal. The film allows us to confuse the two, principally because the power structures in this 'imaginary' republic are deeply implicated with the forces of illegality, and recourse to the law can thus take on some of the characteristics of a revolutionary activity. In *Z* the legal, positive combat is against a corrupt government which is outrageously abusing or more precisely evading an essentially just system: the system itself is never called into question. The Right are clandestine agents of political change, bent on the destruction of the legal framework that they are already subverting. The Left rest their hopes on the survival of that framework, and preferably the advent of other authorities which can better assure its guardianship; their only acknowledged platform, pacifism, is guaranteed to win them widespread sympathy with a minimum of controversy. Since the military bases in question are foreign, they cannot even be said to be taking a stand against nuclear defence. The definition of a 'good' left-wing activist thus involves little rocking of the boat. Although *Z*'s implications certainly reached beyond Greece, it would have needed quite a bit of mental adjustment to apply this pattern to Gaullist France.

The vast majority of Z's supporters are middle-aged members of the liberal professions. Students are conspicuous by their absence, but 'les jeunes' are seen by the *right* wing as a potential source of support. And although ordinary people do appear in both camps, by far the most memorable are the two thugs who carry out Z's murder, Iago and Vago. Those who decide to help Z's cause usually do so by reporting on conversations heard in the course of daily life, thus implying that their regular milieu is infiltrated by the Fascist right. The giving of testimony is always a perilous exercise, or at least perceived as such; both Nick and Coste, the two principal witnesses, feel that in testifying they are going against their peers, and are likely to incur hostility close to home rather than directly from the powerful. In the case of Nick this is particularly clearly true, since his sister is a member of the Fascist organisation.

Support for the 'left', then, is against the norm and in many ways against the interests of the ordinary people, and the motives of those who do testify for Z are individual and humanist.

Solidarity with a victim and an abstract sense of justice, rather than interest in or support for Z's cause, is the norm. Coste is said to be politicised, but it is far from clear what this implies, except that it makes his testimony inherently suspect. The ordinary people that seek to preserve their material interests do so by compromising with the powers-that-be. Iago and Vago are both persuaded into murdering Z by a covert bribe (although they attend clandestine Fascist meetings and thus presumably hold corresponding opinions). Others, more neutral, can easily be swayed into support by the giving and withholding of permits. Nick's sister's involvement with CROC is shown to stem almost entirely from material interest. If there is a 'popular' political ideology (other than vague ideals of preventing a murder) it seems to be that of the right which at least has a physical presence and communicates with the people, even corruptly. Although it is indicated that demonstrations take place in support of both left and right, the relative strengths of the two sides are never compared and we are never privy to the functioning of any alternative to Fascism on the ground, as it were. As a result the film creates two political polarisations which are profoundly pessimistic: the illegal right is politically articulate and aggressive, while the legal left is passive and relatively vague: the power base of the left is among the intelligentsia, while that of the right is in the streets and among ordinary people.

Needless to say, the camps are also divided very firmly into Good and Bad, Heroes and Villains. There is barely any ambiguity in this division; like the female characters, it rests on stereotypes. It would be obvious in any still from the film that Yves Montand is the representative of Good and Renato Salvatori and Marcel Bozzuffi are Baddies. This Manichaean division extends over all the traits represented by each group. There are no real exceptions: if the two investigators, reporter and judge, are initially relatively neutral, they are soon identified, as of right, with the Good through their responsibility to the Law. The reporter's methods are sometimes dubious, but he does not act illegally; and although he may wish for mass action in support of Z, he does nothing to provoke it. And yet, in all but the content of the political discourse, it is the profile of the right which corresponds most closely to the revolutionary left of 1968: highly politicised, prepared to use illegal means if necessary and to take the initiative, based among the young and the working-class; and these traits are therefore stigmatised as dangerous and potentially Fascist.

In fact *Z* is a left-wing political thriller which is profoundly anti-revolutionary; and, in the climate of the times, this may account for some of the delight with which it was hailed by *Le Figaro littéraire*, *L'Express*, or *La Croix*. Claude Mauriac wrote in the first of these: 'Striking with a force as accurate as it is powerful, *Z* is the film which every school and university student, everyone who loves freedom and justice, should see' (*CinémAction* 1985: 23) Jean Rochereau, in *La Croix*, dictated that: 'For anyone who really wants to live, through the cinema, in today's world and to understand it, in its most dreadful realities, it is absolutely essential to see *Z*, this autopsy of a crime' (Costa-Gavras *et al.* 1969: 18).[13] Both quotes contain the same message: *Z* is the film to see (rather than others) for those who really want to understand (so those who gave *Z* a poor reception do not *really* care). Watching *Z*, perhaps, will inculcate a proper respect for legal structures and a *rejection* of direct political action or of any desire to change them.

Z thus satisfied a need for 'progressive' political content while posing no threat to the structures in place in France – on condition, of course, that those structures were in the hands of responsible and enlightened authorities. The situation in France could not but compare favourably with that in pre-putsch Greece and therefore the film implicitly preached grateful acceptance of what legality and democracy was available. Stereotypes clearly recognisable by the right-thinking law-abiding citizen are brought into play, while, at the same time, other signs (Semprun, Montand, or the film's factual base) gave it left-wing credentials. It is a civic film, and, post-1968, highly reassuring. There is a French left which believes in ideals of justice and respects the Law; which takes as its hero not some Maoist student but a gentle doctor in his forties, while the villain is uneducated, unshaven, violent and revolutionary in his own way. The only women of importance are passive or, if not passive, strongly negative. This is a left, besides, which can enjoy the suspense of a good thriller and an apparently wildly

[13] Mauriac: 'D'une force de frappe aussi précise que puissante, *Z* est le film à voir par tous les lycéens, les étudiants et tous ceux qui sont épris de liberté et de justice'. Rochereau: 'Pour qui veut vraiment, grâce au cinéma, vivre avec son temps et le comprendre, jusque dans ses plus terribles réalités, la vision de *Z*, cette autopsie d'un crime, s'impose'.

unlikely car-chase without imbuing these innocent pleasures with political criticism. On the other hand, aggressive Fascism as shown in the film was largely in abeyance in France at this point (which is perhaps how the film came to be made there). To quote Serceau once more:

> It is ... the sensational elements (the plot, the assassination) which have value as an accusation. Extraordinary events are needed in order to judge everyday life ... If something extraordinary is needed to mobilise the masses, won't they be helpless before the 'legal' practices of ordinary fascism? (Serceau 1985: 56)[14]

With the right reduced to its most extreme expression, an uncommitted, apolitical spectator finds that in identifying with the left he or she can feel at one with the political climate of the times. *Z* thus provided reassurance for those unwilling to consider themselves reactionary but intimidated by revolution: or even for those seeking to condemn revolutionary movements without identifying with the 'stuffy and outdated' aspects of the stereotype of the establishment. Even the *Figaro* and the *Express* could thus find reason to support the film.

L'Attentat similarly played down its political criticism and discouraged direct action, and, even more than *Z*, which does set out a bitter analysis of its particular type of society, it functions *first* on the level of the thriller. Leaving aside those critics (Grant 1977; Vecchiali 1972) who panned it simply on the grounds that it was a poor thriller, the importance given to the film's historico-political stance by the critics can be compared very instructively with that which greeted *Z* three years previously; this forms part of a critical development which is characteristic of the whole debate over the *série-Z*.

Z was greeted with almost unanimous critical praise across the political and cultural spectrum, and not only from the daily and weekly papers.[15] On the right and centre, only *Le Figaro* admitted

---

[14] 'C'est ... le sensationnel (le complot, l'assassinat) qui prennent une valeur accusatrice. Il faut de l'extraordinaire pour juger de l'ordinaire de la vie ... S'il faut de l'extraordinaire pour mobiliser les foules, celles-ci ne seront-elles pas démunies devant les pratiques 'légales' du fascisme ordinaire?'

[15] A list of the publications containing highly favourable reviews of *Z* (from the three sources cited, with the exception of *Film français*, 14 March 1969, p. 10): *Téléciné, Le Nouvel Observateur, Le Monde, Le Canard enchaîné, La Croix, Lettres françaises, L'Express, Combat* (with a few reservations), *France-Nouvelle, Réforme,*

to worrying about its politics. Otherwise, praise was divided between the film's political merits and its use of the thriller format. On the first point: 'a universal accusation which denounces with rare virulence the crimes against liberty, the corruption and the injustice of totalitarian regimes' (*Film français*), 'This film wants to act, and it acts. It's combat cinema. Militant cinema' (*Le Nouvel Observateur*), 'The cinema can act on current events like X-rays on an opaque body to reveal to us the structure, the underlying foundations, the pathological symptoms' (*Lettres françaises*). The *Nouvel Observateur* even went so far as to criticise the film for 'the flaws which the needs of the fight, that is of propaganda, impose on it'. As for the thriller form, it was generally welcomed, though with some surprise: 'Why shouldn't the illustration of the glory and the decline of democracy follow the rough road of "thrillers" and westerns?' wondered *Réforme*, noting at the same time that '*Z* is as gripping and exciting as a Hitchcock'. *L'Humanité* defended the method directly on account of its observed effect on the public, 'their applause or their reproachful gestures'.[16]

Two publications expressed doubts – but they were two which could not be ignored in 1968, all the more because in almost every field they were arch-rivals and at opposite poles of critical opinion. In *Cahiers du cinéma*, Jean Narboni provided a careful critique which sought to answer the question posed by *Réforme* from the point of view of a magazine committed to the critique of traditional forms: 'Petty-bourgeois ideology, at work here in the functioning of the film as much as in its consumption, can always be recognised because it neglects the concrete analysis of concrete

---

L'Humanité, Le Figaro littéraire, L'Humanité dimanche, Rivarol, Jeune cinéma, Tribune de Lausanne, Image et Son, Le Soir de Bruxelles, Film français. Le Figaro and *Télé-rama* recorded more reserved verdicts. Unfavourable reviews were limited to *Cahiers du cinéma, Positif, Tribune socialiste*, and *La Nouvelle République du Centre-Ouest.*

[16] 'une accusation universelle qui dénonce avec une rare virulence les crimes contre la liberté, les corruptions et les injustices des régimes totalitaires'; 'Ce film veut agir, et il agit. C'est du cinéma de combat. Du cinéma militant'; 'le cinéma peut opérer sur les événements contemporains à la manière des rayons X sur un corps opaque pour nous en dévoiler la structure, les soubassements, les symptômes pathologiques'; 'les défauts ... qu'imposent les nécessités du combat, c'est-à-dire de la propagande'; 'Pourquoi l'illustration des grandeurs et décadences de la démocratie n'emprunterait-elle pas les voies rugueuses du "policier" et du "western"?'; '*Z* accroche, passionne comme un Hitchcock.; 'leurs applaudissements ou ... leurs mouvements de réprobation'.

situations, the objective study of social relations, the breakdown of political mechanisms' (cf. *Lettres françaises*). 'Militant? Like variety shows can sometimes be, and misleading as they are ... a deflected and degraded form of what – with all ideological reserves – was nonetheless the strength of the American cinema' (Narboni 1969: 54–5).[17] Such criticism was probably to be expected from *Cahiers* with its uncompromising formalism and aspiration to revolutionary politics, but, interestingly, *Positif* also expressed doubts about the appropriateness of form to content.

Dissent from both these magazines could hardly be ignored, and *Cahiers* in 1969 was still the cutting edge of French film criticism; the premises of a debate were therefore launched. The appearance of *L'Aveu* led to a more general criticism of the use of the spectacular to hold an audience. *Cahiers*, of course, renewed its attack, and Comolli's long article could figure as a theoretical manifesto against the '*effet-Z*', but this time doubts were expressed in other quarters. *Télérama* found it necessary to publish two conflicting reports: while J.L. Tallenay represented the favourable opinion, 'a report such as a journalist who has to make the facts known might write', Jean Collet took the film to task for its use of 'dubiously honest procedures, which are just so many low blows to the stomach, an organised beating-up of the public', and he extends the accusation retrospectively to *Z*. *Image et son* took exception to 'its essential flaw: its spectacular nature ... the accent which it puts on dramatic incidents rather than a less superficial truth'.[18]

However, criticism of *L'Aveu* was complicated by the political positions of the various publications which dealt with it, and some reactions betrayed little interest in the film as a film. *Cinéma 70* explicitly congratulated the film-makers for respecting Artur

[17] 'L'idéologie petite-bourgeoise, en oeuvre ici tant dans l'opération du film que dans sa consommation, se reconnaît toujours à ce qu'elle ignore les analyses concrètes de situations concrètes, l'étude objectif des rapports sociaux, le démontage des mécanismes politiques'; 'Militant? Comme peuvent l'être les spectacles des chansonniers, mais comme eux mystifiant' ... 'forme déviée et dégradée de ce qui – toutes réserves idéologiques faites – constituait quand même la force du cinéma américain'.

[18] 'un témoignage comme celui que pourrait écrire un journaliste qui doit faire connaître les faits'; 'des procédés fort peu honnêtes, des procédés qui sont autant de coups bas, coups bas dans l'estomac, matraquage organisé du public'; 'son défaut essentiel: son caractère spectaculaire ... cet accent mis sur des péripéties dramatiques au détriment d'une vérité plus intérieure'.

London's continued support for communism as expressed in the book on which the film was based, while *L'Humanité*, and even *Cahiers*, accused them of eliding this issue. For *L'Humanité* it was London's communism which was betrayed, for *Cahiers* his analytical position. Besides, it is perhaps inaccurate to consider *L'Aveu* as having the form of a thriller: it was associated with *Z* because of its director and star, but its 'low blows' were of a different order. It functions through intense scrutiny of the torture of an innocent man, it was a high-profile film intended for mass consumption, and almost by definition it was open to the charge of trading on voyeurism.

By 1971 comparison with Costa-Gavras was no longer a sign of critical approbation. The term *série-Z* had been coined by *Nouvelle critique* (no. 49) to describe the New Thriller, and adopted by Guy Hennebelle in *Ecran 72* (Hennebelle 1972: 3).[19] Its connotations were hardly flattering and the articles which accompanied its introduction highly critical although the majority of the films surveyed have little in common – certainly with regard to political ambition – with Costa-Gavras' work: both Boisset and Cayatte had yet to venture fully into the territory of political fiction. The New Thrillers were a varied bunch, and Hennebelle recognised that: 'some of them are acceptable despite everything, others aren't'. That 'despite everything' is eloquent, however.

It was with the appearance of *L'Attentat* that debate about the compatibility of politics and thrillers became lively. Here was a film which bore direct comparison with *Z* in terms of ambition and of subject matter, and which was in addition concerned with a *French* scandal. It had clear merits; while a direct descendant of *Z* it was not by Costa-Gavras, and it demanded recognition of the political thriller as a nascent *genre* in French popular cinema. But critical appreciation of *L'Attentat* was much more mitigated than that of *Z*, perhaps more so than the respective merits of the two films can explain. As *Image et son*'s features on the film – a debate followed by a critical article including a review of previous criticism (*Revue du cinéma/Image et son* 1972; 1973) – show, the issue had moved beyond individual films to consider current

[19] Both magazines list as representative of the genre, apart from *Z* and *L'Aveu*: *Un condé* (1970), *Le Saut de l'ange* (1971: both Boisset), *L'Albatros* (Mocky, 1972), *Sans mobile apparent* (Labro, 1971), *Mourir d'aimer* (Cayatte, 1970), and *Les Assassins de l'ordre* (Carné, 1971).

expectations regarding politics in the cinema and the state of the thriller, and the reviews were already analysing reactions as well as texts.

Thus the very existence of *L'Attentat* was seen as important and positive, independently of its merits or demerits, by some critics who saw it as a sign that no subject was henceforward taboo to the popular French cinema. Paul Vecchiali, who largely disliked it, observed in the course of the *Image et son* debate: 'After *L'Attentat*, politically committed film-makers can no longer use censorship as their alibi. Everything has been said and shown, and a vaguely conscientious policeman will not be enough to accuse a film of being pro-government' (*Revue du cinéma/ Image et Son* 1972: 30).[20] The film appeared despite threats to those involved, which at least proved that the market for political fiction was considered large enough to justify the risks of production.

As regards the value of the exposé, however, opinion was divided. For some, all was *not* said. Even a critic who praised the film, Etienne Fuzellier (*L'Education*), did not consider it valuable as an account of the Ben Barka affair, but only as a general exposé of the mechanics of 'disappearances'. Tristan Renaud in *Cinéma 72* is particularly severe on these grounds:

> His [Boisset's] film has completely lost sight of its main subject, the Ben Barka affair itself. No doubt he believed – optimistically to say the least – that this affair was still present in everyone's memory ... Why does *L'Attentat* hide behind a mask of fiction which in the end deceives nobody? ... The answer will no doubt be, because of censorship. OK, it exists, and is always deplorable. But in the end isn't it an easy excuse ... to offer us, under the name of politics, a spy film with multiple plot twists which (since, alas, we know the end) will always lack suspense. (Renaud 1972: 126)[21]

[20] 'Après *L'Attentat*, tous les cinéastes engagés ne pourront plus évoquer la censure comme alibi. Tout est dit, tout est montré et ce n'est pas parce qu'il y a un policier vaguement consciencieux que l'on pourra accuser le film d'être pro-gouvernemental'.
[21] 'Son [Boisset's] film se trouve complètement vidé de son propos, l'affaire Ben Barka elle-même. Sans doute a-t-il cru que cette affaire – ce qui est pour le moins optimiste – était encore présente dans toutes les mémoires ... Pourquoi *L'Attentat* emprunte-t-il le masque d'une fiction qui ne trompe, au bout de compte, personne? ... On répondra, sans doute, la censure. Soit, elle existe, et toujours déplorable. Mais n'est-elle pas en fin de compte une excuse facile ... pour, sous couvert de politique, nous livrer un film d'espionnage aux rebondissements multiples auquel manquera toujours (puisque nous en connaissons, hélas, la fin), le suspense.'

We may find three themes in the above quotation. First there is the uncomfortable coexistence of politics and thriller which dilutes both political bite and the thrill of suspense. *Positif* had said something similar about *Z*, but we have already seen that Boisset's approach created more problems than Costa-Gavras' as regards sustaining dramatic interest. Eventually Jacques Grant was to turn this argument once again on its head, claiming that the film fails politically *because* it is not dramatic enough to retain the audience's interest (Grant 1977: 22).

Renaud's article also raises two points concerning the relation of *L'Attentat*, and by implication all the *série-Z*, to reality. This question was extremely important since the films were presented not only as spectacle, but also as representation and, to some extent, re-appraisal of recent history. The first and basic question is whether they are accurate, even at a superficial level. André Cornand observed that when, inspired by films such as *Z* and *L'Aveu* set reassuringly abroad, the fashion for *films-affaires* extended into domestic politics, they might be led to make small adjustments adding up inadvertently to a major compromise: 'We worry when cinema makes reference to – or takes as its subject – more or less recent events. We saw the results with *L'Attentat,* on the Ben Barka affair: since Boisset could not tell "the whole truth", he made a Gaullist film, a government film' (*Revue du cinéma/ Image et son* 1973: 47).[22] This point became the basic reproach levelled at *L'Attentat*, although *Cahiers* had already raised the issue in the case of *Z* and at the appearance of *L'Aveu* a number of others had joined it. The second point concerned the value of raising renewed public interest in these past incidents, at once jogging the collective memory and providing an abiding record which might also be an inaccurate one. Some, optimistically, held that renewed debate around a forgotten subject was a good thing on historical grounds: others contended firstly that if the information given was insufficient or even inaccurate, a debate on such a false basis was worse than no debate at all, and secondly that the films were not sufficiently gripping thrillers to raise public interest anyway (*Revue du cinéma/Image et son* 1972).

---

[22] 'Nous sommes inquiets lorsque le cinéma fait référence à – ou prend pour sujet – des événements plus ou moins récents. On a vu ce que cela donne avec *L'Attentat* sur l'affaire Ben Barka: comme Boisset ne pouvait pas dire "toute la vérité", il a fait un film gaulliste, gouvernemental'.

Apart from these issues, the formal debate – that radical content required a radical form, and popular cinema needed reconstructing before it could be an appropriate place for politics – was still alive, and had indeed become more common currency since its first formulation in the specialist pages of *Cahiers*. Costa-Gavras at the time of the making of *Z* had justified himself to the sympathetic critics of *Télérama* by citing an American tradition of social cinema, but in 1969 efficacity (or, put another way, success) was the best justification: *Z* had a vast audience. By 1972 the effect of surprise was no longer active, there were other 'political thrillers' around and *L'Attentat* was perceived as one of a kind, and even if good box-office could be expected Boisset could not rely on the film being the sensation of the year. When *Cahiers* applied its theory to the analysis of particular films, it could usually support its criticism by precise demonstration of the ill-effects the form had imposed on any possible radical intentions, and by 1972 its methods of analysis were current practice, if somewhat diluted, elsewhere. François Chevassu therefore rejects *L'Attentat* because 'any film which proceeds through a series of emotional shocks is right-wing, since it's an alienating method and … I consider alienation to be right-wing' (*Revue du cinéma/Image et son* 1972).[23]

Against that proponents of the *série-Z* – critics and film-makers – invoked the advantages of visibility for their progressive agenda: 'A film which is not seen is a film which does not exist. Even more when we're talking about a political film' (Guy Allombert). It was a telling argument, which only the most incorruptible revolutionaries felt they could ignore: thus, in the course of the *Image et son* debate François Chevassu, who in principle disapproved of *L'Attentat*, accepted that: 'In this system which we are obliged to suffer, we must admit this dilemma: a satisfactory political film is a film which can have an impact. Political action, which is seeking a degree of efficacity, always implies compromise.' Another contributor, Jacques Chevallier, commented: 'this type of story is so anchored in public expectations that any film which goes against it risks having no audience' (*Revue du cinéma/Image et son* 1972).[24]

[23] 'tout film qui procède par succession de chocs affectifs est de droite, parce que c'est une démarche aliénante, et … je situe l'aliénation à droite'.

[24] Allombert: 'Un film qui n'est pas vu est un film qui n'existe pas. Plus encore quand il s'agit d'un film politique'; Chevassu: 'Dans le système que nous sommes obligés de subir, il nous faut admettre ce dilemme: le film politique satisfaisant est

However, that debate concluded with a majority negative judgement. The critical reception of Costa-Gavras' *Etat de siège*, in 1973, was considerably more muted than that for *Z*. Even Marcel Martin, despite his defence of *L'Attentat* and continued sympathy for the commercial political genre generally (Martin 1984: 81–5), began to admit doubts: 'The fundamental ambiguity of this type of political cinema seems to me to be the following: in the end it relies in an artistic and dramatic judgement while logically a truly political cinema should rely above all on political judgement' even while he considers that 'if you believe that political cinema has a function, one can only note with satisfaction that a film like *Etat de siège* exists' (Martin 1973: 59).[25] There is also a growing tendency to extend criticisms retroactively.

As the decade advanced, support for the genre declined. *Section spéciale* (Costa-Gavras, 1975), was even less well-received than *Etat de siège*, and *France-Nouvelles* in reviewing it describes it merely in terms of a genre now established: 'a film which confirms both the limits and the relative merits of a certain conception of "political cinema"' (Sauvaget 1977: 35).[26] Audiences too were declining, and Costa-Gavras seems to have been deterred; he made no more films until 1979, and then turned to a very different genre with *Clair de femme*.

The debate continued without him. In December 1977, *Revue du cinéma* published a lengthy feature on his films, despite his two-year silence, which was as much about the critical issues as it was about the films. Daniel Sauvaget's article (Sauvaget 1977) serves as an introduction and description of the current state of play.

Also in 1977, the arguments were reignited by the appearance of Boisset's *Le Juge Fayard dit le shérif*, one of the last examples of the genre in France. At this point the critics were showing no sign

---

le film susceptible d'impact. Une action politique, c'est-à-dire la recherche d'une certaine efficacité, passe toujours par une compromission'; Chevallier: 'ce type de récit est tellement bien ancré dans les moeurs du public que tout film qui va contre risque de n'avoir aucune audience'.

[25] 'L'ambiguïté fondamentale de ce type de cinéma politique me semble être la suivante: il relève finalement d'un jugement esthético-dramaturgique alors qu'en bonne logique un cinéma véritablement politique devrait relever avant tout d'un jugement politique … si l'on croit à l'utilité du cinéma politique, on ne peut que constater avec satisfaction l'existence d'un film comme *Etat de siège*'.

[26] 'un film qui confirme autant les limites que les mérites relatifs d'une certaine conception du "cinéma politique"'.

of winding up the debate. *Jeune cinéma*, which fervently supported the *série-Z*, published (as a preface to an interview with Boisset) a page in his defence which even hails the political merits of *Un condé* and *Le Saut de l'ange*, and concludes in frankly combative mode: 'To declare oneself to be on the left and to spitefully despise the work of the two bravest French film-directors [Boisset and Costa-Gavras] as some people do without the slightest embarrassment, is a detestable and harmful attitude' (Boisset 1977: 8).[27] In contrast, *Cinéma 77* claimed that *Le Juge Fayard* was as likely to be reactionary as progressive, given its source. The story of Judge Fayard was in fact inspired in part by the assassination of a certain Judge Renaud, like Fayard fervently opposed to political corruption, but unlike Fayard of extreme right-wing leanings. *Cinéma 77* considers confusion possible, especially since the apolitical Fayard has recourse to unnecessary violence to further his aims of uncovering justice. He resembles in many ways the maverick police officer of *Un condé*, who beats up the anarchist played by Rufus. Boisset recognises this trait but dismisses it rapidly: 'There is a certain ambiguity in the character of Fayard: he's someone who is perfectly honest but, through coming up against violence, bad faith and compromise, he himself becomes violent and finally loses sight of his ideals.' (Boisset 1977: 13–14).[28] *Cinéma 77*, on the other hand, points out the danger that the public will be led to identify with and to justify not only Fayard but Renaud in his entirety.[29]

---

[27] 'Se proclamer de gauche et mépriser méchamment le travail des deux réalisateurs français les plus courageux [Boisset and Costa-Gavras], comme le font sans la moindre gêne quelques-uns, est une attitude détestable et nuisible.' (Claude Benoit).

[28] 'Il y a une certaine ambiguïté dans le personnage de Fayard: c'est un être qui est parfaitement intègre, mais qui, à force de se heurter à la violence, à la mauvaise foi, à la compromission, devient lui aussi violent, et finit par perdre de vue son idéal'.

[29] *Cahiers du cinéma*, while certainly not approving of *Le Juge Fayard*, is less virulent against it than might have been expected. By 1977, the magazine's political rigidity was beginning to relax, and here it prefers to analyse the way the film relates to the spectator in order to illustrate its relative weakness: 'Le film de Boisset vient s'ajouter à la liste, déjà longue, des films français, italiens, ou franco-italiens, de "dénonciation" ... La fiction de gauche travaille aujourd'hui à faire miroiter d'autres valeurs, d'autres discours, à l'alluvionnement d'une doxa de gauche, d'une nouvelle majorité, c'est-à-dire à la mise en place d'un régime qui confère aux nouvelles idées, *d'emblée*, statut d'évidences' ['Boisset's film is another addition to the already long list of French, Italian or Franco-Italian 'accusatory' films ... Left-wing fiction today is working to show us different values and different

The debate about the *série-Z* took for granted, as a rule, that explicit politics in a thriller would be, at least intentionally, liberal and progressive if not left-wing. However, this was not always the case: *Le Complot* (René Gainville and Agnieszka Holland, 1973) is an example of a right-wing *série-Z*, rarely mentioned by contemporary contributors to these debates – perhaps because it was not successful, a fact which in itself is interesting, since it certainly did not lack star names to draw an audience. The only critic to draw attention to it has been Jean-Pierre Jeancolas (Jeancolas 1979a). *Le Complot*, like its contemporary *The Day of the Jackal* (Zinnemann, 1973, GB/France), deals with the Algerian war, and with a plot hatched by the OAS (Organisation de l'armée secrète), but while the latter film uses French politics more or less as an excuse for a game of suspense,[30] *Le Complot*, a very inferior thriller, is rooted in politics. Jeancolas calls it 'certainly very different, but nonetheless close (as the negative is close to the positive)' (1979a: 201) to the *série-Z*, and indeed it is easy to find correspondences.

Firstly, like *Z*, it centres upon a judicial enquiry. The enquirer (Michel Bouquet) is investigating a plot hatched a little after the end of the Algerian war to kidnap the imprisoned General Challe and continue to fight for French Algeria: the suspense hinges on whether the plot (which it is established exists) will be successfully forestalled. Like *Z* or *L'Attentat*, then, the suspense hangs on the *process* of investigation rather than its results, again as a necessary concession to history since clearly if such a plot existed it was not successful. As in any self-respecting thriller including the *série-Z*, chase sequences and violent action are inevitable: the start of the action is already frenetic, the arrest, after pursuit, of a military officer, an event clearly of more than mere criminal

discourses, to lay down a left-wing doxa, a new consensus, in other words to put in place a regime which gives these new ideas the status of obvious truths *from the outset*'] (Toubiana 1977: 47–8). The criticism that the spectator leaves the film convinced that the battle has been fought and won since the film exists (despite, or because of, the censorship exerted on *Le Juge Fayard* which Boisset made extremely obvious in the text of the film as eventually released) will recur in relation to filmic Utopias (chapter 4). *Cahiers* is unusual here in recalling that the genre is shared between France and Italy, where the irony of reading these films as little victories in themselves was even more evident.

[30] Nonetheless it provides ideological support for Gaullism, simply on the grounds that it is part of the international status quo.

significance even though the audience has no idea yet of the identities of the protagonists. The OAS is identified as a name and a credo defined in two words, 'Algérie française'; there is no attempt to give any background to its existence, as explanation would slow the frantic pace of the plot. Gainville assumes knowledge in his audience – possibly justifiably but nonetheless the film *depends* on background knowledge to avoid confusion to a much greater extent than, for example, *L'Attentat* which was also criticised for assuming too much. Boisset at least gives enough explanation to support his plot. This, again, may account for the film's lack of success; it also perhaps suggests that Gainville or his producers had already located their likely audience.

The principal difference between the opposing sides in *Le Complot* is the degree to which each accepts the use of violence. That Algeria is French and should remain so is an assumption shared by *both* sides, which incidentally means that all protagonists are supporting a lost cause and practically defines the film as designed to appeal to an audience of nostalgic *pieds-noirs*. The *série-Z*, at least, was dealing with general issues which were live. But *Le Complot*'s methods are similar: the summary divide between the violent and the legalistic is similar to the legality/illegality opposition which defines Good and Bad in *Z*, and indicates just how politically neutral a position that is. There is no left in *Le Complot*: but while a left-wing – or even moderately liberal – audience in 1973 might well be alienated by the ideas *named* in *Le Complot*, as a right-wing audience could be alienated by those named in *Z*, the values placed on the behaviour of those who hold those ideas is largely consensual. If violence is established as bad, the Algerian nationalists who exist as an offscreen and largely undefined danger can be discredited simply by being labelled 'violent'. Incidentally, the active villains of the piece are here as in the *série-Z* the extreme-right and not the left: there was presumably a limit to what was considered tenable box-office.

Like *Z* or *L'Attentat*, *Le Complot* depends on the politically neutral, or rather politically ambiguous, central figure, an incorruptible investigator as in *Z* or indeed the later *Juge Fayard*. This figure, played by Michel Bouquet, has more sympathy with his 'enemy' than the *série-Z* usually allowed for, and it grows rather than declines as the action progresses, to the point where he is semi-superseded by an unofficial fellow-traveller of more ruthless tendencies.

Bouquet, ever-reasonable, can only gain from the comparison. The film ends with an individual confrontation in true genre tradition, where this everyday, Everyman figure – he has a photograph of his dog on his desk – becomes the archetype of the hero.

Gainville thus encourages us to identify with Bouquet and to share his divided loyalties, which is one characteristic which the film does not share with the *série-Z* proper. None of the left-wing political thrillers allow much possibility of sympathy with the 'villains', and, as a psychological drama, this trait works to the advantage of *Le Complot*. It works, however, largely on the assumption that the audience forgets the underlying politics in the heat of the action, and even *Z* itself is not immune from that. Here we can sympathise, alternately, with the good-natured *commissaire* and with the noble, but misguided, general heading the plot. The general has a strictly enunciative function. An idealist, he is never shown directly involved in violence. He has a private life, always an incentive to audience sympathy; in the final sequence, he apparently recognises the hopelessness – if not the undesirability – of his position, and surrenders voluntarily to the rule of law. *Le Complot* thus ends with the victory of justice, but also with reconciliation, under the forgiving auspices of Gaullism, of the right and the reformed further-right.

Le Complot is thus an anti-*série-Z*; but it owes its existence to the political upsurge of the early 1970s as much as do its left-wing counterparts. 'This is not Gaullism, but Pompidolism [from de Gaulle's successor, Georges Pompidou], post-69, beating the drum for every conservative ideology and extending pardon to those who have strayed, in order to face up to the peril glimpsed in 1968', (Jeancolas 1979a: 222),[31] in Jeancolas' judgement: and possibly the peril which the *série-Z* represented for a conservative popular cinema was one of the sources of *Le Complot* even though it rides on the back of the success of its liberal predecessors. And its very existence provides a demonstration of many of the criticisms which were levelled against the political thrillers as effective political cinema. Even if *Le Complot* fails in practice through a number of stylistic misjudgements – it is overcomplicated, its clichés are very blatant and the political moral at the

---

[31] 'Ce n'est plus le gaullisme, mais du pompidolisme, de l'après-69, battant le rappel de tous les conservatismes, pardonnant aux égarés, pour faire face au péril entrevu en 1968'.

end is overstated and not really prepared by the body of the film – there is no reason why it should not have functioned excellently as a right-wing thriller. It tends therefore to prove the point made by Gérard Leblanc: '*Z* is political only inasmuch as it brings new themes to the blind emotion which the great cinematic genres play on and continually revive. The way that it presents itself before an audience, with the intention of both scaring and reassuring them, could serve any "cause" – fascist just as much as anti-fascist' (Leblanc 1985: 44).[32]

Disagreement regarding the *série-Z* continued long after it was for all practical purposes exhausted in France. Costa-Gavras and later Oliver Stone continued the tradition in the USA (ironically, *Missing*, produced in America, won the Palme d'Or at Cannes), but French civic cinema went into abeyance with the coming to power of the Left in 1981. The adaptable Tavernier is perhaps the only film-maker who, occasionally, revived some memories of the genre. But the controversy surrounding it remained. Even in historical accounts authors have found it necessary to conclude 'for' or 'against' the genre. When Jeancolas, in *Le Cinéma des français: la Ve République*, reached a largely negative conclusion – 'A cinema which denounced particular abuses, which highlighted privileges and compromises : no doubt a necessary cinema, but in no way a sufficient one' (Jeancolas 1979a: 227)[33] – he was entering a still-open debate. Martin, in 1984, regarded the political thrillers as products of their time, but the terms in which he exposed the arguments for and against them indicate clearly that he con-sidered the question as still potentially relevant. He regretted the decline of the genre, recognising that there was a risk that 1981 might have marked its end: 'we might have hoped for some sort of development, the appearance of more immediately relevant subjects, the emergence of new priorities: clearly, there's been nothing of the kind … it would be a shame if film-makers with

[32] '*Z* n'est politique que dans la mesure où il renouvelle thématiquement l'aveuglement émotionnel joué et perpétuellement relancé par les grands genres cinématographiques. Tel qu'il se présente aux yeux des spectateurs, destiné à leur faire peur et à les rassurer tout à la fois, il pourrait servir n'importe quelle "cause" – fasciste aussi bien qu'anti-fasciste'.

[33] 'Un cinéma qui dénonce les abus individuels, qui met en lumière les privilèges et les compromissions: un cinéma sans doute nécessaire, mais en aucun cas un cinéma suffisant'.

something to say renounced their duty as reporters and critics to become simple providers of popular *entertainment* (Martin 1984: 112),[34] but when referring to the films of the 1970s his assessment is negative, although with qualifications: 'it would be excessive to totally condemn this *civic* cinema' (Martin 1984: 84).[35] This from one of the most outspoken defenders of the genre during the early 1970s. *CinémAction*'s edition on Costa-Gavras (1985), which provided a long-overdue synthesis of his significance in France, still adopted a polemical tone. Perhaps most interesting, however, was the incipient willingness to discuss the genre in terms of *popular* rather than of political cinema: as Gérard Camy suggested, in an article which gave broad support to the phenomenon and especially to Boisset: 'these films should not be judged in comparison with the defunct militant cinema or the very worthy but obscure productions of Jean-Marie Straub or Marguerite Duras but in comparison with films like *Le Corniaud*, *La Grande Vadrouille* or *L'Aventure, c'est l'aventure*. They use the same formal system and reach the same public' (Camy 1985: 126).[36]

Costa-Gavras and Boisset did inaugurate a truly original movement in the mainstream cinema of the 1970s, following perhaps in the footsteps of Cayatte but, it was generally recognised, with greater skill and more daring. Boisset in particular encountered obstruction from the censors to his projects (as, indeed, did Cayatte, more inclined to tackle subjects which were *socially* sensitive than of strictly *political* relevance, and perhaps for that reason given less critical attention except when, as occurred with *Il n'y a pas de fumée sans feu* (1973), censorship difficulties became so great as to amount to blockage of the film). These perhaps give an indication (as both Camy and Martin have observed) that this new departure within the field of mass entertainment could cause

---

[34] 'on pouvait escompter une évolution quelconque, l'apparition de sujets plus liés à l'actualité, l'émergence de préoccupations nouvelles: manifestement, il n'en est rien … il serait fâcheux que les cinéastes qui ont quelque chose à dire renoncent à leur devoir de témoignage et de critique pour devenir de simples fournisseurs du *divertissement* populaire'.

[35] 'il serait excessif de condamner totalement ce cinéma *civique*'.

[36] 'il ne faut pas juger leurs films par rapport au défunt cinéma militant ou aux très estimables mais hermétiques réalisations de Jean-Marie Straub ou Marguerite Duras mais par rapport à des films comme *Le Corniaud*, *La Grande Vadrouille* ou *L'Aventure, c'est l'aventure*. Ils utilisent le même système formel et touchent le même public'.

some official alarm. It certainly introduced a degree of necessary reflection on current affairs into the mass-entertainment market which had previously been given over almost entirely to escapism. By the end of the decade, indeed, a limited relevance to current debates was almost taken for granted in high-profile films: 'current events provide an episode here ... an atmosphere there ... elsewhere an issue to deal with' as Jeancolas observed in an article on some of the biggest-grossing films of 1979 (Jeancolas 1979b: 80).[37] More social than political, these popular films of the end of the decade are nonetheless beginning to show signs of tackling some of the major concerns of the new France, which at the beginning of the decade were present only at the very margins of production: *Les Chiens* dealt with fighting dogs and violence in the *banlieues*, Edouard Molinaro's comedy *Causes toujours tu m'intéresses* ends with a sympathetic and serious portrayal of a lonely Senegalese immigrant in Paris. This change in the current perhaps reflects a real change in French public expectations, an increased interest in their own society which must have been borne by the debates which the early part of the decade had seen ubiquitously raging. If a mass audience could be moved and interested by political content, the big guns of the industry were likely to respond to a new area of demand; Boisset noted in 1978 that he felt that social subjects were more accessible to film-makers than they had been ten years previously, although he also said that 'the only really effective censorship still exists and is stronger than ever: that is economic censorship' (*Film français* 1978: 15).[38]

However the French cinema of the 1970s cannot be reduced to the militant, the 'hermetic' and the broadly commercial: the small-scale, intimate aspirations of a number of first films by

[37] 'l'actualité fournit ici un anecdote ... là un climat ... ailleurs un problématique'. The films concerned were *Les Egouts du Paradis* (José Giovanni, on a bank-robbery which was justified with some vague reference to 68ard ideals), *Un si joli village* (François Périer), *Les Chiens* (Alain Jessua), and *L'Homme en colère* (Claude Pinoteau).

[38] 'la seule véritable censure efficace subsiste, plus forte que jamais: la censure économique'. The magazine presented a questionnaire, of which this formed question 5, to a number of film-makers. Boisset's response was typical of those provided by film-makers with some aspirations to social relevance (Jessua, Miller, Tavernier, Vianney, Labro, Pinoteau, Vecchiali). Kast, Leroy and Tacchella are more pessimistic. Others have clearly never encountered censorship.

young, or at least novice, directors, who approached the portrayal of the realities of post-'68 French life with a relatively discreet, although often skilful, style, allowed for the new interpretations of the experience of being young in France which 1968 had brought to the forefront to be integrated in quite unspectacular, personal human stories. Such films were soon gathered by journalists under a convenient heading, in this case 'New Naturalism', a label which many of the film-makers concerned disliked vociferously and with reason. In the ambit of this 'New Naturalism' the decade developed its own auteurs; it also, not necessarily through the same films and film-makers, began to express in images on screen the political and social state of the nation – that is, the young nation yet to find its place in the fabric of French society. While the impact of the *série-Z* depended essentially on shock-value and the exposure of major scandals, and direct involvement of ordinary people in politics is discouraged, these films, less ambitious although far from unsuccessful, sought to expose the difficulties of everyday life and the possible responses to them of those caught in an uncertain world.

REFERENCES

Boisset, Yves (1977) Interview with Claude Benoit, *Jeune cinéma* 102, avril–mai: 8–16.

Cahiers du cinéma (1974) 'Le Mode rétro', *Cahiers du cinéma* 250, juillet–août: 5–15.

Camy, Gérard (1985) 'Le Cinéma politique "grand public" en France', in *Cinémaction 35*, Paris: Cerf: 124–37.

CinémAction (1985) 'Le Choc de *Z*' (press reactions), *Cinémaction 35*, Paris: Cerf: 23.

Comolli, Jean-Louis (1970) 'Film/Politique II', *Cahiers du cinéma* 224, octobre: 48–51.

Costa-Gavras, Constantin, Perrin, Jacques, Vasilikos, Vassilis, Guiomar, Jacques, interview, *Téléciné* 151/2, mars/avr. 69, 4–16.

Costa-Gavras, Constantin (1969) Interview in *Image et son* 228, mai: 60–5.

Film français (1978) 'La Parole aux réalisateurs', *Film français* 1716, 17 mars: 15–20.

Grant, Jacques (1977) '*Le Juge Fayard*', *Cinéma 77* 222, juin: 21–2.

Hennebelle, Guy (1972) 'Les Prémices d'un nouveau cinéma français', *Ecran 72* 3, mars: 3–4.

Jeancolas, Jean-Pierre (1979a) *Le Cinéma des français: la Vᵉ République 1958–78*, Paris: Stock/Cinéma.

Jeancolas, Jean-Pierre (1979b) 'Le Cinéma des bonnes recettes', *Positif* 241, juillet–août: 80–3

Leblanc, Gérard (1985) 'Cinéma et politique?', in *CinémAction 35*, Paris: Cerf: 36–47.

Martin, Marcel (1973) '*Etat de siège*', *Ecran 73* 13, mars: 59.

Martin, Marcel (1984) *Le Cinéma français depuis la guerre*, Paris: Edilig.

Narboni, Jean (1969) 'Le Pirée pour un homme', *Cahiers du cinéma* 210, mars: 54–5.

Poulle, François (1985) 'Le Cinéma politique de grande audience, autopsie d'un prototype', *CinémAction 35*, Paris: Cerf: 24–35.

Renaud, Tristan (1972) 'Beaucoup de bruit pour rien', *Cinéma 72* 170, novembre: 125–6.

Revue du cinéma/Image et son (1972) 'Réflexions sur le cinéma politique', dossier *L'Attentat*, *Revue du cinéma/Image et son* 266, décembre: 30–47.

Revue du cinéma/Image et son (1973) 'L'Analyse du discours filmique', dossier *L'Attentat*, *Revue du cinéma/Image et son* 270, mars: 38–50.

Sauvaget, Daniel (1977) 'A propos de Costa-Gavras', *Revue du cinéma/Image et son* 323, décembre: 31–6.

Semprun, Jorge (1983) *Montand: la vie continue*, Paris: Denoël.

Serceau, Daniel (1985) 'La Trilogie', in 'Le Cinema de Costa-Gavras', *CinémAction 35*, Paris: Cerf: 48–63.

Toubiana, Serge (1977) 'Sur la fiction de gauche', *Cahiers du cinéma* 275, avril: 47–51.

Zimmer, Christian (1974) *Cinéma et politique*, Paris: Seghers.

3
The New Naturalism

In December 1974, *Télérama* began the publication of a series of four articles on a movement it styled 'Le Nouveau Naturel' (Douin 1974; Rémond 1975; Tallenay 1974; Trémois 1975). This was an attempt to unite under a group title a very diverse collection of films in which the magazine not unreasonably perceived common factors of content and style. The protagonists of the films were generally from a similar modest background: specifically young workers not yet established in the system and attempting to make ends meet with menial or insecure jobs while at the same time adjusting to the adult world. Fiction springs from the links between the private and the socio-economic problems of these main characters.

The films' décor is restricted as the protagonists' environments would be expected to be; places are visually uninspiring if not frankly unattractive, but not spectacularly so, neither by and large is visual capital made of them. The camera enters these locations and explores them, but they are filmed undramatically with no attempt to glamorise. In the fourth article the magazine distinguishes two favoured stylistic models for its new 'movement': either documentary *cinéma vérité*: 'seizing reality as it passes, using the methods of television and improvising the image as it goes along', or a preference for the *plan fixe*. It cites as partisans of the first technique Gérard Guérin, Joël Séria, Jacques Rozier, and of the second (it seems to be assumed that they are mutually exclusive) Maurice Pialat, Jean Eustache, Jacques Doillon, Pascal Thomas (Rémond 1975: 70).[1]

Télérama was not alone in remarking on the emergence of a new current in the cinema. In April of the same year, *Jeune cinéma* recorded the same tendency:

---

[1] 'saisir au vol la réalité, en utilisant les méthodes de la télévision, en improvisant l'image au fur et à mesure'.

A few films since 1968 bear witness to new priorities and a new style … They have the explicit project of expressing reality, which lays them open to criticism both of their authenticity and of their political significance.

Their interest in non-bourgeois characters, and environments which don't belong to the triumphant consumer society … give importance to a certain age-group: those between 17 and 30. These characters are almost always independent … They are situated precisely, in terms of their marginality if such is the case. (Jeancolas-Audé 1975, 1)[2]

This article too notes that the films have stylistic factors in common, in particular their favouring of the televisual or *cinéma direct*.

For both *Télérama* and *Jeune cinéma* the origins of this new current can be traced to May 1968: 'These auteurs and their characters are the children of Godard and May '68. Their heroes are anti-heroes, young people finding a voice, wanting to change life but submitting to it and forced to conform' (Tallenay 1974: 68).[3] The same article also notes what it sees as important developments in the films' treatment of sexuality: 'eros and politics. Two subjects forbidden to the cinema for so long that the first to venture into this territory could not help indulging in provocation'. Or, perhaps, to be *perceived* as indulging in provocation. Here, however, 'when sexuality needs talking about, they talk about it; when it is necessary to explain the injustices which the baker's or carpenter's apprentice suffer, they talk about politics and trade unions. But these characters are not sex maniacs. And the film never becomes a pamphlet or a manifesto' (Tallenay 1974: 67).[4]

---

[2] 'Quelques films, depuis 68, témoignent de préoccupations et d'un style nouveau … Ils ont le projet explicite d'exprimer le réel, ce qui les expose à une critique d'authenticité et de portée politique.

Leur intérêt pour des personnages qui n'appartiennent pas à la bourgeoisie, pour des décors de vie qui ne sont pas ceux de la triomphante société de consommation … privilégie [nt] une certaine classe d'âge: celle des gens qui ont entre 17 et 30 ans. Ces personnages sont presque toujours responsables d'eux-mêmes … Ils sont situés avec précision, même dans leur marginalité quand c'est le cas.'

[3] 'Ces auteurs et leurs personnages sont les petits enfants de Godard et de mai 68. Leurs héros sont des anti-héros, des jeunes qui prennent la parole, qui voudraient changer la vie mais qui la subissent et doivent rentrer dans le rang.'

[4] 'l'érotisme et la politique. Deux sujets si longtemps interdits au cinéma que les premiers qui osèrent s'y risquer ne purent se défendre de tomber dans la provocation' … 'quand il est besoin de parler d'érotisme, on en parle; quand il faut

Cahiers du cinéma, which also published an article on the subject in 1975 (Daney *et al.* 1975), was less impressed with the credentials of the New Naturalism. For them it represented a form of recuperation of earlier ideals, where a true 'prise de parole' is an issue avoided: 'Naturalism performs the magic trick of suddenly including those who were very recently still banned from the screen ... in fiction films (and traditional fiction films) *as if they had always been there* ... What is skated over ... is their *appearance* (and the reasons for that appearance) in fiction films. (Daney *et al.* 1975: 7).[5] For *Cahiers*, the movement is thus seen as a way of responding to the new demands of the cinema-going public without acknowledging the roots from which they sprang, or of changing the cinema while pretending that it was the same as before. Cahiers also noted that the films were political only on the level of an individual experience, and, for these various reasons, considered the current an insufficient response to the challenge posed to the cinema in May 1968.

The 'New Naturalism' movement outlived its connection to 1968, and in the course of its development launched some of the most significant new film-makers to come to prominence in this decade, such as Jacques Doillon, Jean Eustache or Claude Miller. In 1978, *Avant-scène* considered the Nouveau Naturel a living movement in the decade's cinema, while claiming that 'the double rupture represented by the Nouvelle Vague on the formal level, and May '68 on the formal and the ideological level, has now entirely disappeared' (Alion 1978: 23).[6] Since this analysis locates the two defining influences on the aesthetic of New Naturalism (Claude Miller had worked for a long time with Truffaut), it is a little difficult to see what such a movement could become without these references: and indeed, the French cinema of the 1980s was to turn its back so definitively on its ideals and aesthetic that it

---

expliquer les injustices dont sont victimes l'ouvrier boulanger ou menuisier, on parle de politique ou de syndicalisme. Mais ces personnages ne sont pas des obsédés sexuels. Et le film ne se transforme pas en pamphlet ou en manifeste'.

[5] 'Le naturalisme, c'est le tour de passe-passe par lequel ceux qui étaient encore hier interdits au filmage ... sont soudain inclus dans une fiction (et une fiction traditionnelle) *comme s'ils y avaient toujours été* ... Ce qui est alors escamoté, ... c'est leur *irruption* (et le pourquoi de cette irruption) dans la fiction.'

[6] 'la double cassure de la Nouvelle Vague, sur le plan esthétique, et de mai 68 sur les plans esthétiques et idéologiques, est maintenant totalement estompé.'

seemed to be a trend that had run its course. However, in the 1990s a new generation of young film-makers were to revive its style, its themes, its mixture of the personal and political and even its occasional aspirations to the revolutionary.[7]

As a label, 'New Naturalism' is almost infinitely extendable. Eustache, Doillon and Miller, all cited by *Télérama* as significant exponents of the genre, all rejected the label and denied that their manner was in any way 'naturalist'. This is particularly evident in the case of Eustache, whose extremely artful constructions can only be associated with 'naturalism' on the basis of a superficial consideration of their subject matter, but it was not just these leaders of the genre who showed a sophisticated understanding of the potential of filmic language; hardly surprising after the experiments of the Nouvelle Vague, this nonetheless calls into question any suggestion that the 'young cinema' of the 1970s as a whole was technically unsophisticated. If anything, the main difference between it and the 1980s 'cinéma du look' was that the sophistication lay in editing and cinematography, exercised on a relatively simple *mise-en-scène* which was for preference discovered rather than invented. Similarly, the degree to which the directors were interested in the socio-political content of their subject-matter varied considerably.

The extent to which the films broadly grouped by *Télérama* and others in the category of the Nouveau Naturel gave their social observation a politically analytical slant was also very varied. Dominique Noguez considered that in comparison with Italian neo-realism (which seems to have been perceived as a reference more frequently than the Nouvelle Vague), these films'

[7] For information on the 'jeune cinéma' of the 1990s and its links to the post-'68 generation, see especially Claude-Marie Trémois, *Les Enfants de la liberté* (1997), Michel Marie (ed.), *Le Jeune Cinéma français* (1998), and René Prédal, *Le Jeune Cinéma français* (2002). The combination of an aesthetic of the hand-held camera, a preoccupation with the socio-economic and a move towards revolutionary politics is perhaps best seen in the work of Laetitia Masson (*En avoir (ou pas)*, 1995; *A vendre*, 1998), Bruno Dumont (*La Vie de Jésus*, 1997) or, in more dramatic mode, Jean-François Richet (*Ma 6–T va crack-er*, 1997). While several of these film-makers have since moved away from the social and reformulated their aesthetic, the style is still exemplified by the work of the Dardenne Brothers (*La Promesse*, 1996; *Rosetta*, 1999; *Le Fils*, 2002) or Laurent Cantet (*Ressources humaines*, 1999; *L'Emploi du temps*, 2001). The period also saw an explicit revival of interest in post-'68 production, as exemplified for example by *Reprise* (Hervé Le Roux, 1996) which revisited the famous film-tract of 1968, *La Reprise du travail aux usines Wonder*.

chances of political relevance was low: 'The two situations are separated by all the difference between film-makers who are carrying out a certain formal *rejuvenation* in the stagnant cinema of a country under a reactionary government, and film-makers who were witnesses, sympathisers and sometimes participants in a violent liberation struggle' (Noguez 1977: 201).[8] However, some of the films did use their 'naturalism' as a vehicle for contestatory politics, in general adapting images to message by means, at best, of innovatory editing; at worst, of long filmed discussions. Michel Drach's *Elise ou la vraie vie* (1970), Marin Karmitz's *Camarades* (1969), Jacques Doillon's *Les Doigts dans la tête* (1974) and Gérard Guérin's *Lo Païs* (1973) illustrate this attempt to adapt style to a directly political purpose in various ways. The last three are regularly included in lists of relevant films in articles about this new tendency in the French cinema: and if *Elise* is not, the most likely reason is its literary origin, since in terms of style and the skeleton of the story it is clearly within the genre and indeed an important precursor of it. All these films achieve a fair degree of success in using images, narrative, references and even a degree of oneiric fantasy in order to construct an analytical picture of their characters' plight, while other examples linked to them, such as René Gilson's *On n'arrête pas le printemps* (1971) – interesting as an analysis of the *social* impact of 1968 on the education system – show less visual imagination and remained marginal to the consciences of most of France's filmgoers, even those attuned to the new demand for serious analysis of the state of the country. All these films show a tendency to rely on an image based on the conventions of documentary, with little elaboration, despite Doillon's inclusion by *Télérama* in its second category. Drach and Guérin adopt these conventions without insistence, producing a cinema where the technique is subordinate to the activities and the words of the protagonists; Doillon, more sensitive to the poetic possibilities of cinematography and editing but voluntarily restricted in his visual scope by the co-ordinates of his narrative, produces an intimate and discreetly sophisticated portrait of a

---

[8] 'Il y a entre les deux situations tout ce qui sépare des cinéastes opérant un certain *rafraîchissement* esthétique dans le cinéma sclérosé d'un pays à gouvernement réactionnaire et des cinéastes témoins, sympathisants et parfois acteurs d'une violente lutte de libération.' Noguez' emphasis. *Télérama* made the same comparison, and arrived at the same preference, on less political grounds.

group interacting. Karmitz' approach is more militant; his documentary style is characterised by sharp editing and changes of register, dissociation of sound-track and image, quotation, and long takes where the audience is obliged to submit to a reality which becomes aggressive by its sheer persistence. In other words, Karmitz, working under the direct influence of the Godardian collages of the 1960s, adopts televisual 'naturalist' conventions and manipulates them to produce a formalist construction.

To the extent that these films adopted and adapted the style, image-quality and ideals of *cinéma direct*, they established themselves in audience minds as linked to the films of the post-'68 parallel circuit, which for many was an ideal. However, it was the directors whose films betrayed cinematic ambition who were destined to have the most impact on the decade's audiences, and to produce a small but significant movement which acted as a relay to the Nouvelle Vague and kept a tradition of small-scale, naturalistic cinema alive during the 1980s. Pialat, Doillon and Eustache all became major names, bearers of a 'tradition' of artistic realism in French film-making.

A definition of the movement's 'naturalism', however, is difficult to establish with any certainty. For *Télérama* the films are 'naturalistic' insofar as they present a recognisable France, they contain 'no hint of the theatre' (Tallenay 1974: 66) and 'the director refuses all virtuosity in filming or in the image which might draw attention to the technique instead of making it transparent' (Tallenay 1974: 67).[9] For an influential sector of the avant-garde, both these factors were the very antithesis of what was regarded as politically effective and desirable. Naturalism is quite different from the sophisticated version of 'realism' put forward by Comolli and his team at *Cahiers du cinéma*, which demanded that the reality of the film/signifier should be taken into account by the spectator at the same time as that of the supposed reality signified.

But the label 'new naturalism' was of course imposed from outside, and the directors concerned were less than enthusiastic to embrace it, by and large with justification. If the films we have selected include many of the characteristics attributed to 'naturalism', it should not be assumed that all of them wished to

[9] 'le réalisateur refuse les virtuosités de prise de vue ou de photo qui attire l'attention sur la technique au lieu de la rendre transparente'.

'recreate reality'. *Lo Païs*, which *Télérama* cites as a perfect example of the genre, makes use of a wide variety of styles; some sequences are a long way from 'transparent' naturalism, and Guérin declared himself dissatisfied with the category, while Doillon, as we have already said, did not recognise his highly constructed style as in any sense 'naturalist'. Nonetheless, the designation proved durable and the films it was used to describe certainly do possess a visible genre identity, traceable even to those, such as *Camarades*, which were never listed with naturalist films.[10] Other films, such as René Allio's *Pierre et Paul* and much of Tanner's work, have some affinities with the genre although far outstripping it in complexity, while yet others, where 'naturalist' techniques serve a Utopian purpose, form a distinct sub-group which will be discussed in the next chapter.

This chapter will look at some films of the early 1970s which retain a consciously politico-social approach to their protagonists' problems, which conform to the broad description of 'new naturalism' in terms of narrative and protagonist, and which to a greater or lesser extent make use of documentary or *cinéma-vérité* conventions in *mise-en-scène* and cinematography.

Marin Karmitz' efforts to provide a genuinely worker-oriented cinema which could attract a commercial audience led to two films in the direct aftermath of 1968. Karmitz aimed to take a step towards the ideal cinema of the future which would deal with workers' lives and be controlled – preferably made – by those who were its subjects, while avoiding the pitfalls of 'militant' production; and in that ambition he was a pure product of the ideals of the Etats-Généraux. *Camarades*, in 1969, was his first move in this direction, still structured as fiction and employing professional actors, although the fiction slips away in the course

[10] The films cited by *Télérama* in the four articles are: *Lo Païs* (Gérard Guérin, 1973), *Charlie et ses deux nénettes* (Joël Séria, 1973), *Erica Minor* (Bertrand van Effenterre, 1974), *Les Doigts dans la tête* (Jacques Doillon, 1974), *La Coupe à dix francs* (Philippe Condroyer, 1975), *Mes petites amoureuses* (Jean Eustache, 1974), *On n'arrête pas le printemps* (René Gilson, 1971), *La Gueule ouverte* (Maurice Pialat, 1974), *La Maman et la putain* (Jean Eustache, 1973), *Du côté d'Orouet* (Jacques Rozier, 1973). Other articles leave the field vague, or restrict it to one or two films while hinting at an unspecified number of others unmentioned. *Cahiers du cinéma* discusses only *Les Doigts dans la tête* and *La Coupe à dix francs*, and implicates in passing *Rude journée pour la reine* (René Allio, 1973) and *Il pleut toujours où c'est mouillé* (Jean-Daniel Simon, 1975).

of the film and the protagonists disappear into the 'mass'. *Coup pour coup*, three years later, was a 'documentary fiction'. The strike which it recounts is in fact a reconstruction, but the cast, in large part working women and not actresses, had in some cases been involved in similar events. The amount of self-determination given to the workers/actors in *Coup pour coup* was much vaunted, and much challenged by the not inconsiderable ranks of opponents of the film (*Image et son* for example attacked it fiercely). The controversy surrounding *Coup pour coup* put a temporary end to Karmitz' activity as a director, and he turned his energies fully to the cinema/arts centre which he had recently opened in the Bastille area as a showcase for the best of radical cinema made in France and imported from abroad – especially Latin America – and as a site for political and artistic discussions. The success of this independent distribution venture, which eventually became the production/distribution company MK2, decided Karmitz' future career and has had a decisive influence on independent French cinema to the present day.

In 1968 Karmitz had been one of the instigators of the most radical project for a cinema of the future to emerge from the discussion groups of the so-called *Etats-Généraux du cinéma*. A former pupil of IDHEC, he had taken an interest in politics prior to 1968 but had not allowed this interest to inflect his earliest film-work. His first feature-length film, *Sept jours ailleurs*, was actually released in 1968. An attack on the materialist society, it bore a considerable resemblance to René Allio's *Pierre et Paul* in both content and theme: so much so indeed that Karmitz changed his ending after the appearance of Allio's film. From his post-68 viewpoint, Karmitz considered himself to have been 'still cut off from reality' when he made *Sept jours ailleurs*, but the film is already imbued not only with student pugnaciousness, but also with a preoccupation with unconventional form and with a degree of actors' autonomy. The attack on materialism is presented through the medium of spectacle (a ballet troupe), and Karmitz' adoption of improvisation leads to the film's conception as a series of separate 'scenes'. Karmitz' two subsequent films retain memories of this element of improvisation, although it was subordinated to other considerations and *Camarades* superficially at least seems much more related to the Nouveau Naturel which was practically defined by being a long way from theatre in all its forms.

In *Camarades* Marin Karmitz began to transfer to the screen his perceptions of the significance of 1968 for the cinema. Although he was not long satisfied with it, it is also an exemplary product of the post-'68 debates, since it represents an essay in the fusion of the politico-militant tendency which had grown out of the Etats-Généraux with the small-scale auteur cinema which was the legacy of the Nouvelle Vague, and it was from that fusion that 'New Naturalism' developed. *Camarades,* however, also contains signs of a wish to experiment with the form, and, while the early scenes of the film conform quite closely to the tenets of 'natural-ism', its cinematic expression later becomes highly individual and often very far removed from reality.

Camarades is in fact a film in two parts, divided, almost too neatly, by an 'intermission' in the shape of a long passage from Solanas' *La Hora de los hornos,* an exemplary political docu-mentary much admired by the young radicals of post-68 France, and a highlight of Karmitz' own programming. *Camarades* freely, indeed proudly, acknowledges its debt to Solanas. The first part is primarily fiction. The protagonist, Yann, lives in St-Nazaire but refuses a traditional future in shipyard work. His 'contrariness' leads to poor relations with his father, and even his sympathetic girlfriend is worried at the spectre of unemployment. He works for a while in the 'new' trade of market researcher, a shorthand for the consumer society his expectations draw him to; and then, disillusioned but not despairing, he decides to try his luck in Paris. But work in Paris is in very short supply, and when a chance encounter in a launderette leads to an offer of employment in a factory, Yann is in no position to refuse. Conditions there are unbearable, and after a while he gets into trouble, is laid off for two days, and comes into contact with a group of political activists in the workplace.

Yann is the typical Nouveau Naturel protagonist: young, working-class but not yet working, and a provincial just arrived in the big city. Until Yann meets the activists (more than halfway through the film) Karmitz' focus is entirely personal. Although there are few close-ups and many interruptions to the smooth flow of the story, so that we are kept at a certain distance from Yann and his troubles, he is the unwavering centre of the narra-tive, sympathetic and entirely comprehensible. By the end of the first part the story seems about to set up a sentimental tangle between Yann's girlfriend in St-Nazaire and the attractive young woman he has encountered in Paris. Karmitz plays with visual stimuli to remind the audience that behind all this there is politics: apart from the title itself, the colour red is dominant in the credit sequence, and the film opens with a quasi-documentary series of shots of the shipyard, accompanied by a song on the soundtrack. Throughout the first part of the film, indeed, non-diegetic songs are frequent; they are sometimes love-songs, but more often provide ironic social comment. But although once we have begun to get involved in Yann's life we relate the songs to him, the words of (mild) protest are not directly associated with him, any more than the apparently political title seems appropriate to his view of life; and while the rapid montage of Yann's market research interviews provides the audience with a very striking illustration of the contrast between the living conditions of the various subjects and the world of St-Nazaire, there is no hint that this is Yann's observation which we are sharing. In the first series of interviews even his presence is not clear, and the relevance of the sequence to the still rather sketchy 'story' is not immediately obvious, and while later sequences are clearly narratively justified, our experience of them still does not coincide with Yann's.

Thus in the first part of the film the personal story predominates, and socio-political comment appears extraneous to it, and even sometimes as an interruption of it. Karmitz uses inserted sequences in a different idiom – documentary or the incipient comedy of fast montage – to place Yann 'in context'; they provide some explanation to us – an explanation not channelled through Yann – of the world which he is at this point rejecting, while at the same time they keep the audience at some remove from Yann, so that although we are drawn into the film through sympathy with him and interest in his fate, absolute identification is not encouraged.

The change of tone is initiated with the first sequences in the factory, where, as we observe (frequently from a slightly high angle which cannot be Yann's viewpoint, in a series of erratic shots which jump from one procedure to another or meander among the protagonists) the various tests which pass for medical examinations on the queue waiting for work, Yann vanishes from the image. Karmitz allows image and sound to become disconnected, so that the sound-track sometimes relates to the previous shot or to the following one, a procedure which here contributes to a sense of haste and indifference. There is a sequence in the machine room of the factory, which becomes a recurrent motif in the second half of the film. Shots of machines and of men are almost undifferentiated. The human element is fragmented, the movement of the production-line is emphasised. There is little light in the image, and in some cases it is hard to say just what is represented; the camera rests for long periods on slowly moving machinery, the vertical movement of which (apparently due to the camera angle) is unexpected, so that its identity is problematic, and the effect menacing. The sound-track meanwhile delivers the full force of the factory noise. In contrast to the scenes on the production line in Drach's *Elise ou la vraie vie* (1969), much praised for its realism and an important precursor of political naturalism, the sound here is hardly even reduced; Karmitz makes no concessions at all. The result rapidly approaches the unbearable. A description given by a former factory worker in a previous dialogue ('there's the noise, you see … I wasn't myself any more, I was a machine') makes it easier for the audience to relate their own temporary discomfort to the impossible factory conditions, but the scene is only tenuously diegetic. The spectators become conscious of themselves *in relation to* the conditions described (if it is so unpleasant for a few minutes in a comfortable cinema, the thought of unlimited exposure to the same noise in the midst of physical discomfort is hellish), without, yet, relating this consciousness clearly to the narrative or to Yann. After a brief respite, corresponding to a break, the sequence recurs, with some of the same shots replicated, but this time Yann is recognisable among the anonymous human figures. A few more intercalated shots, and it returns yet again, again repeating certain images so that we seem to have been watching a continuous sequence with interruptions.

There follows Yann's laying-off and his encounter with the factory activists, who begin his political education with conversations taking place under portraits of Marx and Lenin; then, without warning, the film becomes both black-and-white and obviously South American, with no mark in the text of the transition to quotation. The sequence from Solanas' film that Karmitz chooses to quote is concerned with the occupation of factories, and incorporates a sequence on the factory floor which reveals the 'source' of the recent sequences and also establishes that Argentina and France are not so dissimilar. It is only after the film comes to an end that the camera withdraws and a sudden light reveals an audience of workers in the back room of a factory. They discuss the methods in the film they have just been watching, and Karmitz thus reveals his own interest in the reception of cinema – especially radical cinema. Screenings in factories were an ideal favoured by the proponents of underground political cinema in the wake of 1968, obviously bearing an assumption that the film was of direct and immediate practical relevance to its audience. Karmitz, at the same time as he was making *Camarades*, was experimenting with this form of audience involvement in a more mainstream context, with some success, and it seems likely that *Camarades* was conceived with this sort of immediate response in mind. The film-within-a-film, then, diverges from a 'naturalist' ideal by suggesting to the audience that they receive the film that they are watching in a similar way – in other words, by reminding them of their position as audience in the cinema, with the ability, even perhaps the responsibility, to reflect on what they see and relate it, dispassionately, to themselves.

From this moment on the film abandons the personal story, although Yann is still the central protagonist, followed at work and outside it, walking with a girl or writing in his room. He has become entirely absorbed by, and into, his own political education and the organisation of which he gradually becomes a part. His conversation with the girl is about politics; shots of him in his room are intercut with scenes on the *chantiers*, while the soundtrack reads, in voice-over, extracts from Karl Marx. Subsequently Yann disappears altogether; we see elements of the more mundane work of the factory revolutionaries (the concoction of a bilingual tract in French and Spanish); then the film returns to the production line, in the most abstract and menacing of all the versions of this scene, a seemingly interminable tracking-shot down the semi-illuminated conveyor-belt, accompanied on the sound-track for a while by a song which protests against the inhumanity of the image. The final sequences chronicle the outburst and spread of workers' movements, first in St-Nazaire, then in Renault: shots of demonstrations and walk-outs alternate with newspaper headlines, and the whole culminates with a massive demonstration in the streets of St-Nazaire.

The individual protagonist has thus undergone the process of absorption into the 'mass' of workers that at the start of the film he had wished to avoid; it is, however, an absorption into a movement for change. The film style has changed also: unspectacular filmed fiction predominates at the beginning, but documentary techniques and even real documentary footage become progressively more important, a change which makes the gradual effacement of the fiction less shocking to the audience. Yann's language also changes, and as he is integrated into the undifferentiated, and inhuman, world of the production line, he also becomes a factor, among others, in a mass movement gathering against that same dehumanising environment. The method is successful to the extent that we do not feel that the narrative has been left unresolved. In scenes where Yann is not visibly present, the relevance of the action to his situation is clear, and an 'ending' (a return to St-Nazaire and the shipyards, but as an activist rather than simply a cog in the machine) can be assumed. We accept that Yann's effacement corresponds to his commitment to a mass movement which is more significant than the personal story not only to the film-maker but also to Yann himself. In any case the resolution in politics will also be a personal dénouement. Nonetheless the film leaves an overall impression of incoherence and some immaturity. The early part employs not only individual protagonists, but actors who are recognisable (Juliet Berto); we accept the film as a fiction while the latter part appears to be documentary; and even though the narrative is closed in an impeccably revolutionary way (and on a high note; the final sequences are extremely dynamic) it is almost as if it ends a different film. Elements of continuity, such as the sequences in the shipyards and the song on the soundtrack (performed by Jeanne Moreau) do exist, but in the first part of the film they are of small importance, apparently no more than introductory sequences. Karmitz was well aware that the two languages of the film had not integrated as well as might have been hoped: he said in 1972, 'the film was constantly hesitating between two styles, two languages' (Karmitz 1972: 5).[11]

   Camarades is an intelligent experiment in the filmic presentation of a political education, conceived with the aim of encouraging

---

[11] 'le film hésitait constamment entre deux styles, deux langages'.

the audience to share Yann's developing consciousness and even (in sequences such as the montage of research interviews) to forestall it, the better to appreciate the necessity of the action which he finally embraces. It is clearly intended to be didactic, and is interesting in that it uses some of the characteristics of 'naturalism' in order to arrive at what is essentially a call to revolution. It is also interesting that the naturalist style proved unsatisfactory as an expression of Karmitz' brand of political engagement, to the extent that Yann's political progress is marked by its gradual abandonment. *Camarades* is in fact a rejection of the very concept of 'political naturalism' and seeks to be a truly radical fiction film. After the making of *Coup pour coup*, Karmitz was very severe indeed on his earlier film, for example con-demning the politics which are 'brought in from outside through texts, phrases and stereotypes'. He perhaps forgets that this exteriority allows the audience to read these elements as a separate commentary on Yann's situation, but it is certainly true that the film's enthusiasm for political organisation is such that it sometimes ignores the decisions and choices essential to the process of developing and acting upon conviction, and thus relegates its budding activist to the status of mechanical part albeit in a revolutionary machine. Less justifiably, Karmitz also subsequently condemned the attention which he and his team paid to style as opposed to content in *Camarades* (Karmitz 1972: 5), although he has succeeded in using the changes of style in order to underline the content of his politics in a quite interesting way. The progress in Yann's perception of his world is paralleled by a change in the perception of the camera. The moments most obviously stylised, such as the frenetic market-research sequence and the grim and enigmatic shots of the production line, also use their language with imaginative force to add to the analytical significance of the content. The frenzied pace of questions put to a series of women regarding their habits of consumption is so great that sound and image become detached, answers are attri-buted to the 'wrong' woman, and we perceive both researcher and interviewer as outpaced by what is expected of them, while the abstract inhumanity of the factory floor is portrayed with real power.

The experiment of *Coup pour coup*, which attracted more critical attention than *Camarades*, was significant as a crossover between ideals most in evidence in the parallel sector and mainstream production and distribution. The manner of its making justified close attention from everyone eager to detect results springing from the Etats-Généraux; in order to make this fiction film about a strike in a clothing factory, Karmitz and his team prepared the bare bones of a scenario, then enriched it first through interviews with a group of striking women, then through active participation in a (different) action, where they filmed the strike as it progressed, on video, and re-projected it for the participants every evening. When the film itself was shot, some of those filmed at this stage in the elaboration of the project took part as actresses; the workers in the film were all played by non-professionals.

The method of preparation went some way towards fulfilling the aim of making a film which was a truly co-operative effort between factory workers and film professionals, and *Coup pour coup* therefore could (and did) claim to provide a wholly authentic account of how a strike is experienced by those taking part, and to put real people on screen in a fictional context.[12] This was fiercely contested at the time; in particular the film's opposition to the mainstream unions, entirely consistent with contemporary radical *ideas*, was still open to criticism when presented as an authentic picture of actual conditions. *Revue du cinéma*, which disliked the film, recorded two interesting facts; firstly that at least some of the women[13] who had come to the film with strike experience had gained it in collaboration with Union representatives, and secondly that when the film was projected to its participants and their colleagues, it was accepted immediately: 'This film is our film … There should be others filmed this way.' The film and its reception thus bring to light an interesting contradiction. On the subject of the *syndicalistes* the film is not realist (Karmitz intended caricature), but it was accepted as being so. Like *Camarades*, but to a more extreme extent, the film is a combination of carefully planned 'naturalism' and obvious artificiality, the latter reflecting the real, but also rapidly mythologised,

---

[12] Jill Forbes has made a very interesting comparison of the representation of the factory workers in this film and in *Tout va bien*, to which it has been much compared, since both came out in the same year and there was a strong coincidence of themes. See Forbes 1992: 30–1.

[13] The magazine does not say what proportion it spoke to, naturally.

hostility of the CGT to spontaneous action in the wake of May. The reaction is probably a clear indication of the limits of naturalism: perhaps no one perceives themselves and those with whom they are in contact wholly naturalistically, and certainly one wants to see reflection on the screen of attitudes to reality as well as its outer appearance.

Coup pour coup was distributed in cinemas, but also semi-underground, and it had reasonable box-office; Karmitz recorded 45,000 entries in six months of commercial distribution and nearly 80,000 during the full season of militant screenings across France (Karmitz 1973: 16) Both *Camarades* and *Coup pour coup* were designed for two alternative markets, in fact. This was not a unique phenomenon in the 1970s; several low-budget, low-profile movies with social themes reached two audiences in this way.

Drach's *Elise ou la vraie vie*, made in 1970, was principally noted as an attempt to touch directly on the taboo subject of the Algerian war and particularly on its effects in France. An adaptation of Claire Etcherelli's 1967 novel, it was thus at two removes from a 'naturalistic' portrayal of contemporary France, and Drach himself referred to it at times as a historical film. Nonetheless it has much in common with the contemporary naturalism which was soon to rise to prominence. *Mise-en-scène* and cinematography are very understated, the image is grainy, much of the action takes place in confined and unglamorous spaces and is dependent on undramatic mid-shots of the main characters. Those characters represent the early appearance in (relatively) 'mainstream' cinema of sectors of French society truly marginalised by the cinematic system. Elise is not only young and working-class but also a woman; Arezki and his friends represent the immigrant workforce whose presence would not be given any true prominence until, in the mid-1980s, Mehdi Charef began the slow process of developing a second-generation immigrant cinema. The beginning of *Elise* establishes several narrative elements which could reasonably be considered 'typical' of the political tendency in New Naturalism. Elise is a young provincial girl moving to Paris in search of work. Her first experience of the capital is centred around the shabby and exiguous living-spaces which young people in her position were condemned to and the workplace environment to which she is introduced, in considerable detail. Although the sequences on the car assembly line where she works are not constructed as impersonally as Karmitz' factory floor in *Camarades*, there is nonetheless a genuine attempt to achieve a sense of documentary footage of the industrial process. Above all, there is nothing which obviously differentiates this factory or these shabby flats and cafés of 1960–61 from those of the early 1970s: if in terms of its events *Elise* is a historical film, in terms of its appearance it is still contemporary with its making. That documentary roughness, in fact, contributes to the immediacy of its condemnation of the brutal treatment of the Algerian population in 1961.

In the course of the film Elise even undergoes a process of political education which includes a direct critique of conventional union politics, as they are represented by her brother Lucien. Lucien, although politically aware and an animator of union meetings, discredits himself by his lack of solidarity with the North African workforce, which even takes the form of direct racism when he is obliged to accept his sister's relationship with an Algerian. All these incidents, of course, are no more than filmic transpositions of the events of a successful novel, but the style in which Drach films is not one which enjoyed much popularity prior to 1968, and the visual insistence on workplace and rundown areas, on the struggle of the young, anonymous and marginal faced with the brutal tactics of the police and their violent reaction to the presence of the 'undesirable' on the streets of Paris, and on political discovery are all elements which would seem both familiar and directly relevant to the audience of 1970. The decision to use unknown actors for the main characters also contributes to identifying the film as a precursor of the naturalist genre, dealing in fact with a subject more explosive than any which the non-militant young directors associated with the current were to approach, a subject which perhaps could only achieve a presence on cinema screens thanks to its literary origins and apparent distance in time.

Made a year after *Coup pour coup* and thus three years after *Camarades*, Gérard Guérin's *Lo Païs*, considered one of the representative films of 'new naturalism', repeats much of the narrative structure of *Camarades*: a young provincial protagonist's awakening to political consciousness in the course of exploitative work in the capital, followed by his return home and active involvement in social protest in an environment the contradictions of which he had never formerly observed. Like *Camarades,* its basically 'naturalist' *mise-en-scène* is varied by cinematographically inventive episodes, and while it is less deeply committed to the primacy of the political and therefore perhaps less representative of the most radical sensibility of the time, it provides a coherent example of the integration of a real commitment to activism with a narrative dependent on personal experience. The principal actor, Olivier Bousquet, provides a link with other films by the new generation of young directors, notably with Jacques Doillon's *Les Doigts dans la tête,* and the hand-held camera and deliberately non-picturesque shots which remain close (but not too close) to the protagonists, together with the modest locations and the age and occupation of the central character, led *Lo Païs* to be seen as a typical example of the new style.

In the pre-credit sequence, the protagonist, Gaston, leaves his village in the Massif Central to come to Paris in search of work; the film observes a number of his experiences and encounters in the capital, as he undertakes a series of different menial jobs. We see him first distributing leaflets among a queue of the unemployed waiting for the first editions of the morning newspaper; subsequently he works behind the counter in a cafeteria, and finally as a billsticker (shades of de Sica ...). In the course of the latter job he encounters a degree of industrial conflict, with his fellow-workers unhappy both with conditions and with the role of the CGT, which they accuse of making no effort to support them and of rigging the preparations for the election of delegates. Gaston is accused of unsatisfactory work because he is afraid to climb a long ladder in a high wind, so that the discussion about conditions relates directly to his experience. He is further taken in hand by two older colleagues, whose stories help both Gaston and the audience to extend their appreciation of the individual case and connect it with others, as well as to connect the 'New Left' of this film firmly to the experiences of the previous generation.

Parallel to these experiences at work, Gaston comes into contact with a group of Bretons and with two Yugoslavian immigrants, through contact with whom he, and we, observe various negotiations between the place and language of origin and the demands of the Parisian present. The Breton group represents at once celebration of a provincial culture and analysis of the particular problems which have made life in Brittany impossible, the Yugoslavians illustrate the different configurations of isolation brought about by, in one case, retreat from the surrounding incomprehensible culture, in the other by total commitment to a new place and the loss of all means of communication with family and friends from the past. These encounters spur him to make an effort to keep contact with his own origins, for example by not losing his accent, and offer a living example of the dangers of losing such contact. His Yugoslavian girlfriend's inability to write to her father, for example, startles him although he has himself been in Paris over two years – as she has – and there is little indication that he has made contact with his family during that time. In the last sequences of the film, he returns to the village, ostensibly for an eight-day holiday, and finds it occupied with demonstrations and protests against the military installation at Larzac; and in the last shot, he is setting off up a country road, armed with a gluepot and a sheaf of posters for the campaign.

This outline of the plot indicates that the film gives considerable importance to the main character's awareness of social problems, and also that it is concerned with the issue of language. Gaston's coming of age involves an awakening to the politico-social implications of his own experience. At first he is only concerned with his individual requirements, be they to find a job, a girlfriend or a flat of his own. As a result of his experiences he gradually identifies himself as a worker and as a *méridional* and finally, it is implied, decides to abandon Paris in order to employ the 'skill' he has learnt there in the Aveyron where he was brought up, and where, the final sequence suggests, he belongs and feels happy. The stages of his political education are abundantly talked through: the long discussion which follows his meeting with the Bretons could convincingly be presented as documentary footage on the subject. The directly personal element is, as in *Camarades* although less radically, subordinate to the social apprenticeship; Gaston's brief relationships are mainly significant for the light they throw on wider issues, and especially on alienation and the difficulty of communication. His encounters with the schoolgirl Mireille, whom he meets at a dance, and with the Yugoslavian are integrated into a personal narrative of the most simple kind; he wants a girlfriend, fails to detach Mireille from her family, spends a night with the Yugoslavian who then disappears from the film.

They have greater significance than this suggests, but only in relation to Gaston's awareness of himself; Mireille, more socially vulnerable even than he, serves as a forceful illustration of the difficulties facing young people just embarking on an active working life, but her subsequent fate does not seem to concern Guérin. The Yugoslavian girl's attitude to her origins serves to define Gaston's sense of his roots.

The majority of the film, including these two principal personal relationships, is 'naturalistic' in presentation. Emphasis is on the characters' conversation, and the camera remains at close-up or medium-shot distances, following their movements rather jerkily as they progress through unassuming streets or circulate in Gaston's minuscule flat. Two other 'personal' episodes represent interludes which open the film to other contemporary approaches to cinema. The encounter with the model who appears on Gaston's posters is filmed in a highly stylised way reminiscent of pre-'68 Godard. The woman invites him to her home, and recounts her life more to the camera than to Gaston, against a blank wall, smiling mechanically. Later she displays to a bemused Gaston her ability to strike twenty different naked publicity poses semi-automatically under the curt direction of her husband/manager. Other speakers, unconnected with the narrative and not present in the flat, intervene as she tells her story; one is identified, in a subtitle, as Pierre Giraudy. This collage is evidently directed at the audience and not at Gaston. It establishes a structured picture of progressive and dehumanising exploitation, dissociated from the rest of the film; nonetheless, like Gaston's other, more realistic encounters, it provides a yardstick for character and audience to measure their situations against. There is a stylistic logic in representing this apparently wealthy and glamorous woman through a different cinematic form, more self-conscious and relatable to 'art cinema' as it was understood in the 1960s: the episode could also be read as a fantasy sequence, in which the Godardian language is revealed as the appropriate visual idiom for an imaginary meeting with a star of consumerism.

The last encounter, uncharacteristically ambiguous, with a mysterious young woman with a fox on a lead who joins Gaston, the Bretons and Gaston's colleague in a café, seems to weaken the film, however; its idiom and its intentions are too unclear. This woman's position is never explained: another fantasy, couched in faintly Buñuelian terms, a glamorous eccentric, a prostitute? She leaves with Gaston's older colleague to Gaston's evident regret, and his return home, which follows closely, is thereby made ambiguous. If it is partly an admission of defeat because he cannot get a girl, then other well-established and more consequent motives are devalued. At most the episode, which certainly has its own quirky poetry, conveys his growing frustration with his almost exclusively passive role, and the extent to which Paris and its ways remain incomprehensible to him – he has more in common with the fox than with its owner.

The film's episodic narrative structure adds to the sense that Gaston's progress is a personal journey; each encounter changes his, and our, perception of his own exemplary situation by a process of comparison. However, it also allows Guérin to approach a surprising variety of issues, integrating them through their various applications to one main character. The problems of rural Aveyron are established in the audience's mind even before the credit sequence; thus we are programmed to assume that they are the main theme of the film, but many other questions arise before the final sequences return to Aveyron and the regional application of Parisian politics.

In all the approaches to these questions, Gaston is scarcely an active participant; his principal role is to listen and in several episodes he is effectively a second audience, acting as a bridge between the 'real' audience and the rest of the film. *Lo Païs* is an account of a *prise de conscience* in the tradition of left-wing narrative from Soviet Russia onwards, the adaptation of a much older tradition of a picaresque apprenticeship in life. The young country boy interested only in finding work and excitement in the city is introduced first to other young people like himself, his fellow-unemployed and the shy schoolgirl Mireille, and he and we become aware of the general problems of being young, inexperienced and without connections. His dealings with an intolerant foreman and a showdown which he witnesses between his colleagues and the Union representatives introduce the issue of solidarity among those in a similar position, and also the potential which it holds for becoming a more active force for change. A series of discussions with other workers allow him, and us, to put his experience in the context of others', always recounted, never shown, but with a certain sympathetic interest for the tellers which the camera transmits to the audience as if through Gaston's increasingly aware gaze.

At the same time, through the Bretons and the Yugoslavians, he is becoming aware of himself as an 'internal immigrant'. It is eventually a regional issue that will move him from passivity to action, but it is made clear that the problems faced by the 'immigrants' are work-related. The very necessity of moving, often reluctantly, to Paris is an economic one, and the Bretons are effusive about the impossible working conditions in Rennes or Nantes. The meal and political discussion with the Bretons, filmed in semi-documentary style, is in fact central to the film. As the camera passes from face to face the various participants contribute their particular comment on the Breton situation; the whole sequence, rounded off with a song, could be an extract from an underground film by some regional collective to which Gaston is the audience, not directly concerned nor directly contributing yet able to apply what he hears to his own situation. Thus he is introduced to the concept of collective action based upon the region through a group of people with *different* concerns to his own, but the audience is already primed to make the link with the Aveyron of the pre-credit sequence, as we assume that Gaston himself is making it.

Subsequent episodes reinforce or adapt his response, always in the direction of identification with the workers' and the regional causes, for example when his older colleague recounts how he was obliged to leave his native Pyrenees, and how his politicisation decreased as a result of having to survive in Paris during the war. The progress of Gaston's experience leads him more and more to see Paris as a source of alienation. The model, driven to success in the city, has allowed herself to be manipulated into a pure object, a 'real mechanical doll', and even Gaston is implicated in that process since he has innocently taken a job pasting her image on the city billboards. Her erotic posturing at their meeting is not even provocative, since there is no communication between performer and audience.

Gaston's colleague sees his own father, who had remained in the Pyrenees fighting Spanish fascism, as a hero-figure (recalling the struggles of the left's heroic past), but he has little faith in his own capacity for action. He tells Gaston: 'If you do what the kids did in '68, I'm with you.' In that sentence, it seems that the quiet and hitherto passive Gaston is being asked to create a revolution on his own, but '68 is twice relegated to irrelevance. On the one hand, it is as irretrievably in the past as the Occupation which the older man has just evoked, with no sign that such a movement still exists in Paris; on the other, it was created by 'kids' – although, it is implied, Gaston too has the potential to revive such action simply because *he* is 'a kid'. But Gaston is alone between a number of different small groups who have each taken charge of part of his experience. The best he can apparently hope for is solidarity between sympathetic individuals, and even there he will encounter passivity born of disillusion; the older man is resigned to his compromises.

The film is thus pessimistic regarding the results of 1968. It has made no difference to the lives of Gaston's colleagues in Paris, while life there has led them into numerous compromises which betray their pre-'68 social ideals. On the other hand, for Gaston the implication seems to be that the best hope for social progress lies now in regional solidarity rather than a Paris-based protest, although within that regional solidarity lie questions of class, economics and power. Two issues – the quality of working life, prominent in 1968, and the importance of regional survival, an issue renewed and re-formulated by the general demand for *prise de parole* in the aftermath of the events – are here linked, and Gaston learns both simultaneously, but in a context which discounts any achievements of four years previously in favour, if anything, of an older tradition of activism – linked to the Spanish Civil War – and of an earlier tradition of activist cinema, that of the Italian neo-realists whose particular concerns *Lo Païs* recalls.

Gradually, however, Gaston moves from a passive to an active role. In the café with the Bretons, he merely listens, but the effect of his reflection on that conversation is that he gives up trying to lose his accent. When the Union is shouted down, he is still a passive listener, but afterwards he actively seeks out one of the participants and buys him a drink in order to talk to him further. His increased understanding of the difficult situation he finds himself in is both dependent on a more active involvement, and as it develops implies it. His attitude is contrasted with that of his girlfriend, who takes little interest either in her own colleagues or in what he tells her about his. Her lack of curiosity is linked to her total severance from her roots and so an interest in one's own origins is presented as indissolubly linked to an interest in present surroundings.

By the time Gaston returns home he is well-prepared to translate what he has learnt into action, and he does so effectively. His conversation with the older man has taught him (perhaps unfairly, but it has a positive effect) that there is little to be hoped for from the older generation, even its most radical representatives – another clear sign of the times. The nature of the action which Gaston chooses is less important than the fact that he chooses it; we learn very little in the film about the Larzac issue. What is important is to see Gaston participating in demonstrations, carrying posters as the Bretons were doing when he first encountered them. The audience understands that this is 'his' fight, with which he identifies, but Guérin avoids any implication that it is the only action which is worthwhile; so that the film potentially leaves it up to the audience, if they have followed Gaston's development, to find the action which relates most directly to them.

Gaston's development, then, is a political education couched, more or less, in a 'naturalist' idiom but still aspiring to implicate the audience. Precisely because he is so passive for the majority of the film, we follow his education with him, hearing and seeing what he hears and sees. There is little indication of what conclusions he has drawn, except for his growing tendency to solicit encounters which promise some enlightenment rather than simply to talk to whoever talks to him. As a result the audience is, apparently, free to analyse events; although the conclusion that some form of action is a necessity is practically imposed. The film is a singularly successful adaptation of the new narrative to a didactic function; the central character is likeable and amusing and there is never any sense that the message is being forced. It embodies an ideal of cultural action both entertaining and exemplary, well understood by the activists of 1968. It also, of course, raises questions regarding the possession of language and the means of communication. Gaston has very little chance of getting his voice heard in Paris, he is too young, too anonymous, and, symbolically, speaks a 'different language'. He believes that in order to attain a voice he has to learn the Parisian language (lose his accent); in the course of the film, he gradually learns the value of retaining his own 'language'. Those who have given up their origins have mostly remained unheard. The model can no longer communicate even through eroticism, Gaston's colleague no longer tries to make his voice heard other than to individuals, while his girlfriend has paid for her ambition to succeed by the inability to communicate any more with her own family and an apparent disinterest in talking to anyone else. When Gaston returns to his village, he seems to check that he can still success-fully communicate with his own people, both in conversation and through gestures – his exuberant participation in the farm-work is proof that he is still at home in his home.

The film also embodies the idea that, in order to attain 'la parole' (in the sense of a discourse that is listened to), the impor-tant factor is number and solidarity, which can make a hitherto unfamiliar language audible. The Breton group can project their identity because there are several of them in agreement, not because they have accepted to change what they say.[14] When all the work-force unite to criticise the Union representative, the latter is stripped of his legitimacy and obliged to defend himself. There are at least two occasions in the film where the authori-tative voice of one individual is discredited by the combined voices of those who, individually, have little influence. Thus the move from the individual to the collective is a central issue in *Lo País* as in *Camarades*, but Gaston is depicted not as losing his identity in the group but as sharing it, a more powerful approach.

Lo País' very structured organisation and reference to parti-cular issues are in fact traits which it shares with many militant fictions from the parallel circuit, and so, like *Camarades*, it illustrates the influence of this cinema on the new generation of young commercial film-makers. However, the launch of the central character into action is the result of a gradual process, and it is that process which the film chronicles, not the action, allowing the personal to take priority over the political. Interesting also is that Gaston's increasing militancy brings with it a *return* to the social order, from which he was excluded in Paris, and not, as in *Camarades*, absorption into an alternative, revolutionary society. When Gaston commits himself to action, he is not going against society or breaking with tradition, but rejoining a traditional

---

[14] Admittedly, they speak French not Breton, but this is vital in that they are extending solidarity to all regional groups; hence their 'adoption' of Gaston. The *content* of what they say is not compromised.

community (his co-fighters are in some cases elderly peasants) and, at the same time, returning home. Since practically everyone with whom he is in personal contact is disaffected or excluded, every social interaction is favourable to the more radical Gaston who is emerging; even the foreman and the Union representative take awareness and activism for granted. By contrast, the 'system' is faceless and voiceless. Bretons, workers, Aveyronnais alike are opposed to a *situation*, for which the film provides no defender. The 'bosses' are abstract figures who appear only in anecdotes, if at all; the human agents responsible for offering lower pay in Brittany than in Paris, for example, are referred to only as 'ils' or 'on'. Activism, or at least disaffection, is thus presented practically as a human norm; although for the most part it is on the level of talk only, everyone defines themselves politically, even in casual conversation, few are yet resigned, and for the vast majority self-definition and awareness goes along with other preoccupations and pleasures. Such a representation would have been improbable in France before 1968 (except if dealing with a small and rarefied milieu): neither, perhaps, would it have found favour with the most politically rigorous critics of the post-'68 era, and *Cahiers* is indeed silent on *Lo Païs*. But in many ways *Lo Païs* is exemplary as an embodiment of post-'68 ideals. It is both approachable and committed. It is not Utopian: it proposes only action, no solutions.[15] Its picture of socially acceptable activism is made credible by the film's unassuming style and because this atmosphere is taken for granted in much the same way as 'established' values were defined as taken for granted in films perpetuating the dominant ideology. Its disinterest in its female characters – whose only function is to aid Gaston to discover his own path through the traps they have fallen into – is certainly a flaw in its general awareness of the issues surrounding him, but it is not untypical of the period.

Lo Païs is probably exceptional in that the 'system' or the 'situations' the characters live in are refused as a frame of reference by such a varied section of society. While revolt is a common feature of the genre, and not only in those films where there is a

---

[15] Guérin observed 'On m'a déjà reproché de ne pas donner de solution. Ca me met toujours en colère car, hors d'une époque révolutionnaire, ce n'est pas au cinéaste à donner des solutions ... Les solutions, de toute façon, ne peuvent intervenir qu'à travers l'évolution d'un personnage' (Guérin 1973–74: 47).

more-or-less explicit political agenda, the normal pattern is to restrict it to the individual (*La Coupe à dix francs*) or to a small distinct group (*Les Doigts dans la tête*; René Gilson's *On n'arrête pas le printemps*, directly concerned with a mini-'68 in a Parisian *lycée* in 1973). Even in *Camarades* it is restricted to the extent that Yann's social world is comparatively homogeneous, although *Camarades* aspires to a rigorous political analysis which *Lo Païs* eschews. And perhaps the most lasting legacy of New Naturalism came from those film-makers whose debt to *cinéma-vérité* and militant fiction was less pronounced than their affiliation to the Nouvelle Vague and to auteur cinema, and as the decade progressed, while the style and the basic choice of milieu remained in favour, the themes of 1968 gave place more and more to individual histories, and a concern with form which definitely transcended any observational, 'naturalist' ideal. The career of Jacques Doillon, from his first film *L'An 01* (see next chapter) through the personal story with wider implications of *Les Doigts dans la tête* to the intimate psychological portraits of the end of the decade, illustrates this graphically. However, within the individual histories, a basic critique of the power structures of wider French society and their inability to adapt to the realities of individual identity remained a central theme. The subversive energy in *Les 400 coups*' subject matter, an energy which Truffaut's subsequent films drifted away from, was the most visible relic of the Nouvelle Vague in these films which had decided against the formalism of the Godard model.

Chris, the protagonist of Doillon's *Les Doigts dans la tête* (1974), is practically interchangeable with Karmitz' Yann or Guérin's Gaston: the same age, the same uprooted existence – although Doillon shows little concern with his origins, and certainly does not see a return to traditional roots as a likely, or a desirable, direction for this new generation seeking among other things its own independence and autonomy. The same dissatisfaction with his absolute dependence on his boss impels Chris to launch a 'strike', but Doillon's interest in it is entirely in the microcosm of an independent community that Chris and three friends establish and struggle to sustain within the four walls of his upstairs room. Arguably, even at the stage of *L'An 01* Doillon's main interest was in the possibility of a parallel universe, and in his first two films the rhetoric of '68 serves him as a suitable starting point for separating his protagonists from the current 'adult' world in order to explore ways to reproduce it with a difference. Five years – but only three films – later, a similar microcosm is established in a forgotten rural stable, in *La Drôlesse*. In this case the crack in the smooth surface of adult society which allows the two young protagonists to escape is caused not by aspirations to a revolutionary future which cannot yet be brought under control, but by the oblivion of French civil society to a remote world where even the young are living in the past. But the two films have in common the fact that Doillon's central concern is the spontaneous establishment of intimate relationships, apart from any immediate social pressures other than to remain closed in and separate. In 1974, *Les Doigts dans la tête* was well-received particularly because it dealt honestly and unspectacularly with the developing sexuality of its characters at the same time as, to some extent, with their fragile social situation. Such recognition of the mutual interference of private and public in any attempt to 'think historically' about the predicament of Chris and his friends was not unique; by 1974 new approaches to sexuality had become the locus for much of the revolutionary energy still at large in the French cinema. Doillon's film was unusual in being consciously low-key and unprovocative: proceeding largely through multiple close-ups emphasising the characters' lack of space and the details of their interactions, shot in a grainy black-and-white which gives it an appearance of documentary footage, perhaps even made by the friends themselves (an effect increased because the lack of space in Chris' flat obliges the actors frequently to look into the camera), it is discreet and often amused. The social environment of the 'new naturalism' is used as the background for an intense and precise exploration of the problems of relationships in a culture in the process of change, a problem otherwise almost exclusively explored in the context of established couples of adult intellectuals similar to the film-makers themselves, and rarely with the acute sense of a new formation of class differences which Jill Forbes locates in this film (Forbes 1992: 202–4).

Claude Miller's début feature, *La Meilleure Façon de marcher*, in 1976, represents a further development of a current which, having been identified, was now beginning to lose its boundaries. While Miller's style was compared with the leading lights of the 'new naturalism' movement, it was generally accepted that he was a stylist: *Positif* referred to him as a 'classicist'. Certainly, although he did not make his first feature until quite late in the decade, Miller's career began among the Nouvelle Vague directors; he had worked with Truffaut, Godard, Demy and ... Bresson. When the scenario of *La Meilleure Façon de marcher* was published in *Avant-scène*, Truffaut wrote an introduction in praise of the film, as, two years earlier, he had spoken out in favour of *Les Doigts dans la tête*. The extent to which the most visible elements of the New Naturalism movement were drifting towards the Truffauldien style of cinema is if anything underlined by Truffaut's own 1976 film, *L'Argent de poche*, which if it had been made by a young director would almost certainly have been perceived as pertaining to the genre, with its provincial setting, non-professional actors, apparently spontaneous action, slim plot and social message. Miller, on the other hand, rejected the 'New Naturalist' label firmly: 'for critics who talk about the 'new naturalism', it's a good way to write a paragraph, but it doesn't correspond to reality. Because no, it doesn't interest me' (Miller 1976: 33). All that he would recognise was that the film might attract the label because it dealt with 'young people and children'.

Certainly, Miller's film never uses images which recall documentary or *cinéma-vérité*, still less militant cinema. The story of *La Meilleure Façon de marcher* is set in the early 1960s, partly perhaps to correspond with the director's own formative years – although he insisted that it was autobiographical in only the slimmest of senses – but more importantly to predate 1968 and thereby to avoid the implications of staging his story in the era of *prise de parole*. The environment of the *colonie de vacances* in which it is set is the very epitome of a regimented and conventional mini-society, a characteristic underlined by the song from which the film takes its title, with its confident announcement that 'ours is the best way to walk': a celebration both of the sporty physicality which the all-male 'colo' is encouraging and of its conviction that the majority is right. In this environment Miller's protagonist is set apart as an indoor intellectual, interested in drama and auteur cinema (Bergman), even before the most aggressive of his colleagues surprises him dressed in women's clothes and make-up. The centre of the film is the duel between the two young men at the centre of the story, but Miller leaves no doubt that the pressure of conformity is all against Philippe, who believes himself open to blackmail and seals his own misery – as several episodes make clear – by his inability to find a way of expressing himself against the surrounding pressures. The apparent resolution of the film involves, in fact, a kind of *prise de parole*, or at least *prise en charge*, of the situation: Philippe uses the pretext of a fancy-dress party – a pretext, however, which he has himself provided – to appear in women's clothes 'legitimately' and confront his principal tormentor. If this is a *prise de parole*, it seems, as Forbes suggests, to be in large part a theatrical one: although Miller never commits himself or his protagonist as to Philippe's sexuality, the aggressive advances he makes to Marc at the dance are unambiguously spectacular, couched in ritual moves, costumed and culminating in a melodramatic – but minor – blow with a knife which announces to the audience both within and outside the film that by establishing his *right* not to conform he has destroyed Marc's power over him.

The construction of *La Meilleure Façon de marcher* encourages the audience to read this as an entirely personal story, with all references to current events or even to social issues wider than the closed institution carefully obliterated. Philippe's dilemma is however, primarily a social one, and the *colonie* is a not ineffective model of the oppressive power of conformity. And, despite the aggressively celebratory announcement of the presence and legitimacy of a different approach at the dance, Miller added a second ending or epilogue. In this, for which he was much criticised, he shows the two protagonists meeting again a few years later; Philippe and his girlfriend – a supportive presence in the film – now a newly married couple, are ushered round an anonymous new flat by Marc, now a sales-rep for the building firm. In contrast to the flamboyant colours and movement, not to mention the dramatic action, of the previous scene, the sequence is filmed carefully 'flat', the actors politely exchanging platitudes in a practically monochrome environment. Miller defended this ending on the grounds that, outside the microcosm of the *colonie*, neither Marc nor Philippe is able to impose his identity faced with the absolute social assumption that they will conform or, at least, be passive: 'a sort of voluntary "peaceful coexistence", because one wants to avoid violence, because violence is a nuisance, uncomfortable'. And, from this, he draws a precise, social and political conclusion. 'It's a "practical" power relation. It's based on comfort. So that everything doesn't break up!' (Miller 1976: 30). Miller felt that it was the only 'honest' way to end the film ('if the idiots lost, it would be marvellous, it would be the golden age') and that decision marks a decided disillusion with the potential 'golden age'. *La Meilleure Façon de marcher* ends with a passive pessimism which the young cinema of the early 1970s still eschewed, and reflects the growing weariness of the advancing decade.

'Naturalism' was always a questionable description of the work of these young film-makers, and it is significant that it was a label imposed from outside and not an ideal which the directors themselves endorsed. The films mostly had modest ambitions to match their modest budgets, in terms of the size of audience they expected to draw: if 'naturalism' meant anything, it referred to a common desire to show the social and physical environment of France as it was experienced, rather than in the idealist or dramatic terms which the popular French cinema presented; to use unknown faces, if not non-actors, for the main roles so as to allow the audience to read the characters directly without the imposition of a star persona; to eschew the temptations both of glossy, carefully constructed images and of allowing formal deconstruction to overshadow the narrative and content; and finally to reacquaint French cinema with the experience of being young in France. The majority of the 'New Naturalist' directors were young, and all were making their début in the cinema.

The 1970s has gained a reputation as a fallow period for new directors; certainly, the French cinema landscape was still dominated by the great names of the Nouvelle Vague and by the prolific directors of comedies and thrillers who marshalled the most massive audiences: Yves Robert, Jean Girault, José Giovanni. Nonetheless, by 1971, as René Prédal has pointed out, the proportion of début films among all French production had risen to 28 per cent (from 9 per cent in 1954), and although the inclusion of porn films in the years from 1973 to 1982 distorts the statistics to the point of making them hard to use, it is likely that this percentage remained more or less stable (Prédal 2002: 1). René Prédal has classified the new arrivals as a continuation of the Nouvelle Vague rather than a genuinely new generation, but a number of the younger directors had a very different agenda from their predecessors, and that agenda was certainly inflected by the language and the demands which had shaken the streets in 1968. In this, it may seem that the generation of the New Naturalism is a true forerunner of the much-noted wave of new films which flooded onto French screens in the second half of the 1990s, the product of those film-makers who, in 1997, declared a brief collective identity in signing the 'appel des 59' calling for a campaign of civil disobedience against the harsh new immigration laws of the Interior Minister Jean-Louis Debré. In that year the current generation of new film-makers – along with two very diverse products of the 1970s, Bertrand Tavernier and Patrice Chéreau – announced its political identity, in an unambiguous declaration which certainly owed more to the ideals of the early 1970s than to the strictly cinematic rebellion of the Nouvelle Vague, to which their films are often compared.

Claude-Marie Trémois, in the first book about the new cinema of the 1990s (Trémois 1997), located the connection astutely, citing Alain Tanner as an exemplary forerunner of the new current. Later writers, such as René Prédal, have tended to relate the spirit of the 'new French cinema' directly back to the Nouvelle Vague, while dismissing the new currents of the 1970s as simply an extension of the latter. However, the preoccupations and the constitution of the new generation of the 1990s have aspects which recall the situation twenty-five years rather than thirty-five years previously. The timid but noticeable emergence, in the 1970s, of women behind the camera, film-makers with an interest in the immigrant experience, and especially of a concern with the regions represented an exponential increase on such representation in the preceding decade. The late 1990s saw another such exponential increase, from a somewhat healthier starting-point: Trémois claimed that, in 1997, 33 per cent of the new film-makers were women, and among those with a high profile, the proportion rose, she claimed, to 50 per cent. Of the selection chosen to illustrate the new current in Cinéma 128's overview of the new generation (Marie 1998), the proportion is 35 per cent.

The language used by these young film-makers in the mid-1990s is also reminiscent of the post-'68 search for a new representation. Their appreciation of the social and the political was couched in terms of 'class struggle' which represented a startling departure from the assumptions of the 1980s both in France and in England, and this was the case not only of the outspokenly political, such as Jean-Pierre Richet (*Ma 6-T va crack-er*) or Laetitia Masson – but also of those apparently closer to the Parisian relationship dramas of Rohmer or later Truffaut, such as Arnaud Despleschin. For Masson's first film, *En avoir (ou pas)* (1996), an aesthetic of poverty was a prerequisite: 'I didn't use a make-up artist because it didn't correspond to the logic of the characters, I wouldn't have wanted to make this film, which deals with work and workers, with a big budget' (Aubenas 1996: 44).[16] For a few years, disaffected young people in marginal spaces were once again prominent on cinema screens – and in the process a new generation of young actors came to the fore. Admittedly these directors, when questioned about their antecedents, most often quote the Nouvelle Vague, along with the American cinema of the movie-brat generation (particularly Scorsese) as their direct influences, but the most durable directors of the Nouveau Naturel, such as Pialat and Doillon, are also cited. The young cinema of the 1990s was politicised as the Nouvelle Vague in its youth never was, and concerned with protagonists in movement from precarious work-place to precarious work-place. What was paradoxically absent was the sense of optimism which pervaded many films of the 1970s. In fact, in the ambit of New Naturalism several films were made dealing with the direct counterpart of 'naturalist' representation; the naturalist style and subject-matter proved a fertile and popular base for the representation of Utopian transformation, something which the French cinema of the 1990s eschewed.

[16] 'je n'ai pas pris de maquilleuse, parce que cela ne correspondait pas avec la logique des personnages, je n'aurais pas voulu faire ce film, qui parle de travail et d'ouvriers, avec de gros moyens'.

REFERENCES

Alion, Yves (1978) 'Dix jeunes cinéastes français: vers un nouveau romantisme', *Avant-scène* 208, 15 mai: 23/I–24/II.

Aubenas, Florence (1996) Profile of Laetitia Masson, *Libération*, 17 janvier: 44.

Daney, Serge, Kané, Pascal, Oudart, Jean-Pierre and Toubiana, Serge (1975) 'Une certaine tendance du cinéma français', *Cahiers du cinéma* 257, mai–juin: 5–21.

Douin, Jean-Luc (1974) 'Le Cinéma de chef-lieu', *Télérama* 1302, 18 décembre: 70–1.

Forbes, Jill (1992) *The Cinema in France after the New Wave*, Basingstoke: Macmillan.

Guérin, Gérard (1973–74) Interview in *Cinématographe* 5, décembre/janvier: 46–7.

Jeancolas-Audé, Françoise (1975) 'Du nouveau dans le cinéma français', *Jeune cinéma* 86, avril: 1–7.

Karmitz, Marin (1972) Interview in *Ecran 72* 3, mars: 5–8.

Karmitz, Marin (1973) Interview in *Cinéma 73* 181, novembre: 15–16.

Marie, Michel (1998) *Le Jeune Cinéma français*, Paris: Nathan.

Miller, Claude (1976) Interview in *Positif* 179, mars: 27–34.

Noguez, Dominique (1977) *Le Cinéma autrement*, Paris: 10/18.

Prédal, René (2002) *Le Jeune Cinéma français*, Paris: Nathan,

Rémond, Alain (1975) 'Ça traîne, ça se balade, ça batifole', *Télérama* 1304, 9 janvier: 68–70.

Tallenay, Jean-Louis (1974) 'Vive le Nouveau Naturel!', *Télérama* 1300, 4 décembre: 64–8.

Trémois, Claude-Marie (1975) 'La Vie on peut la tuer la recréer ou la happer', *Télérama* 1303, 2 janvier, 64–5.

Trémois, Claude-Marie (1997) *Les Enfants de la liberté*, Paris: Seuil.

1 *L'Attentat* (Yves Boisset, 1972): Saddiel (Gian-Maria Volonté and Darien (Jean-Louis Trintignant)

2 *Lo Païs* (Gérard Guérin, 1971): Yann (Olivier Bousquet) and his Yugoslavian girlfriend

3 *Themroc* (Claude Faraldo, 1972): the fate of the police

4 *La Cecilia* (Jean-Louis Comolli, 1976): Maria Carta as Olimpia counsels a comrade

5 *Les Camisards* (René Allio, 1970): Camisard costumes

6 *Moi, Pierre Rivière...* (René Allio, 1976): the rituals of peasant life and death

7 *L'Affiche rouge* (Franck Cassenti, 1976): the Brechtian performance

8 *Mister Freedom* (William Klein, 1968): Mister Freedom triumphant

9 *Charles mort ou vif* (Alain Tanner, 1968): François Simon as Charles Dé

10 *Jonas qui aura 25 ans en l'an 2000* (Alain Tanner, 1976): the eight Mas share a meal

4

Filmic Utopias: imagining the new society

The protagonists of the new naturalism tended to stage small, credible and often ultimately futile or self-destructive revolts; the films discussed in the previous chapter, the most activist of the genre, still only arrive at a hesitant optimism. Inevitably, not all film-makers were satisfied with this. The slogans of 1968 positively encouraged the imaginary creation of new societies, and a number of films were made on the principle of 'taking desire for reality'; that is, presenting a utopian society created either by a small group of like-minded people or, in the most euphoric representative of the genre, *L'an 01*, by all the human race. The vast majority construct their Utopias around a small and closely knit group (Serceau 1983a). The encouraging implication is that even if it has proved impossible to engineer a change in society, all is not lost; one or two people may still succeed in creating within the current society a microcosm of the ideal.

This current in the post-'68 cinema may well be introduced in the words of Jacques Chevallier:

> This – this desire, this demand for a different life – is the most direct fall-out from May '68 in fiction films. The failure of the 'different way of life' on the collective level with the return to 'normal life' in June 68 did not make the desire for it disappear. It withdrew to the individual, to the group. Failing a great upheaval, why not have little ones? And why not begin to live in twos and threes the life we had hoped for for all? Take one's desires for reality: another message on the walls of '68. (Chevallier 1983: 39)[1]

---

[1] 'Cela – ce désir, cette exigence de vie autre – c'est la retombée la plus directe de mai 68 dans le cinéma de fiction. L'échec du "vivre autrement" sur le plan collectif avec le retour à la "vie normale" en juin 68 n'en a pas fait disparaître le désir. Il se replie sur l'individu, sur le groupe. A défaut du grand chambardement, pourquoi pas de petits? Et pourquoi ne pas commencer à vivre à quelques-uns ce qu'on avait espéré pour tous? Prendre ses désirs pour la réalité: encore une parole sur un mur de 68.'

The creation of filmic Utopias was often criticised as actually reducing the inclination of the audience to seek change or as underestimating the difficulties involved. The latter accusation was often, but not always, justified; the best of the 'Utopian' films, such as Tanner's *Jonas qui aura 25 ans...* (see chapter 8) make no secret of the problems their realisation might cause, and they are by no means all purveyors of unjustified and mindless optimism. Chevallier notes a propensity for 'gentle [i.e. non-violent] rebellions'. However, a certain amount of violence is always present, even if it is sometimes hidden; for example in Claude Faraldo's *Bof!*, which Chevallier considers, wrongly in my opinion, to be gentle. As to the first criticism, the exhilaration which enters into the constructing and acting of many of the films reduces its force.

This discussion will concentrate on the two very different cinematic Utopias imagined by Claude Faraldo (*Bof!*, 1971, and *Themroc*, 1972) and on the exuberant universal renewal created by Jacques Doillon and his numerous collaborators in *L'An 01* (1972). These three films create a sample of widening scope. In *Bof!* the action is restricted to a small group, a reconstructed 'family' of five; *Themroc* begins in one household whose influence spreads until Utopia, if such it can be called, embraces a whole neighbourhood; *L'An 01* finally posits a world-wide reformulation of society, such that the limits of Utopia are no longer spatial but temporal – it is contrasted not with 'outside' but with 'before'. However all three have an important factor in common; they were conceived first and foremost as comedies, and although they adopt the idiom of the new naturalism to the extent that Faraldo's work could almost be called exemplary of it, they do not pretend to reproduce the world but flaunt their impossibility. Two other, rather later, films with clear affiliations to the theme, which will be discussed in other contexts, show that it was perfectly possible to treat Utopianism seriously. Tanner's *Jonas...* (the most relevant of this film-maker's work, which all uses and sheds light on the utopian ideal), which is dealt with in chapter 8, using the same understated idiom and characters very similar to Faraldo's, brings the aspirations of the utopian comedies into a genuinely credible framework. It is the most accomplished cinematic Utopia of the decade. Jean-Louis Comolli's *La Cecilia*, dealt with in chapter 7, analyses the apparently inevitable failure of a utopian microcosm. It is worth noting that these films were made in the later part of the decade, and their more serious treatment of the theme prohibits the exuberant optimism of the earlier films. Even in *Jonas...* the group's self-sufficient alternative society has to reformulate itself in order to survive in a hostile – or, rather, indifferent – world. Other films, such as *Qu'est-ce que tu veux, Julie?* (Charlotte Dubreuil, 1976) pose similar questions.

Apart from the above we may cite, among mini-Utopias restricted to small groups: *Ça va, ça vient* (Pierre Barouh, 1970), *Les Valseuses* (Bernard Blier, 1974: this achieved audience figures of 5.7 million (Frodon 1995: 833), and was the second most successful French film of the year, after *Emmanuelle*), *Violette et François* (Jacques Rouffio, 1977), *Pourquoi pas!* (Coline Serreau, 1978), and even *Cocktail Molotov* (Diane Kurys, 1979). Not all of these make any pretence to be more than individualistic, but all are characterised by an effort on the part of the protagonists to create something positive rather than simply expressing anger against the system. The genre was not confined even to the young and the Left-inclined: *La Chute d'un corps* (Michel Polac, 1973) has its New Age Utopia ruled over by a Master who must be obeyed. Films which posit the possibility of renewal spreading to encompass the world are much rarer, indeed *L'An 01* may well be the only example. Admittedly the cinematic challenge is much greater, both with regard to narration and to the establishment of a relationship between film and audience that will not lead to outright rejection of the 'impossible' fiction. It will be seen that *L'An 01* meets the latter difficulty triumphantly.

Among the films dealing with individual Utopias, *Bof!* stands out firstly in that its subject is the formation of the community in revolt, rather than its functioning, secondly in that its protagonists are firmly anchored in an ordinary working life. The early part of the film could be a typical product of the New Naturalism, although without that movement's concern for the psychology of its characters. The full title of the film, *Bof! ou l'anatomie d'un livreur* [Bof, anatomy of a delivery-man] suggests that it is going to analyse its young protagonist with regard to his socio-economic role.[2] He

---

[2] 'Anatomie' is not as significant a choice of term as it would be in English. It announces a close analysis, but not necessarily a relation to the physical. Luc Moullet's *Anatomie d'un rapport* (1976) uses the term and plays on it, but *Bof!* does not.

conforms to the profile of the New Naturalist protagonist: he is shown in his environment, at work and at home. The filming, as in the New Naturalism, is competent and unspectacular, the style is straightforward, and the occasional filmic indulgence – such as pronounced high or low angles – is always justified narratively. The gradual establishment of a Utopia does not involve any stylistic change in the film, or indeed in the surroundings, and neither are the incidents shown spectacular. Change and re-formulation takes place within an unremarkable flat, and the creation of the new society is achieved through hesitant conversations around a meal-table, filmed by an unobtrusive camera.

In *Bof!*, Utopia is a family affair. The first few scenes establish the unnamed protagonist in his parental home, only to separate him from it, in quite conventional style: he meets Germaine, marries her, acquires a flat, moves out. Shortly after this they attend the funeral of the young man's mother, which symbolically marks the end of that family unit. The early sequences also establish him in his job as delivery-man to a wine company. He is shown, in true New Naturalist style, on his first day at this trade, in the course of which he meets and makes friends with a black road-sweeper of a similar age. The introduction of this character suggests that the film's social span will reach further than the general run of new naturalist work; representations of African – as opposed to 'internal' or European – immigrants is in fact extremely rare in all this cinema, and when it happens it is invariably the narrative centre. *Bof!*'s understated inclusiveness (the sweeper will eventually enter the 'family' unit) is perhaps its most innovative feature.

In brief, the early part of the film appears to promise a generational renewal that will perpetuate the social status quo: the parental home is replaced by that of the young couple, while a new working life is also shown beginning at the bottom of the ladder (literally, in one shot of the young man at work). After a time-lapse, he takes the next step up the ladder, when he is allowed to drive a lorry. Significantly, this comes about because the majority of the work-force is on strike; our 'hero', however, is unconcerned with this, as is the film. His boss informs him that if he accepts the lorry in these conditions he is effectively cutting himself off from his workmates; his acceptance establishes him very explicitly as apolitical. On the other hand, the attraction of the lorry is shown to be the immediate pleasure of control of it, rather than its status value in his work, and as soon as he has it he drives off, not on his rounds but to show it off to the sweeper.

Revolt from the status quo arrives, in fact, not through the protagonist but through his father, a factory worker. Even as the protagonist achieves 'promotion' with the acquisition of the lorry, his father, after arriving at the factory gates to clock in, opts to turn away instead. Again, this action is seen as separating him from his colleagues, who follow each other on the obviously accustomed path into work, while the father makes no attempt to suggest that anyone join him. Instead we have parallel montage of the three major protagonists – Germaine, the young man, and his father – spending their day in three different, but all apparently pleasurable, ways. Finally, they are reunited in the young man's flat, where the father announces that he has left his job and, with minimal fuss, the young couple accept him in their home.

We now have the beginnings of a substitute 'family' which already constitutes a change from the presumed norm. The next step, which transforms it into a *ménage à trois* placing father and son on the same generational and sexual footing, is set up through a series of conversations – father to son, father and son to Germaine; by the next morning the situation is shown as established, with the young man leaving for work and his father replacing him in Germaine's bed. He kisses both goodbye, and another series of parallel montage contrasts his working day with Germaine and his father having leisurely breakfast in bed. The images adopt a series of clichés of family life, but the roles are confused: the son acts as the stereotypical father, with links to the outside world. Father and son's wife act out, at different times, the image of the parental couple (intimate breakfast in bed) or of the children, kissed good-bye by the departing worker.

This mobile nuclear family is not however allowed to stabilise, since the film soon introduces a second young woman, whom the father helps to steal a dress from a shop and afterwards brings home. The manner of their meeting makes it clear that she is at least a disaffected consumer; she also proves to be the daughter of the father's ex-boss. She is integrated into the new family unit, and leaves the house with Germaine on the following day while the two men remain behind to do the housework, once again turning foreseeable roles on their heads.

Alone in the house, the father tells the son that his mother's death was not an accident. The conversation is hesitant, as the son blocks the story at first, but the father explains how he had 'taken the responsibility' for turning on the gas, an action justified by his wife's lack of zest for life: 'she was tired, not happy, she complained you see ... She whimpered, poor thing.' The son assures his father that he understands, the women return and a small party is thrown in honour of the father's birthday. The subject is forgotten. The next morning's activities, also shown in parallel montage, lead to the culminating establishment of a new society. The son goes to work, in the flat the father and the two women have breakfast, the boss's daughter fetches her record player. We see the young man beside a country road looking at the scenery, then his lorry with its nose in a ditch. He hitches back to Paris after a brief inspection of the wreckage, and returns to the flat, picking up the sweeper on the way. This group of five constitutes the full complement of the new family/Utopian microcosm, which decides in the course, once again, of a conversation in the flat, to leave for the South the next day. The visual fulfilment of this decision, a shot of the group walking down a wooded path beside a river, ends with the camera focussing on Germaine as she announces, to general delight, that she is pregnant.

If the small events of *Bof!* have been narrated in such detail, this is because the narrative is entirely dependent on small and unspectacular episodes, with no occurrence which is, in itself, unusual or startling. The revolutionary impetus comes from the sequence of the events, and especially from the changing roles of the participants. The image is extremely discreet, and without the sound-track, the action could be assumed to be banal. Similarly, despite the occasional hesitancy, the dialogue flows without noticeable rupture over every eventuality. Once anything is expressed verbally, there is no need to consider it further. Both Faraldo's films, in fact, in their different ways interrogate language, and we shall return to this. For the moment we will note only that the assumption that once a thing is said it is as good as done together with the understated visual style mean that no action in the film is analysed, either by the characters in their discussion or by the image. Events occur in a logical sequence (as a consequence of the father's giving up work, he is left alone in the flat with Germaine and so on) but each incident is ascribed only the cause and the consequence shown. Other possibilities are simply ignored, and problems which the briefest reflection might lead one to expect are left aside, non-existent in this film's world. The strict probability of everything that we see means that it is relatively easy to accept the film's false naturalism as valid; to assume, temporarily, that what looks so possible – and is, clearly, physically possible – is as unproblematic as it seems.

Total exclusion of the problems does not, of course, apply in all cases, but it is essentially true of everything that touches on economic or social constraints, the most obvious of which is money. Rarely mentioned, its necessity is occasionally accepted – 'Si Papa veut sortir, donne-lui un peu d'argent' – occasionally explicitly rejected, but never becomes a problem. If the young man goes to work regularly, his motives seem to be as much pleasure as profit; after the first sequence, shots of him 'at work' mostly show him at rest, talking, eating, or taking his friend for a drive, and he can allow himself to accept or refuse payment for a delivery. He finally chooses to give up his job, without wondering how the group are going to eat afterwards.

Social constraints are no more in evidence than economic ones. There is no police to make stealing a hazardous occupation, which incidentally removes much of its subversive power.[3] There is no authority who might threaten investigation into the death of the mother, or enquire into the fate of the abandoned lorry. The factory manager has just enough existence to be named as his daughter's father, but not enough apparently to actively look for her.

This blithe disregard for the realities of existence can be explained away as quite justifiable since, despite appearances, Faraldo is not making a serious film. However, when compared with other films of the same genre, the choice made in *Bof!* may seem surprising. After all, the potential of setting up authority figures, policemen particularly, as an unequal and opposite force in comedy has been known since the days of music hall and Punch and Judy, and probably earlier; and it could be argued that

---

[3] Shoplifting as a form of revolt features in *Violette et François*, *Jonas qui aura...*, *F comme Fairbanks* (Dugowson, 1976), to name a few, but the sense of the action comes from the knowledge that it is carried out against official repression. The phenomenon is given full political significance at the end of *Tout va bien*. Some of the spirit of the filmic supermarket-actions of the 1970s reappears in Robert Guediguian's *Marius et Jeannette* (1997) with undiminished energy.

the very nature of subversive social comedy (which is what *Bof!* is all about) lies in ridiculing the representatives of social order. Faraldo was soon to exploit this to its fullest extent. Here, however, outside order seems to be ensured by no one, and the comedy comes, in fact, from the audience's confrontation with their own, internalised, taboos, which are overridden without the slightest acknowledgement of their existence. It is in many ways a radical choice, and to the extent that it is genuinely uncompromising it is effective, as comedy.

However, the Utopian element of the film suffers somewhat, and arguably so does the social subversiveness of the film. The latter perhaps only poses a problem to the extent that Faraldo is not quite consistent in his abolition of outside sanctions. The protagonist is threatened with a call to order once, when he takes over the lorry at work as a result of an unexplained and unexplored strike. Then, a minor boss – making a statement for the one and only time – warns the young man that 'in a month or in six years, if you go on strike, we'll take the lorry away. No one will defend you'. It is a negative call to order, admittedly, and voiced by the director, but the implicit threat comes from the idea that in taking the lorry the young man is breaking a taboo, one imposed by his workmates. Strikebreaking is the only subversive activity which might conceivably have a consequence in the film, and the perhaps unintentional result is to give it a slightly increased value as compared with the subsequent acts, such as leaving work without clocking in or wrecking the firm's property and abandoning it. These apparently free and unopposed decisions are taken *against* nothing (except perhaps the audience's work ethic); while a little courage is required to act against the wishes of one's fellow workers. The resultant image of social order would probably have been rejected by most of the participants in and sympathisers with May 1968, of whatever persuasion.

This, however, is a problem of detail and seems, indeed, to have been unintentional since the spirit of the film is largely contestatory. A more serious consequence of the total absence of outside sanctions is to threaten, ultimately, to destroy the sense of the Utopian project altogether. If the heterogeneous individuals concerned can elude the forces of society so easily, and reformulate their relationships in ways which one must assume are more desirable, it becomes incomprehensible that everyone has not already rejected their 'normal' lives long ago. The last reticences of the group become senseless. There is nothing to explain why escape is restricted to five people rather than extended to the whole world, as in *L'An 01*: outside society seems profoundly unnecessary.

If, as we have suggested above, the intention is to confront and challenge the audience with the consequences of their own inhibitions, the effect can be salutary within the limits of the experience of the film: however, if that challenge is intended to have some outcome in the audience's relation to reality once outside the cinema, such total lack of outside resistance is self-defeating. No sooner is the question 'Why not?' posed, in fact, than a flood of obvious objections arise, which the film has deliberately chosen not to deal with. *Bof!* is thus irredeemably confined to its own fantasy space. Even within that fantasy space, however, there are problems. In the absence of any power invested in the old social structures which can enforce their maintenance, we are compelled to assume that their survival must be due to some intrinsic merit. Since the only imperative ruling any individual's action seems to be that of maximum pleasure, we are left with only two feasible explanations for the fact that people work: either they enjoy their work, even when it seems to have no redeeming features (and in fact, the protagonist's experience of his job seems to afford him more pleasure than pain), or no one has had the intelligence to make a break which requires neither effort nor sacrifice. The first amounts to a defence of the social structure for its own sake, the second leaves little possibility of actually constructing anything.

Themroc, which Faraldo made the following year, has its protagonist break free from a much more repressive structure, and encounter a number of problems as a result of doing so. Its well-known plot concerns a middle-aged maintenance worker, who revolts after being hauled up before the boss for spying on him through the window as he fondles his secretary. Themroc (Michel Piccoli) breaks out of the factory, returns home to sequester his mother and convert his flat into a cave-dwelling by knocking a large hole in the wall. All furniture is thrown out into the courtyard. Here Themroc lives in sexual bliss with his sister, in full view of the neighbours who react with tentative attraction or repulsion. Journalists invade the courtyard where he lives, the police come in to bring him to order. The woman in the opposite flat follows Themroc's example, with the support of her timid husband and enthusiastic children. As the police become more desperate and more violent, Themroc's influence spreads in the surrounding buildings. Tear-gas proves ineffective, machine-guns even more so. The neighbourhood becomes a cave-colony, nourished in suitably primitive style by prey brought in by the hunters – the game being the policemen, cooked on spits. As a last resort, workmen arrive to wall the irreducible inhabitants into their homes. The film celebrates the joys of animal pleasure, with the final sequence setting a rising orgasmic cry against rapidly cut images contrasting the built environment (the dereliction of the old working-class Paris and the inhumanity of the new) with the ecstatic faces of the actors. However, despite the seduction of the workman dealing with Themroc's own flat, the walling-in is semi-successful. The very last image is of the arms of the female neighbour reaching desperately out from the intermittent bricks of a completed, if ventilated, wall.

Themroc has a good deal in common with *Bof!*, many of the tendencies of which it picks up and takes to further extreme lengths. The reformulation of the family is again central, but the violence and sexuality which are (interestingly) occulted in *Bof!* are brought to the screen in the second film. *Themroc* is much darker, literally and figuratively, but its dark side is already implicit in *Bof!*. In the first half of the film at least the comedy is very broad – all in all the film is less subtle than *Bof!*. Faraldo is here working with a group of actors from the *café-théâtre*, several of whom were also involved in *L'An 01* the same year (Romain Bouteille, Coluche, Miou-Miou, to name only the best-known). They had worked together before and their anarchistic group-spirit had developed in spontaneous comedy in front of live audiences. Thus, this Utopia is violently outrageous, and the working environment is parodied rather than reproduced. The delivery-man's job is perfectly real but Themroc's is an exemplary invention. The characteristics of New Naturalist style are themselves carried to the point of parody, with an extreme poverty of image as of environment. On the other hand, this parodic society subjects Themroc to recognisable constraints, external as well as internal, and it is not only from his own and the spectator's personal inhibitions that he has to free himself. In fact, the premise of *Themroc* is that inhibitions have little or no hold, and that a substantial public and private police force is needed to prevent the satisfaction of the animal instincts.

By and large, the common-sense objections that could be opposed to Themroc's revolt are incorporated into the narrative, albeit sometimes by way of comic magic which subverts them by transformation. Thus the Parisian police force is visible and visibly repressive, as the participants of May 1968 had found; a scene of a young man being beaten up in the courtyard is shot after the manner of the most politically committed examples of New Naturalism, that is to say not very far from the style of news footage, and would almost be believable as documentary footage of 1968 vintage. Some of Themroc's strategies of resistance are not only naturalistically shot but also physically credible, the policeman-hunt notably. At other times the film indulges in its privilege of comic spectacle: tear-gas canisters are used by the rebels to get high. However, while the total evacuation of all resistance in *Bof!* produces a perceptible lack in a necessary element in the diegetic world, without which it can only be insubstantial, such changes in function of given objects, for all their impossibility, are credible within the confines of the film because they take place within a complete world where all elements which might be expected to be present are indeed physically, or visibly, there.

If there is any resistance to utopian developments inscribed in the text in *Bof!*, it comes – as might be expected – from the protagonists themselves and it is expressed through their use of language. More precisely, it is expressed by their reluctance to use language. Developments in *Bof!* take place as a result of conversations which will them into being, and in two cases an important development is preceded by a long conversational hiatus, during which the new situation apparently cannot be named. This applies firstly to the sexual relationship between the father and Germaine, secondly to acceptance of the father as killer of the mother.

The implied resistance bears no relation to any external social constraint. It is internal to the group and affects (or risks affecting) only its internal equilibrium, and one accepts it as inspired by individual conscience and the risk of bruising conventional sensibilities. In both cases it is the father who is the pivotal point:

it is he who proposes the breaking of a taboo, but it is also he who creates that taboo since, once again, he encounters no external resistance once his own silence has been overcome. Even individual, psychological resistance is thus presented as entirely contained in one person who negates it even as he creates it, so that it can only appear, in the end, as illusory.

Hesitation and resistance exist, in fact, not so much to the accomplishment of the resisted action but to its expression. They last only so long as the action is not named, nor identified explicitly by the listener. Reticence therefore seems to apply not to actions – one of which, after all, has already occurred – but to words. As long as the act remains unnameable, each taboo seems absolute. The father skirts around a gap in his text, which his listener (be it his son or Germaine) takes care not to fill. The audience, helped by a few visual clues, certainly understands what he wants long before he succeeds in expressing it, and so, we assume, does his listener; however, the visual clues remain just that, a visual equivalent of the father's hesitant equivocations and not a straightforward illustration. The film, too, avoids the direct representation which would be the equivalent of *naming* the act, until the taboo is discounted by a word or act of acceptance on the part of the listener. Although the father's account of the mother's death requires a certain amount of verbal formulation, and this is accompanied by a discreetly oblique image of the lavatory where the father took refuge from the gas, the vital words 'Je l'ai tuée' [I killed her] are not pronounced until the son has already indicated forgiveness. Once accepted, the taboo can be named freely, and the action itself is either unproblematic or relieved of its significance by the phrase which accepts it. Reasonably enough since naming the acts was so important, their only consequence is to change the name of the perpetrator: 'Don't call me Dad any more. I've killed your mother; I've made love to your wife; call me Paolo!' To change his name, but also to finally destroy the family relationships with all their archetypal significance: the substitution of a first name suggests that father and son are now in a relationship of equals and friends.

That re-formulating of the family also takes place in *Themroc*, and in a similar way. The mother, though not killed, is sequestered in her own rigid little world, where, as the father in *Bof!* says of his wife, 'she is tired, without happiness … she whimpers'. By sleeping with his sister Themroc destroys the most basic family taboo and also redefines their relationship, which is now ambiguous. It is intriguing to note the condemnation which the mother receives in Faraldo's films – the old ladies are portrayed as the keepers of the joyless, rigid structure of an ultimately pointless society, unfailingly negative although ultimately powerless. They are a reactionary, indeed a death-like, force, filmed in dirty greys, and the suppressors of the instinctual pleasures which their children, without them, return to. In *Themroc* at least, this repressive death-giving mother is contrasted with the 'good mother', the neighbour who participates wholeheartedly in the barbarian joys Themroc initiates and pushes juicy morsels of roast policeman into her children's mouths. Yet at the end of the film this mother – indeed, one must assume, all her family – is walled up and weeping. One cannot help but wonder, in the circumstances, about the final scene of *Bof!*. The sunny image, and the joyful progress down the path which follows Germaine's announcement of her pregnancy suggest the obvious reading of it as a sign of hope for the future of the little group; yet, given Faraldo's image of motherhood, in this and in his subsequent film, the cliché becomes ambiguous.

If in *Bof!*, verbalising the new situation is all-important, in *Themroc* it is the utopian rejection of language which is paramount. This is somehow appropriate to the unrealistic, over-simplified concept of society which *Bof!* presents, and the dark, parodic but solidly repressive version which surrounds Themroc. *Bof!*, in fact, is a conceptual Utopia where what the characters, and the audience, must learn is how to formulate in words and images family relationships and family destructions which contradict all preconceived social notions. *Bof!*'s revolution takes place in the realm of the symbolic, and amounts to conquering the ability to order its symbols differently. In *Themroc* the realm of language is rejected altogether, as repressive but also as ultimately unnecessary. Verbal language expresses nothing. At the level at which Themroc and his companions live, *before* his re-appropriation of barbarianism, there is no need for abstract language – there are innumerable images to suggest that he is already living in a world approaching the animal. Social exchanges can take place without any comprehensible words, they function to create appropriate links and, crucially, the audience too have no problem understanding these sub-verbal communications. The only user of recognisably verbal language, the boss, is quite incomprehensible as regards content, but, once again, the *form* – tone and gesture – is sufficient to communicate his bad temper and his rejection of Themroc. His discussion with the foreman in front of Themroc adds the vague menace of an incomprehensible conversation which will have immediate consequences on a third person. Language, spoken language, in fact serves only a repressive function.

In order to attain the satisfactions he craves, Themroc has no need of words because within his own world people make themselves understood by gesture and look. And yet those satisfactions are, explicitly, of the sort associated with the 'bourgeois' lifestyle which he envies at the beginning of the film. The film was, in fact, criticised in the climate of the time for portraying Themroc's ultimate aim as bourgeois pleasures, and this is how Piccoli interpreted his role (Piccoli 1976: 248). The advantages which the boss gains from his use of language, then, are not even those concerned with the pleasures of existence: its only function is to confer repressive power. Concurrently, Themroc's rebellion is expressed in a series of growls mounting to a shriek, expressing the fury and frustration which conditions his repressed life. He succeeds in making himself heard, but this is not, as the walls of '68 would have had it, a 'prise de parole'. Words are unnecessary, Themroc can fulfil his life without them.

The film's greatest triumph is perhaps its unveiling of the superfluity of much of our use of language, and the doubt that it casts on the use which can be made of it. There is never a moment when the spectator is not perfectly aware of what is being communicated. The greatest triumph, perhaps, is a scene in the workers' locker-room where everyone is talking at once; the teasing which goes on across the wall which separates the 'inside-fence' team from the 'outside-fence' team comes very near to degenerating into a fight before the tension subsides into good-humoured joshing once more, and within the teams there are also small tensions. Without allowing a single word to be distinguishable Faraldo makes clear not only the changes in mood among the group, but also the natures, and even the different origins, of individuals. The scene is full of language, and yet there is no language.

However, the enterprise is, of course, founded on a 'cheat'. Our understanding is entirely dependent on the structuring of the image, which allows for example a montage of close-ups from Themroc's morning routine to intrude into his journey through the Metro in order to make us understand what is going through his mind. Themroc's concerns can, certainly, be expressed in images – but it is not the character, only the film-maker, who can convey them. Similarly, the film-maker makes use of written subtitles to introduce the characters – subtitles which establish, precisely, those relationships which it was so vital to subvert in *Bof!*: 'the mother', 'the sister', 'Themroc, son and brother'. Even if we accept that the characters have no need to communicate these to each other, they nonetheless have to be formulated in order to be subverted, and that formulation is necessarily abstract, verbal or not. The function of the subtitles is further complicated when Faraldo introduces irony ('superior shapely secretary'). The notices on the factory doors – 'gentils prolétaires', 'gentil gardien' – are pieces of wordplay which the film-maker is directing at the audience 'over the heads', as it were, of the characters. ('You and I know that this isn't a bit like a holiday camp...'.) If the function of spoken language is to be emptied of its sense and used as a weapon of repression, the written word is used to establish a second level of communication, between film-maker and audience. If Faraldo uses this only in the first part of the film, to satirise Themroc's dismal unreconstructed world, it nonetheless allows audience and film-maker together to laugh at the content of the image in ways which would seem to be beyond the characters. Irony always implies a certain superiority in its detachment, at least the superiority that comes from a general, commanding view. If the boss in the film is shown using his contentless, articulated speech to establish his power over Themroc, the access to meaningful words which is available to those outside the film is used to construct, and to mock, the world without language which is presented. Finally, *Themroc* does contain within itself the proof that language is not quite so superfluous as it seems to suggest, and the hedonistic Utopia which is achieved by disposing of it is, finally, probably doomed to become as confining as the world which has been rejected. The final sequences are ambiguous. If in the enigmatic game which Themroc plays with the plasterer (Patrick Dewaere) there is a suggestion of a possible complex exchange which the protagonists understand while the audience do not, the last image of the film is desperate, unlike the last image of *Bof!*. One wonders if, having decided to refuse the 'prise de parole' to his protagonists, Faraldo had any option other than pessimism.

In both Faraldo's films, the subversion of language and the symbolic order cannot be achieved without violence, and even if in *Bof!* it is never visualised, the threat of it is. A very early sequence shows Paolo looking down at his wife asleep in a chair, and in that look is contained the threat of destruction which, with her death two sequences later, we understand has been realised. Throughout the film the characters – foreshadowing *Themroc* in this – look at each other rather more often, and rather more expressively, than they speak. Unlike in *Themroc*, where hostility is expressed in open violence, the gaze here often seems danger-ous or unnerving; the interplay of looks suggests aggression beneath the surface, and the effect is disturbing rather than care-free. The lack of any open opposition which would justify latent hostility increases disturbance. In fact, this re-formulation of the world, limited to a small group and to the level of symbols and abstract relationships, forces the members of the group to assume in any unknown watcher an un-reconstructed conceptual framework which will reject their new one. This is illustrated in the relations between characters: Paolo's hesitancy is due to a presumption, and fear, of rejection; Nana takes Paolo's gaze as a threat when he sees her shoplifting. Germaine particularly occa-sionally gazes at the audience with a similar suggestion of hostility. The liberation that comes from being able to say the unsayable is predicated, in fact, on finding others who 'speak the same language', and mistrust is therefore inevitable.

It is therefore probably also inevitable that such an intimate reappraisal should remain restricted to an intimate group. *Them-roc*'s non-linguistic return to the instinctual is paradoxically much easier to communicate; since communication is reduced to the lowest common denominator, everybody *can*, on condition that they *will*, participate. And it is in fact in the renewed possibility of human closeness, in an authentic, if limited, communion, that the world of Themroc finds its attraction. From a small beginning, this Utopia spreads like a contagion, but whether it is genuinely desir-able is more open to question. Doillon's *L'An 01*, made the same year and in a not dissimilar atmosphere, leaves no such doubt. It proposes a re-formulation of society across the whole world, simultaneously, and it presents itself as part of a project dedicated to its own fulfilment. The spectator is drawn into the film not, as in *Themroc*, as the recipient of the film-maker's jokes, but as a potential actor in the present which the film is foreshadowing.

L'An 01 is really a series of sketches revolving around the central idea that, spontaneously at a given date, the entire population decides to inaugurate 'L'an 01' ('We're stopping everything. And it's not all gloom'). There is a broad chronological sequence, from 'preliminary exercises' to the settling of the date and its consequences. The first sequences are more or less clearly set in France, then the film broadens its base, while one sketch indicates that the idea had appeared spontaneously in Argentina. Resistance is minimal. The financial world of 'Bank Street' [sic] naturally cannot cope, and the astonished population gathers to watch broker after broker leap from the skyscrapers. An unidentified authority figure wonders, at the start of the movement, whether the tide can be turned by a mobilisation order, but he is dissuaded by his own aide. A group of marketing experts meets to discuss possible ways of 'recuperating' Year 01; the meeting ends with a unanimous declaration of support for the un-recuperated version. Latterly, a small conspiracy of diehard conservatives is revealed, but they propose gentle subversion rather than force, and in any case their plot is efficiently bugged and the plotters broadcast as a harmless joke to the population.

Presenting Utopia on a global scale might seem like over-reaching ambition for a low-budget first feature. Much of the film, however, gives the impression of small-scale intimacy, with black-and-white filmstock and sequences shot with a shakiness of camera and exposure reminiscent of news footage or, more appropriately, of the work of the roving camera-teams during May '68. Such footage is interspersed, in an exuberant amalgam, with musical numbers, constructed titles, spectacularly aesthetic visuals (courtesy among others of Alain Resnais), and even animation. Thus *L'An 01* establishes a fluctuating relationship with reality; at times it is as credible as newsreel (no more, no less), but the intrusion of very different episodes means that the film plays with the audience, snatching the Utopia away at the crucial moment. While the near-documentary episodes, and a general concentration on small and apparently insignificant incidents within what we understand to be a world-wide movement, create a sense that the Year 01 is a reality close to everyday experience, the visible, and entirely deliberate, *poverty* of the film is so inadequate to its universal ambition that the two cannot be reconciled completely. It is impossible not to notice the rough edges; they make the audience acutely conscious of the existence of the object-film, and aware that this object is not appropriate to its content. Thus even in the apparently *cinéma-vérité* sequences, the form functions in an unconvincing way. It is at once convincing and unconvincing, realistic and an agent of distanciation.

Although the *cinéma-vérité* New Naturalist sequences constitute a 'dominant' style in the film, there is considerable variation within it, from the level of low-budget commercial cinema, as in the first sequences, to something nearer the style of a home movie. And some episodes break the pattern completely, creating a New Naturalist film which is, as it were, constantly interrupted by other genres. Resnais' Bank Street sequence, with its oblique shots up the walls of tall buildings and its human element subordinated to the décor, is an elegant modernist construction like the skyscapers themselves. A sequence on a factory floor where a group of welders inform the foreman that they are about to stop work is treated as slapstick, a couple discuss their sexuality silhouetted against a blank background after the manner of 'Godardian' art-house work, and two sequences make use of the theatre.

All this generic variation contributes to our awareness of the film as a film, perhaps even as a game with the medium. The first and last sequences, which act as a framing device, confirm this and give it its sense. The film is introduced by its credits, all presented on one hand-written board. Since *L'An 01* was a collaboration from its inception, the number of people involved is immense, and the credits are totally illegible, but they remain on screen for a while as two voices-off comment on the film and its construction. Their comments are banal ('No music?' 'Yes, there's a song or two later') but, as with the much more sophisticated procedure in *Tout va bien*, we are reminded that the film had to be created and choices had to be made. At the same time the illegible credits draw attention to the sheer number of participants and to their unhierarchical anonymity – a characteristic which is shared by the event which the film will evoke.

In the last sequence, a group of office workers, relaxing in their work-place, discuss the beginnings of Year 01. One recounts that he had first noticed the change in his father. At this point the image leaves the office to constitute the only flashback in the film, illustrating the young man's words. When he refers to 'the third cyclists' demo, 14 July (which was a real incident), a sketch of the demonstration appears adorned with a large arrow to indicate the notional whereabouts of Father. The voice continues that he has lost track of his father but is sure that he's well and happy somewhere (sketch of a little man buzzing through a wood powered by his own propeller). 'Then, there was the film *L'An 01*, and my father was in the first row.' Another sketch illustrates this.

Thus this final sequence replaces the film in the context of the *bande dessinée* which was its origin – the concept first saw the light as a series of cartoons in the satirical magazine *Politique Hebdo* – while, at the same time, anchoring the film in the audience's reality. Up to this point it is possible to read *L'An 01* as a narrative comedy, believable in its own coherent world, but with 'no road through to reality'. Its heterogeneous style ensures that separation, which could have been read as a decision on the film-maker's part to avoid the trap which Daniel Serceau describes in *CinémAction*:

> The 'revolution' seems to be accomplished in the fiction, even if not in the real world ... The spectators who agree with the project see their daydreams realised. While the film lasts, they achieve the illusion of liberation. They belong to a simplified world where one only has to wish for something for it to occur ... More worryingly, [these films] make us live on an idealist level ... Does not this cinema betray its deepest tendencies, beyond its deliberately sensualist declarations? Does it not aspire to another human nature, stripped of contradictions, ruled over solely by the pleasure principle? ... The creative imagination is at the service of this myth. By this measure, doesn't any consideration of 'realism' appear superfluous? (Serceau 1983: 123, 125)[4]

[4] 'la "révolution" paraît achevée dans la fiction, à défaut de l'être dans le monde objectif ... Les spectateurs en accord avec ce projet assistant à la réalisation de leurs fantasmes. Le temps d'un film, ils conquièrent l'illusion de leur libération. Ils appartiennent à un monde simplifié où il suffit de vouloir une chose pour qu'aussitôt elle se produise ... Plus gravement encore, [ces films] nous font vivre sur un mode idéaliste ... Ce cinéma, par-delà ses affirmations volontiers sensualistes, ne trahit-il pas ses tendances profondes? N'aspire-t-il pas à une autre nature humaine, dépourvue de contradictions, et placée sous l'emprise unique du principe de plaisir? ... L'imagination créatrice est au service de ce mythe. A cette aune, toute considération "réaliste" ne paraît-elle pas superflue?'

This reproach, addressed to the 'Utopian' current in general, might certainly be applied to Faraldo's work, as well as to other films which affirm the successful existence of their fantastic Utopias (the piece was written largely about Coline Serreau's *Pourquoi pas?*, in many ways not quite as simplified as *Bof!*). Although we have argued that Faraldo's engagement with language requires the outside world of *Bof!* to be simplified, one does not necessarily read this superficially 'naturalist' film at that level, and it is certainly possible to argue that Faraldo, and also perhaps Serreau, is rather airily assuming that humans are capable of re-writing the fundamental psychological relationships that form their existence, and presenting the result in a 'naturalistic' way. *L'An 01* is too fragmented, and too playful with regard to the cinematic medium, to be read as anything other than a fantasy. The only possibility it assures is that of its own, filmic, existence, and of an audience's consequent exposure to it. Now, with this last sequence, that very exposure is brought into the ambit of the fantasy, and the act of watching the film is given a potential positive value. The revolution is not 'accomplished', but to be accomplished, and it is the audience of this film who will go out and do it. This is a clever twist to the Utopian mechanism criticised by Serceau.

It is, of course, a joke. Since the action in the film can only be taken as a fantastic projection, something in the nature of an extended daydream, it doesn't give the spectator much clue as to what action to take. *Cahiers du cinéma*, believing in the very serious role of the cinema as an ideological structure in re-shaping the conceptions of the audience, were derisive: 'In *L'An 01*, ... we are assured that the intention is to find a place in the immediately historically practicable, on the side of need and not desire' (Kané 1973: 36n).[5] Clearly, on the level of content, this claim would be ridiculous. However, as regards the impulse to real, and *enjoyable*, action which was expressed by its making and by its appearance in its own narrative as a catalyst, it did correspond to a real need in 1973. The ideas expressed in May were still current in many fields, some structural changes had been taking place and discussions of reform – not to mention recriminations –

---

[5] 'Dans *L'an 01* ... on assure vouloir se situer dans l'opérable de l'histoire immédiate, du côté du besoin et non pas du désir'.

were omnipresent, but the exhilaration of the events was as irreplaceable as it had been, inevitably, ephemeral. Occasional, minor events might evoke a pale shadow of it for those involved – the cyclists' demonstrations, forerunners of the Reclaim the Streets movement, were an example. *L'An 01*, which at one point refers to 'desire considered as potential energy', perceived, and expressed, the need to reinject energy into the political and analytical discourses to which May had given rise. It does not provide a blueprint for social change, but a reminder that in order to accomplish anything it is necessary to desire not only the result but also the process of change.

Even outside the puritan culture of *Cahiers*, the film suffered from the critics' tendency to analyse its revolutionary vision and find it wanting. 'Miraculous', 'idealist', 'evading all questions' – such were the accusations levelled at it. In general terms such criticisms (though justified in their own terms) ignored the fundamental fact of its fragmentation. It is not a coherent whole, but a series of propositions, ideas and essays. Dominique Noguez, one of the film's principal critics, did finally recognise, not only that: 'Like any Utopia, however, it has great negative value: for by suggesting that everything could be different, it highlights the arbitrariness, absurdity and finally the intolerable nature of a "developed" society such as ours'[6] but, more importantly: 'As for what *L'An 01* suggests or evades, there would be enough to talk about for a year and I can well imagine a philosophy teacher building a whole class around this film' (Noguez 1977: 197, 195).[7] Such potential for discussion is no small advantage.

While Faraldo, Serreau, and other Utopianists present, by and large, one strategy, more or less coherent, for living differently, which the audience can accept or reject, *L'An 01* opens a field of possible alternatives which, if not necessarily practicable, allow endless opportunities for manipulation. It invites active participation not only through its final challenge, but also because its loose structure allows for imagining further episodes which can simply

[6] 'Comme toute utopie, il est cependant précieux négativement: car en suggérant que tout pourrait être différent, il fait ressortir la contingence, l'absurde et finalement le caractère intolérable d'une société développée comme la nôtre'.

[7] 'Sur ce que suggère ou qu'escamote *L'An 01*, il y aurait de quoi dire pendant un an et j'imagine fort bien un professeur de la classe de philosophie bâtissant tout son cours à partir de ce film'.

be added mentally to what is provided. If, as Serceau suggests, the likes of *Bof!*, *Themroc*, or *Pourquoi pas?* are unconstructive to the extent that when the problems which they evade are recognised, or the drawbacks of their ideals exposed, they provide neither alternative roads to the desired result nor any enquiry into the causes of difficulties or their possible solutions, *L'An 01*, at least, establishes a Utopia of infinite variation, and encourages the audience to exercise its imagination joyfully. The graffiti of 1968 had given due place to the importance of this primary freedom.

However, a real interrogation of the utopian dream, its attractions and its pitfalls, was probably beyond the scope of these low-budget comedies. Even if the *café-théâtre* troupes and the *Charlie-Hebdo* satirists who were involved in *Themroc* and *L'An 01* were one of the most enduring repositories for the street-humour of May – Coluche, who appears in both films, embodies its legacy perhaps as well as any other single personality – their exuberance did not allow for any kind of exploration of a failed ideal. It is in the exploration of qualified failures that the cinema best came to terms with the problems of such re-formulated social experiments, and arguably best came to terms with the legacy of the May experience itself. We will find several examples in subsequent chapters.

REFERENCES

Chevallier, Jacques (1993) 'En France: Révoltes tous azimuths pour vivre autrement...', *CinémAction* 25: 30–42 (first published as 'Mai 68 et après', *Revue du cinéma* 326, mars 1978: 67–84).

Frodon, Jean-Michel (1995) *L'Age moderne du cinéma français: de la nouvelle vague à nos jours*, Paris: Flammarion.

Kané, Pascal (1973) 'Et c'est pas triste', *Cahiers du cinéma* 247, juillet–août: 36–9.

Noguez, Dominique (1977) *Le Cinéma, autrement*, Paris: 10/18.

Piccoli, Michel (1976) *Dialogues égoïstes*, Paris: Olivier Orban.

Serceau, Daniel (ed.) (1983a) '60–80: Vingt ans d'Utopies au cinéma', *CinémAction* 25, Paris: Harmattan.

Serceau, Daniel (1983b) 'Du messianisme prolétarien à la transformation des consciences', *CinémAction* 25: 118–29.

5

Revolutionary form in theory and practice

The films we have considered in the first four chapters derive from 1968 primarily in terms of content. Their styles remain modelled on pre-existing cinematic conventions, even if they have introduced innovations in emphasis and sometimes even in form. While in the 1940s and 1950s naturalism could be associated with a politically inspired break with previous production, notably in the early days of Italian neo-realism, by the 1970s it was both traditional and depoliticised. The implied low budget and social honesty did dissociate those films which opted for it from the more extravagant compromises with a dominant production system, but they were hardly a rethinking of the actual structure of films.

There were many in the aftermath of 1968 who held that such a rethinking was the only appropriate response to the demands of a new cinema. All forms of traditional narrative and indeed documentary had, in their opinion, been associated for too long with the old order, and elements in the very nature of their functioning made them unsatisfactory. The inherent tendency to carry the audience passively along the path of the story, or to impose (or worse assume) an interpretation of the images of documentary, were, according to the 'formalist' critics in the aftermath of 1968, in themselves alienating, and the new cinema had to reinvent not only the subjects it treated but also its ways of telling.

Chief among the proponents of this school of thought were the two most radical cinema magazines, *Cahiers du cinéma* and *Cinéthique*, the latter having strong links with similar publications in literary criticism such as *Tel Quel*. The theories of these two magazines became the focus for a great deal of critical study and have been outlined very lucidly in Sylvia Harvey's *May '68 and Film Culture* (Harvey 1978: 33–40): they had considerable influence on film theory and on the most innovative sector of production, and it seems appropriate to consider them in some detail here. We have chosen to do so with reference to one of their main proponents, the *Cahiers du cinéma* critic Jean-Louis Comolli, who (unlike many of his colleagues on the *Cahiers* board at this time) was a fairly productive director as well as a theoretician of cinema.

Jean-Louis Comolli was the chief editor of *Cahiers du cinéma* from 1966 to 1971, and remained on the editorial board for several years afterwards. Thus it was under his supervision that the magazine approached 1968, and his work was central to the elaboration of *Cahiers'* new editorial policy after the events.

Comolli was deeply involved as a critic and theorist in the renewal of thinking about the cinema. During the Etats-Généraux at Suresnes he had formed part of a team which had formulated Project 16, which was the first restructuring project retained by the general meeting and seems to have been the principal source for the compromise plan eventually arrived at. *Cahiers* published a (fairly) full account of the EG in its August issue, together with a summary of the action taken as a result and a list of the films made under its auspices.

Comolli's theoretical articles, even before 1968, were written from a Marxist/materialist standpoint. His analyses and discussions use, more or less explicitly, the essential concept of a dominant ideology as developed by Louis Althusser in France. Both *Cahiers* and *Cinéthique* recognised Althusser as influential to them. According to Althusser, the dominant ideology of capitalism tends to present the capitalist economic and social system as natural and totally desirable. Acceptance of the dominant ideology implies acceptance of prevailing conditions and a willingness to participate in them. Such a theory gives to ideology (which Marx saw as a superstructure built on and determined by the economic base) a much greater importance in reproducing relations of production. By extension, something could be gained in a revolutionary sense by attacking the dominant ideology, cracking its certainties or disseminating alternatives. This, as we saw in the introduction, was clearly interesting to those involved in film production.

Much of Comolli's theoretical work was devoted to considering how cinema could escape its long-standing role as purveyor of the dominant ideology, into which its development had directed it. (The ideological reasons behind the development of cinema, as Comolli sees them, are set out in the very important series of articles 'Technique et idéologie' (Comolli 1971–2).) The materialist approach seeks to subvert the illusion of reality, seen as the major factor in the ideological role of the cinema, by drawing attention to the fact that it is only an illusion, and that the film is an artefact, an object that has been worked on. Comolli's critical articles before 1968 already concentrated particularly on films which drew attention to their artificiality. The function of cinema, he wrote in 1967, should be to emphasise the 'difference which is fundamental, and given from the start as a constitutive element of cinema: the difference which the film itself represents with respect to the world. And to want a film to confirm the world by conforming to it is to give up without any decisive struggle the idea that the cinema should create its object rather than illustrating it' (Comolli 1967b: 56).[1]

This sentence, in an article on new Canadian cinema, is an admirable expression of two of the central themes of Comolli's theoretical work. On the one hand, he rejects the theory (propounded most notoriously and fervently in France by André Bazin in the 1950s) that the aim of cinema is to approach as much as possible a perfect image of reality (while considering that the main developments of commercial cinema have been in this direction). Not only is perfect realism impossible (the film is an artefact) but as a stated aim it is dangerous, tending to reproduce the status quo uncritically, to 'confirm the world by conforming to it'. On the other hand, Comolli was to consistently argue for a reciprocal relationship between film and reality: 'the cinema should create its object rather than illustrating it'. In these circumstances, instead of serving to bolster the status quo, a new cinema should question what it records, seek to awaken in an audience other reactions than simple acceptance and, in fact, create a new reality, or at least throw a new light on what it shows.

If this theme was already appearing in Comolli's work before 1968 (and, of course, he was not alone in his preoccupation), after the events it took on much greater importance. *Cahiers*' commitment to considering cinema as a possible agent for ideological change was taken up by the new publication *Cinéthique*. In the

---

[1] 'différence fondamentale, et donnée d'emblée comme constitutive du cinéma: cette différence c'est, déjà, le film lui-même au regard du monde. Et vouloir que le film confirme le monde par conformité avec lui, c'est renoncer sans lutte décisive à ce que le cinéma doive créer son objet plutôt que l'illustrer.'

October/November issues of 1969, Comolli and his fellow-editor Jean Narboni jointly wrote and published two articles, entitled 'Cinéma/Idéologie/Critique' (Comolli and Narboni 1969), which attempted to define an approach to film criticism appropriate to their political thinking. Films were to be discussed in an uncompromisingly materialistic way: 'a criticism ... based on the study and comparison of the factors which determine a film's production (such-and-such an economy, such-and-such an ideology, such-and-such a demand to be supplied) and of those equally tangible ones which produce the meaning and the form of the film' (Comolli and Narboni 1969: 14).[2] The film's relation to the dominant ideology was to be an important factor in assessing it. The first article elaborates a skeleton 'structure' of cinema in order to approach this kind of analysis. The authors begin by pointing out that all films are political in that they are in some way related to the dominant ideology and therefore aid in the acceptance or refusal of the current (capitalist) system. Comolli and Narboni then propose seven categories of film based on different positions with regard to capitalist ideology: each category demands a different line of approach from the critic.

Inevitably, in defining these categories and the appropriate critical responses to each, the article goes far enough to indicate what kind of film production Comolli and Narboni prefer. Thus among the seven categories mentioned three are singled out as worthy of particular interest. Category (b) includes films which are both political in content and revolutionary in form; (c) those where the form is untraditional even though the content is not specifically political. The article claims that 'for *Cahiers* these films [b and c] are the essential part of cinema and will take up the essential part of the magazine' (Comolli and Narboni 1969: 13)[3] although they do attribute a positive role to their category (g) – the more militant version of *cinéma direct*, in which documentary footage is accompanied by a (revolutionary) political message, as in for example *La Rentrée des usines Wonder*.

---

[2] 'une critique ... fondée sur l'étude et la comparaison des données de fait qui président à la production du film (telle économie, telle idéologie, telle demande-réponse) et de celles, tout aussi tangibles, de la production des sens et des formes dans le film'.

[3] 'pour les *Cahiers*, ces films [(b) et (c)] sont l'essentiel du cinéma et font l'essentiel de la revue'.

Comolli and Narboni thus consider the form of the film more important than its content in determining whether or not it really calls anything into question. Films in category (b) are defined as having an active revolutionary content: 'a political act necessarily linked, in order to be at all effective, to a critical de-construction of the system of representation'. Still referring to category (b), they stress that 'only this double action (at the level of the signified and of the signifiers) has any chance of being operational against the dominant ideology: a double, indissoluble economic/political/formal action' (Comolli and Narboni 1969: 13),[4] but they recognise considerable interest in films where the formal action is not coupled with an explicit message (category (c)), while condemning as reactionary those whose political content is expressed in a traditional form (category (d)). Arguably, the political credentials accorded to category (c) were more a reflection of the personal interest of the writers than of honest analysis; there had always been an experimental avant-garde in France, which did not need but could easily integrate an ideological, or counter-ideological, *raison d'être* (see *Ecran 78* round table, especially the contributions of Noguez and Eizykman). There were, however, also film-makers already working in France who carried out formal experiment with the expressed aim of ideological subversion. The most uncompromising and best known were probably the duo Jean-Marie Straub and Danièle Huillet, who duly became exemplary figures for *Cahiers*. Straub and Huillet's reputation in France was undoubtedly much heightened as a result of the new critical criteria, but the events of 1968 and their subsequent critical elevation were little more than a marginal incident in a mutual career that had long ago selected its course. Their projects often had long histories, so that, for example, a work such as *Othon*, begun in 1968 and much discussed at its appearance by the newly sensitised publications, had roots going back six years previously.

This stress on form was essential to most discussion on film immediately following 1968 and *Cinéthique* was even more uncompromising than *Cahiers* in its insistence on formal innovation. Comolli had always given particular critical attention to films

---

[4] 'cette seule double action (au niveau des signifiés et à celui des signifiants) a quelque chance d'être opérante contre (dans) l'idéologie dominante: action double, indissoluble, économique/politique/formelle'.

where the form called attention to itself, and thus to the film's artificiality. He had also, for example in the article on Canadian cinema already quoted, declared his interest in, and begun to formulate his ideas on, the methods and forms of *cinéma direct*. In this article he had attacked the traditional notion of *cinéma-vérité*: 'recording what makes life resemble the film, as the Anglo-Saxon "cinéma-vérité" aims to do, is not basing the film in life, but selecting within lived experience those few *spectacular* moments' (Comolli 1967b: 57).[5] On the other hand he defends a series of films made in one community using real characters from a charge of lack of creativity: his point here is that the real people, once they are on film, have a cinematic existence (and *only* a cinematic existence) for the spectator. That is, reality becomes an artefact when transferred to the screen.

This phenomenon is re-explored more deeply after 1968 in the articles 'Le Détour par le direct' (Comolli 1969), which start from the observation that the techniques associated with *cinéma direct* on the one hand and fiction film on the other are coming together. The two categories are beginning to overlap, to their mutual benefit. Comolli argues from this premise that *cinéma direct* needs redefinition, since '[it] is breaking out of the frame originally assigned to it by strict reporting in every direction'. The definition which Comolli arrives at reiterates the idea of a two-way relationship between film and reality: 'a system not of re-production but of reciprocal production ... their [the real events filmed] reflection – of them and on them – and their critique' (Comolli 1969: 53).[6] That is, neither *cinéma direct* old style, based on the fallacious notion of reporting without manipulation, nor 'fictional cinema' in the sense of 're-presentation. Socially coded game with a view to setting up a spectacle parallel to life'.

Having redefined *cinéma direct* in a dynamic sense – essentially as manipulated documentary footage, with the emphasis on the manipulation – Comolli remarks that this method of filmmaking has always been marginalised by the industry. Its relative cheapness allowed it to escape financial censorship. A technique

---

[5] 'enregistrer ce par quoi la vie ressemble au film, comme c'est l'entreprise du "cinéma-vérité" à l'anglo-saxonne, n'est pas fonder le film en vie, mais opérer à l'intérieur du vécu une sélection de ses seuls moments *spectaculaires*'.

[6] 'un système non de re-production mais de réciproque production ... leur [les événements réels filmés] – à et sur eux – réflexion et *leur* critique'.

favoured by independent and penniless experimenters (and, of course, especially those whose convictions left them particularly disfavoured with regard to getting funding) came to carry a political charge automatically, and thus its introduction into mainstream cinema brings a political element into those films which include it. This idea also had been propounded by Comolli prior to 1968 (Comolli, 1967a).

Comolli's final definition of *cinéma direct*, as a cinema acting on, and acted on by, the real world, is opposed to the fiction film, which, in its pure state, is limited to reproducing a previously set-out (and ideologically fixed) copy of 'reality'. It is the tension between the two categories at the point of overlap which really interests Comolli, and where he sees the most interesting developments in contemporary cinema (where, for instance, layers of fictional representation and of 'documentary' are superposed, as in Rivette's *L'Amour fou*, or where a fiction film is made in an entirely improvised manner, as in Jancsó's *Csend és kiáltás*; both these films are discussed in detail in the second article).

Although Comolli is writing these articles primarily as a critic, attempting to rationalise a phenomenon he has observed at work in contemporary cinema, it is obvious how positively he views this tendency, and in the working notes for *La Cecilia*, his own major feature film, we see that he has remained faithful to the idea of a reciprocal relationship between the reality of a film's making and its fictional content. The action was – according to Comolli – largely dependent on the discussions between the actors during the filming, and almost a third of the film was improvised 'on the set itself' (Comolli 1976a).[7]

Comolli's most important – or, at least, his longest and most detailed – theoretical work after 1968 was the long-running series of articles 'Technique et idéologie'. This is essentially a historical review – or rather, a critical review of cinema history, since Comolli questions in these articles both the relation of practitioners of cinema to certain techniques and the attitudes of previous historians who have attempted to explain them. The series began as an attempt to refute the proposition of Jean-Patrick Lebel, in his book *Cinéma et idéologie*, that the technical apparatus of cinema is based purely on scientific principles and has no ideological

---

[7] 'sur le plateau même'.

implications. This was a regressive position which was already discredited in the more advanced circles of cinematic theory, but it had rarely been subjected to so rigorous an attack as Comolli was to produce. He argues firstly that the technical apparatus is totally irrelevant *until it is made use of*, but that as soon as it is put to use it enters the field of signifying process, which is by nature ideological: 'absolutely blinded by his desire to make cinema (or the camera) into a *scientific object*, a simple technical system, he can do no better than to compare it to another technical system like an aeroplane' (a comparison which Lebel had, in fact, rather rashly made), 'it's simply to exclude cinema from the field it operates in … that of processes of signification, of ideology itself' (Comolli 1971–72, I: 11).[8] Secondly, Comolli claims that the invention of the cinema, and the technical advances which marked its development, resulted from ideological demand. Most of cinematic technology could theoretically have been developed long before it in fact was: 'The 'scientific' preconditions for the production of the definitive movie-camera were in place more than a century before one was developed' but 'it was at the moment when production of a movie-camera was written into social demand and economic reality that things leapt forward and efforts multiplied.' (Comolli 1971–72, I: 15).[9]

Comolli suggests that the reasons for such a demand might be found in the powers recently discovered in photography, which at once reaffirmed and denied the exactitude of the human eye as sensor of reality. Its effects were 'a reinforced confidence in a perspective-based, analogical representation of the world (the photographic image is beyond doubt: it shows forth the real in its truth) and a crisis of confidence in the organ of vision which had reigned supreme hitherto' (Comolli   1971–72, I: 13).[10] Popular

---

[8] 'proprement aveuglé par son souci de faire du cinéma (ou de la caméra) un *objet scientifique*, pur système technique, il ne voit pas que le comparer à un autre système technique comme l'avion' … 'c'est tout simplement exclure le cinéma du champ où il se joue … celui des procès de signification, celui même de l'idéologie'.

[9] 'Les conditions "scientifiques" de la production de la caméra définitive étaient réunies plus d'un siècle avant sa mise au point' … 'c'est à partir du moment où la production de la caméra s'est inscrite dans une demande sociale et dans une réalité économique que les choses se sont précipitées, les efforts décuplés'.

[10] 'un renforcement de la confiance en la représentation perspective et analogique du monde (l'image photographique est indubitable: elle manifeste le réel dans sa vérité) et une crise de confiance dans l'organe de la vision qui jusqu'alors régentait'.

cinema developed entirely in the direction of reproduction of visible reality (reaffirming the status of the eye), but Comolli points out that this was far from scientifically inevitable: indeed scientific use of film essentially concentrated on manipulation, in order to reveal the non-visible.

The reproduction of the evidence of the senses, the article continues, may be by no means an ideologically innocent aim. The added authority of a 'scientific' technique was given to the world 'as it is': that is, the familiar reality immediately visible, but also, by implication, the status quo as maintained by the dominant ideology. The camera records what it 'sees', the recorded message corresponds to what we might see, therefore we accept it without question. The technology of increased realism continually reinforces this myth. Seeing, in fact, is believing; the audience loses all impetus to doubt. It is clear that this situation is potentially very favourable to the reproduction of a dominant view of the world. Following a similar line, the written history of cinema technology usually concentrates on methods of recording and projecting the visual (and, since sound development followed the same course, the aural). Techniques of manipulation of the filmic material – laboratory work, sound mixing – normally received much less attention. They are relegated to the invisible and conveniently forgotten.

Having set out his argument that the quest for ever-increasing realism corresponds to the interests of the dominant ideology, Comolli in the rest of the series of articles uses the example of 'deep-focus' technique to reinterpret cinema history, taking as his starting-point two apparently opposed French approaches, those of André Bazin and of Jean Mitry. The first approached the history of cinema in general as a search for perfect realism, and heralded the general use of 'deep focus' as the widespread adoption of a more 'realistic' technique – which he even claimed (implicitly) was less ideologically loaded: 'it literally shows more things, more "reality", it allows once more for the play of that "ambiguity" which leaves the spectator free' (Comolli 1971–72, I: 18).[11] Mitry on the contrary holds that 'between the real world and us, there is the film, there is the camera, there is the representation' (quoted

---

[11] 'elle montre littéralement plus de choses, plus de "réel", elle permet de nouveau le jeu de cette "ambiguïté" qui laisse libre le spectateur'.

in Comolli 1971–72, I: 19),[12] a view which corresponds to Comolli's. However, he still fundamentally accepts greater realism as an aim (although, unlike Bazin, he considers it unrealisable); his explanation for the rise and fall of deep focus is exclusively technical.

Comolli takes the further step, proceeding dialectically from the opposition of Mitry and Bazin, of observing that, even if Mitry is right in recalling that the film is always an artefact, the cinema's development tended to hide that fact, and that this is ideologically significant, as explained above. Comolli is in fact arguing for a new approach to cinema history, starting from a Marxist standpoint in order to consider the cinema as 'signifying practice', contrasting 'the multiple actualisations of the cinema as an ideological apparatus, vector and transmitter of ideological representations where the subjects of the ideology (the spectators of the spectacle) cannot but recognise themselves' with those films where 'work in the signifier changes the status of the meaning' (Comolli 1971–72, III: 44).[13] Once again, Comolli is returning to the idea of using film form as a means of breaking down the dominant codes. As regards deep focus, its use is ideological both in cause and effect: 'depth of field is the mark, in the primitive cinematic image, of its submission to codes of representation and to the histories and ideologies which of necessity determine these codes and make them function … but more generally it signals that the ideological apparatus called cinema is itself produced within these codes and by these systems of representation' (Comolli 1971–72, IV: 42–3).[14] The historical thesis of these articles could be summed up as follows. The effect obtained (in the event, deep focus) is determined by technical factors (Mitry's argument) and by a desire for correspondence with visual reality (Bazin's argument), but that desire is itself determined by an ideological

---

[12] 'entre le monde réel et nous, il y a le film, il y a la caméra, il y a la représentation'.

[13] 'les multiples actualisations du cinéma comme appareil idéologique, vecteur et diffuseur de représentations idéologiques où le sujet de l'idéologie (le spectateur du spectacle) ne peut manquer de se reconnaître' … 'le travail dans le signifiant modifie le statut du sens'.

[14] 'la profondeur du champ est la marque, dans l'image cinématographique primitive, de sa soumission à ces codes de la représentation et aux histoires et idéologies qui nécessairement déterminent et font fonctionner ces codes … mais plus globalement elle signale que l'appareil idéologique cinéma est lui-même produit dans ces codes et par ces systèmes de la représentation'.

demand which directs technical advance (Comolli's contribution). By 1972 the articles have almost abandoned their concentration on deep focus and are discussing the history of cinema in general in the context of the search for realism, concentrating for example in article 5 on the introduction of sound.

These are theoretical articles rather than an attempt to formulate an improved practice for the cinema. Interestingly, in a later version of these articles, 'Machines of the Visible' (Comolli 1980), Comolli referred to his use of deep focus in *La Cecilia*, which he claims springs from different aims: 'Paradoxically, this was not in order to strengthen the realism of the image (deep focus as "more real") but in order to make the shot theatrical: to act along the verticality of the image in the same way that in the theatre one can perform along the vertical axis of the stage' (Comolli 1980: 137). He describes the mechanics of this in some detail, but it is hard to see how this *practical* decision (which works, I think, as he wants it to) fits with his theoretical position.

The conclusion of this English summary also refers to another concept taken from a much later article (Comolli 1977). Here Comolli adds that the mystification constituted by the illusion of reality implies an actual effort on the part of the audience, an effort which is willingly furnished. However, it is implied in 'Machines of the Visible', the desire to concur with the illusion is itself the result of preconditioning, the audience having already become accustomed to a prevailing world-view which the realist presentation reinforces. That reinforcement gives the audience the security which it unconsciously desires. However, this last passage of 'Machines of the Visible' has been removed from its original context within 'Un corps en trop'. Originally it specifically related to historical film and the discussion of the audience's concurrence in the film's illusion has no derogatory tone, it is simply an explanation of how the audience of a historical film appreciates the fiction. This is interesting because, although most of Comolli's theoretical work is preoccupied with the ideological implications of film form, in the films that he made his formal innovations are never very great. Formal innovation was, in any case, indissolubly linked for Comolli to political statement, and as his political commitment became more complex, so apparently his interest in the form of film somewhat waned.

The first of Comolli's films, *Les Deux Marseillaises*, was made in 1968 with another member of the *Cahiers* team, A.S. Labarthe, 'en hommage à Renoir et aux événements de mai' (Passek 1987: 93). Eight years later, he released *La Cecilia*, the story of an anarchist colony set up in Brazil in the nineteenth century; in 1981 *L'Ombre rouge*, concerned with two Stalinist agents during the Spanish Civil War, and in 1983 a thriller, *Balles perdues*. The series of films provides a chronicle of the political evolution of a committed left-wing theoretician in the course of the 1970s; a somewhat discouraging record, although Comolli by no means disappeared from sight in the 1980s and 1990s.

At the time of the making of *La Cecilia*, Comolli had apparently renounced none of his political or theoretical preoccupations. The film, a joint French and Italian production shot in Italian, was accompanied at its release by a large dossier, in French, including not only the complete screenplay but also a number of documents relative to the historical events the film was concerned with, a commentary on them, and a few pages of 'Notes de travail' in which Comolli gives some clues as to the film's intentions and the way in which it was made. It was generally well received at its appearance. *Ecran* said of it 'its success surpasses that of a mere first film, rising to the level of an ideological reflection directly inscribed in life' (Braucourt 1976).[15] *Image et son*, in one article, praised it as 'a fine film and an exciting one' (Cornand 1976: 74),[16] while *Le Monde* (15 janvier 1976) gave up its whole cinema page to an interview with Comolli and to a cautiously positive article.

La Cecilia is the story of a revolutionary experiment that fails. The little group of anarchists, let by the idealistic Giovanni Rossi, who set up their colony on land granted to them by the liberal emperor of Brazil fail to contend with the forces which bind them to traditional values. This criticism of Utopianism, perhaps a wry comment on the relative failure of the ideals of 1968 to produce any lasting change, binds the film to those which, as we have seen, were produced to celebrate an imaginary alternative society, but also to the various attempts at Utopian communal experiments which were made in reality, with varying degrees of success, but no progress towards a general social revolution (the

---

[15] 'une réussite qui dépasse largement celle d'un premier film, pour s'élever à celle d'une réflexion idéologique directement inscrite dans la vie'.

[16] 'un beau film et un film passionnant'.

ideal, after all, of 1968). A similar tendency within the cinema, where groups opted to work outside the system, had been rejected by Comolli in the 'Cinéma/Idéologie/Critique' articles, as not only idealist, but impossible. A better strategy, in his opinion, is to work within 'the system' but against it, since an economic-ideological system has so many ramifications that it is inescapable.

It is precisely this kind of criticism that Comolli intended to imply in the film with reference to the colony of anarchists. Surrounded on all sides by traditionally ordered society, dependent on the government for land and on the local storekeeper for agricultural supplies, the group is forced to compromise. The film is intended to raise questions rather than to express Comolli's opinion, but in the dossier he makes it clear that he considers that an experiment like that presented in *La Cecilia* is necessarily doomed to failure. Nonetheless in the course of the film questions of all kinds are raised. The reasons presented for the colony's failure are complex. The film's development was influenced by the discussions which took place among the actors, and thus all the problems which the film raises have a relevance to debates which were alive in the late 1970s. Apart from the viability of an isolated communal experiment (which in fact can only survive so long as the surrounding society feels strong enough to tolerate it) problems raised include the conflict between necessary internal organisation and anarchist ideals, the division of labour and the product of labour, the role of intellectuals, the status of women and the social effect of the family. Since *La Cecilia* is a historical film, there is further tension between the terms of 1976 and those of nineteenth-century anarchism, available to the historical protagonists. Comolli said in his *Le Monde* interview: 'Our ambition was to present all the possible discourses of the time',[17] and published documents by the founder of the historical colony in the dossier to the film. However, there are questions addressed by the film which were ignored by the historical Rossi, while nonetheless appearing, as it were, between the lines of his pamphlets, for example the value of the Utopian experience itself, and the status of the women (Rossi's attitude to women having been idealistic and sentimental). Such questions, of obvious contemporary relevance,

[17] 'Notre ambition était de faire tenir des discours, tous les discours possibles à l'époque'.

visibly also *existed* for the nineteenth-century colony even if they
went unrecorded. Comolli remarks: 'We tried to analyse Rossi's
silences. He is an author who censors himself, who doesn't want to
see things which are happening before his eyes' (Comolli 1976b).[18]

Comolli claimed that his aim in making the film was not to
make statements about the questions he raised, but merely to
pose the problems (Comolli 1978: 44),[19] and in this way he separates himself from what he defines as militant cinema. It is true that
in watching *La Cecilia* one becomes aware of the problems
gradually: they interweave with one another, increasing in complexity and in importance until in the end the whole edifice falls
apart under their combined action. The departure of the peasant
families, for example, is a result of disagreements over the division
of produce, over the right or lack of right to personal property,
over the general attitude to women and over the clash between
traditional moral values and the anarchist ideal of free love.
Tensions build up to explosion point as a result of all these factors
which combine and develop. Never does the film make absolutely
evident what the 'correct' attitude should be, although Comolli
does give some indications, perhaps involuntary, as to the attitude
he favours. However, taking the film as a whole, the eventual
failure of the colony throws implicit doubt upon *any* action
actually taken – including, of course, setting it up in the first place.

This issue can serve as an example of Comolli's method of
presenting the parameters of a debate. The film sets up the
experiment firstly as desirable (despite the contradictions of its
existence within a despotism, enlightened or not), because of the
enthusiasm and very positive idealism of the little group. The
contrast which they present with the other inhabitants of the
region, who are shown either as hostile (the plantation owner) or

[18] 'Nous avons tenté d'analyser les silences de Rossi. C'est un auteur qui se
censure, qui ne veut pas voir des choses qui pourtant se produisent sous ses yeux.'

[19] 'When cinema is transitive and intensely assertive (didactic) that, so far as I
am concerned, objectifies the audience, so I am trying to ask political questions
through the use of a fictional style and thus to push the spectator towards
questioning his/her own mode of political speech and expression.' In 1981, on the
appearance of *L'Ombre rouge*, he made a comment which can be applied very easily
to *La Cecilia*: 'ce que j'essaie de faire, c'est moins de délivrer des messages ou des
analyses que de mettre en scène des contradictions en partie politiques, de façon
que le spectateur … tire de là surtout une sorte d'énergie pour se reposer lui-même
les questions' (Comolli 1981–82: 24).

enslaved (the Italian field labourers) only serves to reinforce them for the audience. However, we also register their isolation, their lack of concern for the plight of their compatriots who work for the neighbouring rancher, and their dependence on the emperor. When Rossi receives a letter from Italy condemning him for evading his responsibilities, all those previously accepted facts influence the spectator's reaction to the accusation, and one is aware that the doubts were there all along, but were simply set to one side while the colony's enthusiasm and energy carried conviction. The group, however, immediately contests the letter hotly. It is an important step to prove that a community can survive without the oppressive rules of society as it has developed. Rossi's plans for the colony are once again justified; to prove that a dream can be realised seems a worthwhile exercise. Throughout the film the question will thus recur, posed first from one side then from another, and eventually developing into the new problem of whether the colony is to attempt to exist permanently or whether the 'experiment' can be closed. The argument coexists with the other issues which will eventually divide the colony. Comolli treats these debates as a number of strands, as he says in the interview quoted above (this time with explicit reference to *La Cecilia*): 'at the start, there are scattered strands which we tie to each other and in the end it makes a braid' (Comolli 1981–82: 27).[20]

Comolli claims that this structure of interacting debates marks a break with traditional narrative: in the *Cinétracts* interview he further described it thus: 'The narration appears to be linear without gaps or ruptures or breaks but it is in effect a narrative that contains many holes, gaps, and that as a result is missing many logical connections' (Comolli 1978: 45). However, given that Comolli's theoretical work placed extreme – almost exclusive – importance on the role of film form, the form of *La Cecilia* may seem surprisingly traditional. So much so, indeed, that one critic (A. Cornand, *Image et son*) found the film very disappointing: 'To say that *La Cecilia* breaks with traditional working methods like it breaks the story, to say that it's outside the usual codes of cinematic representation, is either to be ignorant of cinema or to take little account of everything which has been done in the last few

---

[20] 'au départ, il y a des brins éparpillés qu'on noue les uns aux autres et après ça fait finalement une tresse'.

years' (Cornand 1976: 76).[21] One of the few 'unfavourable' criticisms received by *La Cecilia* (but not, apparently, motivated by party feuding despite the major differences between *Image et son* and *Cahiers*), Cornand's article highlights a gap between Comolli's theory and his practice. It concludes: 'It all holds together. Giovanni Rossi's failure when he moves from theory to practice becomes the metaphor for the failure of the theorist of cinema when he moves into direction.'

Certainly *La Cecilia* does not indulge in such extreme formal disruption as that which Godard, for example, was engaged with well before 1968, although this is the kind of cinema that Comolli the critic praises most. But neither does the film comply with those codes of realism which Comolli traced in 'Technique et idéologie'. The use of sound, for example, is not 'traditional'. The anarchist songs which recur at key moments function as a metaphor for the idealism which supports the colony and as a unifying force in the narrative which triumphs, at least in the early stages, over the forces of dissension. As problems increase, the singing becomes rarer. These songs, not demanded by the narrative although integrated into it to some extent, form a theatrical interruption to the development of the action, as in Brechtian spectacle. Comolli certainly intended the music to play an important role as a kind of secondary discourse (Comolli 1976a: 96).

The filmic technique favours long tracking shots, lasting well over a minute in many cases; this is unusual enough to call attention to itself, as is the alternate editing between Rossi's address to an anarchist meeting in Italy and the colony in discussion beside the river, where the audience is required to contrast not only the situation but also what is said. However, it is certainly stretching a point to claim that the form in *La Cecilia* was so adventurous as to consistently undermine the illusion in the way which Comolli seems to advocate in his essays. And in 1981, thirteen years after 1968 and five years after *La Cecilia*'s appearance, he commented thus on *L'Ombre rouge*: 'I like things which can't be seen, I try to manage things so that my work is seen as little as possible and is as it were forgotten by its product;

---

[21] 'Dire que *La Cecilia* rompt avec les méthodes traditionnelles du travail, comme il casse le récit, dire qu'il sort des codes habituelles de la représentation cinématographique, c'est ou bien ne pas connaître le cinéma ou bien afficher un certain mépris pour tout ce qui a été fait depuis un certain nombre d'années.'

it disappears behind what I am making' (Comolli 1981–82: 27).[22] This from the writer of one of the most detailed and famous expositions of the idea that the audience must be 'demystified' by being made aware of the choices made and of what has been left unsaid. Comolli after all had even criticised the history of film technique specifically because its emphasis on the visible led to the effacement of work!

Even in discussing *La Cecilia*, Comolli felt obliged to defend the traditional as well as the experimental aspects of his work, first by the need to 'place' the spectator: 'to give the spectator a place and to generate codes of representation that the spectator can identify with ... so my strategy is to create a conventional code of representation with which the spectator can easily identify in much the same way as the mystifying experience of the Hollywood film. The work is to make sure that the identifications are not fixed and are incessantly called into question' (Comolli 1978: 45). Expressed theoretically, this strategy may sound rather a disappointment, in comparison with the ideals of mixed form which Comolli praised in his theoretical work. However, the concept of shifting identification is quite effective when Comolli presents different aspects of the problems facing the group. Comolli intends the spectator to identify with the group as a whole, rather than with any one of its members, and this aim meets with a qualified success. At best, it allows one to come up with a personal opinion or a personal doubt. However, he does undoubtedly favour certain characters. The principal ambiguity concerns the woman, Olimpia, who eventually becomes – along with one of the men, Luigi – the guardian of the colony's ideals in their original pure state.

Olimpia is singled out from the start as an exceptional being, and Comolli's treatment of her was criticised in the course of an American debate on the film, at which he was present, as 'conventional and sexist'. Rather surprisingly, Comolli did not contest this, observing only that Olimpia '*represents* all that is traditional in the representation of women' (Comolli 1978: 46). This leads to two separate lines of defence: firstly, that he means to inscribe the dominant code (as he puts it) in order that afterwards 'the

[22] 'J'aime bien les choses qui ne se voient pas, j'essaie de faire en sorte que mon travail se voit le moins possible et soit en quelque sorte oublié par ce qui est produit, disparaisse derrière ce que je fabrique.'

inscription can be played with, must be played with' (Comolli 1978: 45), secondly, that the characters are not to be read psychologically, but as a system of logical signs.

Cinétracts found the first argument somewhat spurious, but Comolli defended it firmly. The second is convincing, although whether it is a progressive decision remains open to debate: Olimpia's role is that of ambiguous symbol rather than living character. Her status in the film is central, and scarcely seems to change from her first entrance, when, as *Cinétracts* protested, in carrying water to the various groups of men she 'walk[s] and gesture[s] in the classical manner of WOMAN as she has been represented in classical Hollywood film'(Comolli 1978: 46). She is the unifying force, as the camera follows her from one group to another; she is the bearer of refreshment, rest, relaxed conversation, even music since the little group around her are singing. They have even lightheartedly substituted her name for the word Anarchia in the song's first line: 'Quando Olimpia verrà'. She is fêted and her entry is ceremonial. She is almost an allegory.

She will not lose this status *throughout the film*. On the one hand, she is continually played off against the male members of the group in their weakest moments. She serves to highlight Rossi's egoism, Alfredo's sexism, or the narrow-mindedness of the peasant families. At the same time she is the constant centre of the group's celebrations and reconciliations and she instigates their singing (a sign of temporary revolutionary unity). Thus, despite Comolli's intention to have the spectator identify with the group as a unity rather than with one individual, Olimpia is constantly indicated as the proponent of the view likely to be right, the holder of the privileged position, almost beyond question and not subject to human failings. The arguments which she supports are implicitly reinforced merely because she supports them. However, on a practical level, she is marginalised. She takes very little part in the frequent debates on the colony's immediate future. Her work in the community appears limited to teaching, a function which reaffirms her position as aside and apart. (According to the dossier her original counterpart was a nurse. To remain faithful to this would no doubt have been to give her a stereotyped female role, but her apartness would not have been so apparent.)

Olimpia is thus outside the (male) order of the colony, but also outside the human order. In her semi-observer's role she has something in common with Rossi, the instigator of the experiment; however, Rossi's opinions are thrown into doubt by the letter from Italy, by Olimpia or by Luigi. Olimpia – even though at one point she is made to say that with all the others she is 'in the thick of it' – is much nearer to an omniscient (Olympian) point of view; and in the process she has become a conventional portrayal, not a woman but the goddess of reason. The other women in the film, with one exception, are a reactionary force. Even though the dialogue points out that the men too have repressive attitudes, we are left with the impression that it is the women who are responsible for the reversion to old habits of property rights and repressive morality on the part of the peasant families. The *Cinétracts* audience thus have some justification for their protest regarding the status of women in the film.

Comolli's claim that: 'To me these relationships (between the characters) are never situated on the psychological level exclusively but essentially are found within the logic of the form. We could ascribe to each of the characters a logical sign and the combination of these signs would give the spectator the scenario' (Comolli 1978: 46) provides some justification for the treatment of Olimpia: the problem, perhaps, is that we do not on the whole experience these people as a group of logical signs; they have too much psychological realism to be simply mouthpieces in the way that Godard's protagonists are. Comolli referred to his intention to use theatricality as a way of reducing their psychological fullness. He told the *Cinétracts* interviewer; 'A further way of dealing with this problem (the dispersal of identification) is to denaturalize the codes of representation, that is, to bring into the foreground the way the artifice operates, notably by the performance of the actors which has to be a consciously theatrical one' (Comolli 1978: 45).

An interest in theatrical codes as a way of breaking cinematic convention was a strong element in the cinema around 1968, and Comolli's critical work had already betrayed his interest in it. However, *La Cecilia* is not obviously a theatrical film, except regarding the role of Olimpia. Many of the scenes where she appears have an air of unreality. Her costume and general appearance are consciously picturesque. She is placed consistently towards the centre of the frame and somehow never quite blends with the scenery, as the other characters normally do, remaining a Figure of Womanhood in a Landscape (frequently idyllic, as in the scene by the waterfall). But while Godard's Eve Democracy sketch in *One + One*, for example, uses similar elements to inscribe a criticism of the mythical figure of the oracle, Olimpia's status is merely established by these images.

Elsewhere the film seems to tend towards a kind of realism. In an article already cited ('Un corps en trop', written a year after the appearance of *La Cecilia*), Comolli discusses the credibility of historical reconstruction in the cinema in general, and specifically the identification of a historical personage with a present-day actor. The approach Comolli describes in the *Cecilia* dossier – 'the characters entered into the actors and identified themselves with them – were identified with this or that actor' (Comolli 1976a) corresponds to that which, in 'Un corps en trop', he identifies as being the most 'realist' strategy available to historical film. The protagonists of *La Cecilia* are largely anonymous, with the exception of Rossi, and even he is hardly familiar – this, according to Comolli's own theory in this article, allows illusion, if not perfect play, at least ideal conditions. (See the article in question, Comolli, 1977, which refers to an anonymous character in Renoir's *La Marseillaise*.) In the same article Comolli refers to the danger, in these conditions, of the appearance of stereotypes: 'We learn to guess what the character will do ... and since every effort is made to make them foreseeable we end up knowing them almost too well: we come up against overdetermination' (Comolli 1978: 11).[23] In *La Cecilia*, to a large extent, the individuals are successfully integrated into a group and no one is allowed to develop such importance as to risk a worrying stereotype – but Olimpia does take on importance, and does not change. Thus in the terms of this article she is an anomaly, even if, reading the film as spectacle and artefact (and the characters as logical signs) she has a clear poetic function.

That said, the theatre as metaphor does have a presence in the film. The terrain of *La Cecilia* lies somewhere between the search for realism and the materialist uncovering of the illusion, and in that space Comolli places performance. The film begins in a theatre,

---

[23] 'Nous apprenons à deviner le personnage ... et comme tout est fait pour nous le rendre prévisible nous finissons par le connaître presque trop bien: on tombe sur le surcodage'.

where Rossi meets the emperor of Brazil who is to guarantee him the land for his colony. This scene constitutes a kind of prologue, and at its end the camera homes in on the closed curtain as if to indicate that the play is about to begin. This is what Comolli intended to convey, as he makes clear in the dossier: 'The theatre at the beginning, the theatre at the end of the fiction: what launches it and what stops it' (Comolli 1976a: 104).[24] The last scene of the film shows a reduced colony about to perform *The Death of Danton* when they are interrupted by an army officer, who informs them that a revolt has broken out and that as Brazilian citizens they are liable for conscription. It is as if all their experiment had been a performance, finally brought to an end by the bitter realities of real power: are the actors about to be used to quell a true revolution? Comolli had, in fact, intended the whole story of the colony to be envisaged as a kind of play, with Rossi, the instigator, as at once actor and audience. The theatrical analogy was to emphasise the colony's isolation: 'The starting-point for the fiction which puts in place a system of repressed consciousness (the imperial protection is supposed to iron out all difficulties, spare the colony any struggle: *La Cecilia* at once begins with paternal authorisation and presents itself as the realisation of a dream); its final block, the explosive return of the historical repressed' (Comolli 1976a: 104).[25] However, the device is used quite timidly: a slight tendency to caricature, the music used as a sign of unity, some (rare) use of texts or recitation, that is all. Hence the effect is muted, although Comolli's statements in the 'Notes de Travail' indicate that he envisaged a much greater role for the theatrical element: 'The theatre as a disturbance of the fiction, the superimposition, desynchronisation, detachment of two representations (the filmic and the theatrical stage), one on top of the other, one against the other. The inscription of theatre in the film breaks the fiction, sets it out of joint, inverses the places, the spectators become actors, the *metteur-en-scène* (Rossi) finds that the troupe have assigned him the prompter's role, the spokesman

---

[24] 'Le théâtre au départ, le théâtre à la fin de la fiction: ce qui la lance, ce qui l'arrête.'

[25] 'Ce qui lance la fiction en mettant en place un dispositif de refoulement (la protection impériale est censée abolir les difficultés, épargner les luttes: *La Cecilia* à la fois commence par une autorisation paternelle et se présente comme la réalisation d'un rêve: ce qui la bloque, le retour éclatant d'un refoulé historique.'

has had speech taken from him and only commands a mockery of it any more' (Comolli 1976a: 104).[26]

These comments recall Comolli's interest in Rivette's *L'Amour fou*, which uses 'direct documentary' footage of theatre to break up and comment on its fictional drama. However, in *La Cecilia* it is perhaps not evident that the theatrical representation 'breaks the fiction'. It does serve to underline the colony's isolation and the theatrical element in the group's situation, and the metaphor of Rossi as director/audience for whom the colony's tribulations are a kind of spectacle is also – with hindsight – successful. Rossi's detached position (Olimpia accuses him of treating the group as an *in vitro* experiment) in fact could be taken as analogous to that of the cinema audience, as well as to a hypothetical theatrical one: and to the extent that it is unjustified, it incriminates the audience's neutrality towards this group of people confronting problems of concern to all. Rossi (and also the audience) forgets that he too is involved in this society and that the questions raised are directly relevant to him (us). In fact, he (we) is (are) perhaps in a position to do something about them, but responsibility is refused.

Theatre was also present in the *making* of *La Cecilia*, which adhered to the collective ideals of 1968. The actors, Comolli said, were like a theatre troupe because: 'the practice of acting in the theatre is of necessity more collectivist than acting in the cinema' (Comolli 1976a: 101)[27] and the collective atmosphere meant that at least to some extent the film was created organically in the course of the work: 'what happens among the group of characters is connected to what happens in the group of actors, it's not its reflection but a product or an echo of it' ... 'Discussions with the actors mostly turned on the political analyses which worked on the film-project, on the political status of the fictional characters, on the debates and the political issues through which the

---

[26] 'Le théâtre comme bousculement de la fiction, comme superposition, décalage, déboîtement de deux représentations (la scène filmique, la scène théâtrale), l'une sur l'autre, l'une contre l'autre. L'inscription du théâtre dans le film casse la fiction, la déboîte, fait changer les places, les spectateurs deviennent acteurs, le metteur en scène (Rossi), se voit attribuer par la troupe la place de souffleur, le porte-parole s'est fait prendre la parole et ne la porte plus que dérisoirement'.

[27] 'la pratique de l'acteur de théâtre est nécessairement plus collectiviste que celle de l'acteur de cinéma'.

"characters" defined themselves.' (Comolli 1976a: 101).[28]

This committed approach to the film's creation is reminiscent of the collective practice of more militant cinema, but Comolli's brief comments on his relations with the actors in *L'Ombre rouge*, in 1981, betray a very great change: 'It was a great pleasure to work with all the actors in the film, not only the stars who were wonderful and whose work I love, but also the actors who played the small roles and who I tried to find outside the usual channels' (Comolli 1981–82: 29).[29] The appreciation is banal, and where is the collectivity in this evocation of 'stars' and 'small roles', not at all the kind of vocabulary which would fit in the 'Notes de Travail' of *La Cecilia*?

In fact, everything about *L'Ombre rouge* bespeaks political disillusion and a change in attitude so profound as to be practically the reverse of all Comolli's principles of 1968/1969. The film traces the progressive disillusion of a Comintern agent in Spain in the 1930s as he finds himself in greater and greater disagreement with Stalin's policies. Comolli refers to his protagonist's dilemma in the heartfelt tones of one describing his own experience: 'One of the themes of the film is belief and the difficulty of leaving it behind. When one's a believer how does one stop being one? It never happens ... in a clear and precise way. It's always much more complex, a mass of little things which you don't really notice, but you begin to notice, which means that at a certain moment you turn round and see a whole picture that you hadn't known was in formation, but which is there' (Comolli 1981–82: 25)[30] ... 'The real

[28] 'ce qui se passe dans le groupe des personnages est lié à ce qui se passe dans le groupe des acteurs, n'en est pas le reflet mais bien le produit, la résonance' ... 'Les discussions avec les acteurs ont porté pour la plupart sur les analyses politiques qui travaillaient le projet du film, sur le statut politique des "personnages" de la fiction, sur les débats et les enjeux politiques à travers lesquels les "personnages" se définissaient'.

[29] 'J'ai eu un très grand plaisir à travailler avec tous les comédiens du film, pas seulement avec les vedettes qui ont été formidables, dont j'aime beaucoup le travail, mais aussi avec les acteurs qui ont joué les petits personnages et que j'ai essayé de trouver hors des sentiers battus'.

[30] 'Un des thèmes du film, c'est la croyance, la difficulté d'en sortir. Quand on est croyant, comment ne plus l'être? Ca ne se passe jamais ... de façon claire et nette. C'est toujours beaucoup plus complexe, un ensemble de petites choses qu'on ne voit pas vraiment, mais qu'on commence à voir, ce qui fait que, à un certain moment, on se retourne et on voit un tableau entier qu'on n'a pas vu se constituer, mais qui est là.'

subject of the film is these phenomena of belief, conviction, a crisis at the heart of this belief, and how to come through it or not to manage to come through it' (Comolli 1981–82: 28).[31]

Beneath this kind of language there lurks a bitter attitude to the director's own past beliefs which is perhaps not untypical of the ex-68ards fifteen years afterwards. It also bears a considerable resemblance to the language with which ex-Communists of a preceding generation, such as Montand and Semprun, referred to their shaken political certainties. When the flurry of creativity which had surrounded *Cahiers* at the time had led to such a fruitful theoretical approach as Comolli's, it seems an anticlimax. In 1976 he still envisaged film-making as work with actors and production team on a common problem, and he was still preoccupied with using the film's form to raise political questions in the audience: 'to push the spectator towards questioning his/her own mode of political speech and expression and not only the political *content* of that position' (Comolli 1978: 44). The Comolli of *L'Ombre rouge* seems to see political film-making more on the lines of the once-despised category (d) of 'Cinéma/Idéologie/Critique' – as having an explicitly political content but a perfectly traditional form, and, indeed, despite Comolli's claims that it is not as 'straightforward' as it appears: 'It's not really linear, there are holes, gaps, pieces of a jigsaw to put together' (Comolli 1981–82: 27),[32] it would not be out of place in the *série-Z*, its low budget apart. By 1981, the *série-Z* too had run out of steam, and *L'Ombre rouge* did not do well. Politics is a notion relevant only to the content: 'it seems to me that among the great subjects which should be dealt with today political subjects or those which have to do with politics are essential, it would be limiting both one's ambition and what one has to say not to take this political dimension, which is omnipresent in our lives but often absent from the cinema, into account' (Comolli 1981–82: 23).[33] Where is the unremitting political

[31] 'Le vrai sujet du film c'était ces phénomènes de croyance, de conviction, de crise à l'intérieur de cette croyance, et comment en sortir ou ne pas réussir à en sortir.'

[32] 'Ce n'est pas vraiment linéaire, il y a des trous, des lacunes, des éléments de puzzle à recombiner'.

[33] 'il me semble que parmi les grands sujets à traiter aujourd'hui il y a essentiellement les sujets politiques, ou qui ont à voir avec la politique, ce serait restreindre à la fois son ambition et ce qu'on a à dire que de ne pas prendre en compte cette dimension politique qui est omniprésente dans notre vie mais souvent absente du cinéma.'

analysis of 'Cinéma/Idéologie/Critique' ('all films are political')? The Comolli of the early 1970s could scarcely have even imagined not taking the political dimension into account.

As for Comolli's next film, *Balles perdues*, the theme of disillusionment continues but within the form of a detective film from which all explicit politics have apparently been excluded. The only ideological message the film contains appears to be an invitation to resigned acceptance. Henceforward Comolli entered a long unproductive period, before returning to the fore with television work and critical articles in the 1990s to the present. His documentary for the ARTE channel on the architect Pierre Riboulet, *Naissance d'un hôpital*, in 1991, marked a return to some of the formal themes of 1968, and a thoughtful re-evaluation of them which recognises the great value the debates of the 1970s had on a personal level and also as a groping towards a form of cinema which was both socially and imaginatively satisfactory. Comolli's interest in the politics of creativity has never entirely died, despite its low period.

Comolli, the principal editor of *Cahiers* at the time of the events, was perforce primarily a theoretician, but in any discussion of the relation of critical theory to cinematic practice in the aftermath of 1968, it is impossible not to deal with the position of that other ex-*Cahiers* writer who had long couched his theory in the form of films, Jean-Luc Godard. In fact, it would be tempting to fall into the opposite trap and present his experience as in some way the most significant, representative or exemplary of all the theoretical–political responses to the events expressed through film. This is not the case, although Godard's case *was* significant because of his immense reputation, which meant that even his non-presence (the most noticeable result of his reaction to 1968 for most audiences) was cause for comment, analysis, admiration or criticism. We have decided therefore to limit the space devoted to Godard here, partly because most of the work which he produced during the 1970s, and especially in the early years post-'68, was not commercially distributed at the time and therefore falls outside our remit; partly because Godard has been more studied than any other film-maker mentioned in these pages, even if his militant 1970s work has long been unfashionable. The commercial film that Godard drew from his experiences in 1968 and his experiments in the years that followed, *Tout va bien*, does however require some discussion, and we will consider it in the light of the body of theory established by the militant films which preceded it. Jean-Luc Godard is an intriguing exponent of cinematic theory; he almost never wrote books on the cinema, and expressed a certain friendly disdain for theoretical discussion. After he made his first film in 1959, he practically ceased publishing articles; most of his published 'work' relates to specific films and is in the form of interviews (see Godard, 1985). His comments on the cinema are frequently cryptic, and not always consistent; Godard's theories seem to relate to specific work in progress or just completed. As his *montagiste*, Agnès Guillemot, comments (Guillemot 1990: 62):[34] 'I admire Godard enormously for his total sincerity which makes him cheerfully contradict himself as his ideas develop. When someone says to me "Godard said that ..." I ask for the date, it's normal that someone's ideas develop. I think that it's rarely the same people who manage to make films and to theorise about them, and I have a great admiration for Godard's ability to practise his craft and to reflect on it concurrently.'

This last phrase is the key to Godard's relation to theory. While in the case of Comolli, theoretical writing was followed by an attempt at practice, Godard expressed his theory in the form of practice, and never more than from 1968 to 1970; each of his films is in itself a reflection on the meaning and aims of the cinema (as he sees it). Although the Dziga-Vertov group occasionally gave interviews, the majority of their theory was worked out on the screen, which accounts for the criticism that their films are inward-looking, and has also probably contributed to their 'disappearance'. They were searching for the best way to 'make a film politically'. The inquiry into cinematic method is all-pervading in *Vent d'est*, for example. Godard once described himself as an 'essayist' (Godard 1985: 215),[35] and the films which he made with the Dziga-Vertov group from 1969 to 1971 are the cinematic equivalents of articles in political or critical magazines; they are all theory. In

[34] 'J'admire énormément Godard pour sa totale sincérité qui le fait allègrement se contredire au gré d'une pensée qui évolue. Quand on me dit que "Godard a dit que…" je demande la date, c'est normal qu'une pensée évolue. Je crois que ce sont rarement les mêmes personnes qui arrivent à faire les films et théoriser dessus, et j'ai une grande admiration pour Godard qui arrive à mener de front la pratique et la réflexion sur son travail.'

[35] 'Je me considère comme un essayiste, je fais des essais en forme de romans ou des romans en forme d'essais: simplement, je les filme au lieu de les écrire'.

principle *Tout va bien* should be the culmination of that series; in fact it was a disappointment to all concerned, and an examination of the reasons for its failure to make any real impact may illustrate the difficulties of translating into practice even theories constituted in the course of reflection on work in progress.

The Dziga-Vertov films are certainly less studied than they deserve; while the new *Cahiers* criticism set a new fashion in ways of reading film, which survived the politics which underlay it, Godard and his colleagues' attempts to find political ways of using sound, image, and the time structure of the film (which allows self-criticism within the film, as in *Pravda*'s three 'false starts' or the structure of *Vent d'est* as a 'work in progress') were largely ignored or rejected outside their own political field, and one of the most potentially important cinematic offshoots of May 1968 was, paradoxically, cut short by its very politicisation, and perhaps by the difficulty of adapting the non-analytic discourse of images to expressing complex political theory.

It seems that the aim of the Dziga-Vertov group was always to produce films of such quality that they could convince a non-Maoist audience of their political desirability. Godard's remark 'films which are badly produced, as is the case of most of those distributed like this [through the parallel circuits], preach only to the converted' (Godard 1985: 346)[36] suggests a desire for mainstream distribution born of quality. And although it has regularly been described even by its most fervent champions as difficult, although the images are often accompanied by soundtracks reciting apparently rather arid political theory, with less apparent irony than in the 1967 *La Chinoise*, even the most dogmatic of Godard's post-'68 work is cinematically stimulating and, despite the intense seriousness of the projects, the films depend very much on humour to engage their audience. However, Godard and the Dziga-Vertov group seem to some extent to have worked in a void. In a politicised parallel cinema which flourished after 1968 their work was never really accepted. All the group's films were made as commissions for television companies, but not one was broadcast after being produced – a perhaps not surprising result. Uneasily balanced, with too many different interests to be restricted

---

[36] 'les films qui sont mal produits, et c'est le cas de ceux qui se diffusent ainsi [par les circuits parallèles] ne prêchent que les convaincus'.

by the priorities of politics, of formal experiment or of public acceptability, the cinematic essays constituted by *Le Gai Savoir*, *Un film comme les autres*, *British Sounds*, *Pravda*, *Lotte in Italia*, *Vent d'est* and *Vladimir et Rosa* were little seen by any audience (other than the Maoist intellectuals of *Cahiers*), and therefore when *Tout va bien* appeared the theoretical work it sprang from was hardly known. Latterly it has been fiercely attacked and has drifted even further into obscurity: in a special edition of *Cahiers du cinéma* in 1990, Joël Magny wrote of *Tout va bien*: '[*Tout va bien*] retains the heavy didacticism of the Vertov period and its "lessons-in-Marxism-Leninism" side ... From *La Chinoise* to *Vladimir et Rosa*, the language is the language of authority, of power, the language of the Father, the new fathers ... with, at their back, willy-nilly (and Mao for his part made no secret of it) the genial silhouette of the "peoples' little father", Joseph Stalin' (Magny 1990: 121).[37] This indicates the extent to which the materialist Marxist-Leninist theories expressed by all these films had fallen from fashion; in all the numerous articles in the rest of the magazine, only Luc Moullet proposed a positive approach to the 'militant period' (Magny 1990: 107). And yet the films take some trouble to avoid the definitive authority of 'the voice of the Father', incorporating doubt and change into their construction.

All the Dziga-Vertov experiments put great emphasis on the analysis of the process of production. A series of modifications of a piece of work, so that the audience is actually watching the progress of its creation, produces the continual reassessments of *Pravda*, the sequence of meetings and discussions which in *Vent d'est* decide the form of the film and the conduct of a strike (simultaneously, or alternatively), and, of course, the previous year, the rehearsals which punctuate *One + One*. These latter are not progressive, they are, as the French word suggests, repetitions, with modifications, and Godard deliberately avoided including a final version of the Rolling Stones' song (which was added by the British distributor). Throughout these films Godard avoids a

---

[37] 'De la période Vertov, [*Tout va bien*] conserve en effet le didactisme pesant, le côté "donneur de leçons de marxisme-léninisme" ... De *La Chinoise* jusqu'à *Vladimir et Rosa*, la parole est une parole d'autorité, de pouvoir, la parole du Père, des nouveaux pères ... avec, derrière eux, qu'on le veuille ou non (et Mao, lui, ne s'en cachait point), la silhouette bonhomme du "petit père des peuples", Joseph Staline'.

definitive, perfect copy; rather than accepting what they see, the audience is encouraged to discuss how it could have been improved.

When in 1972 Godard and Gorin returned to commercial distribution to make *Tout va bien*, they still gave great importance to the analysis of production, but its function has subtly changed. It no longer implies self-criticism in relation to defined aims and ideals, but sets out to expose the system. Such is the primary sense of the first sequence, where the concept of the 'film' is elaborated from the total vagueness of 'I want to make a film' through all the constraints and considerations which have to be taken into account. Prime position is given to the financial considerations which limit the content; the long sequence of cheques (not realistic, in that some are made out for percentages) with which the film starts indicates how much this work costs, and also all the necessary ingredients, such as film-stock and locations, which must be paid for. For a general audience, the film needs, before it can criticise the development of its work, to point out that the work is there – which is something that the avant-garde productions of the previous two years take for granted.

The first sequence of *Tout va bien* follows the development of the conception of the film, and as such it follows the pattern of repetition with variations, refocusing and deepening what has already been said. The 'film' of the start is situated first in the world of its production – 'We must have money' – then its content is discussed. It must have a story – a banal love-story is sugges-ted, where only the protagonists themselves are fully portrayed. Then, the film-maker is reminded that the characters cannot exist in a vacuum – they need a social setting, which is provided, with relation still to the principal characters only. But there must be a wider social context, and stationary images are provided of social classes applicable to the France in which the film will be set. Asked to provide movement, these images are reportrayed in action, each engaged in 'typical' class activities. (The bourgeoisie, when set in motion, projects its media image in the form of a press conference with President Pompidou.) In response to a third request for change, the action becomes expression of revolt, no longer typical but with intention to break down the boundaries; the 'paysans' who 'paysannent' (milking a cow) are now por-trayed burning their crop.

Here, we see the concept of the film gradually developing and broadening. The process is articulated, as it was in the Dziga-Vertov experiments, by the off-screen dialogue of two voices, one male, one female; only here, unlike in, for example, *Pravda*, one voice is clearly more authoritative. The woman advises and the man produces (we suppose) film sequences in accordance with that advice. We are thus prepared for the dialectical process which will occur in the main part of the film, where Susan (Jane Fonda) will consistently show Jacques (Yves Montand) the way.

The two protagonists in the film proper are both engaged in the production of sound and/or image but not in the production of the film we are watching. In *Tout va bien*, faced with the necessity of a coherent plot, Godard no longer shows his own film in the process of development, apart from in the prologue-like first sequence. Nonetheless, the theme of the film is an enquiry into how to produce representations adequate to their subjects, be they news reports or films; the enquiry is carried on through the two characters' developing dissatisfaction with their own productions as a reporter and a film-maker who has voluntarily, but very negatively, opted out. In this investigation, Susan, the American reporter, makes the discoveries, and acts as political initiator to the more confused (although well-intentioned) Jacques. Susan, however, is not presented as the source of all wisdom; she too is confused and comes to her conclusions gradually and with difficulty. As in the previous films, the problem of how to produce satisfactory representations is not resolved, although the two protagonists do reach some conclusion that politicisation and a sense of historical circumstance is necessary.

In fact, the film ends at the point where the Dziga-Vertov enquiries began. The conclusion: 'il faut se penser historique-ment' ('we must think of ourselves historically') which Susan reaches in the last reel is so self-evident to the Marxist-Leninist perspective that in their previous films Godard and Gorin scarcely felt the need even to express it, certainly not to spend an hour and a half proving it. On the other hand, the penultimate sequence, when Susan is faced with making a report on a super-market and feels unable to formulate it, indicates the beginning of an enquiry into satisfactory production from a politicised point of view, which is what the Dziga-Vertov films were all about. In a sense, *Tout va bien*, made at the end of Godard's Marxist-Leninist sequence, is best approached as an introduction to it, an effort to create an audience who would understand the questions which the previous films were trying to answer.

However, the film was not a success. It received a mediocre critical reception. Formally it is less experimental than Godard's immediate pre-'68 production; the story is relatively straightforward and the characters are coherent; there are none of the poetic interruptions of wandering philosophers which interlard *Week End* (1967); there is no obvious street theatre (and what there is was often taken literally by commentators); there are very few titles (Godard's obsession with the written word seems temporarily in abeyance, although 'May '68' imprints its existence on the film through an early red, white and blue lettered card) or references to literature, not even to the political texts which the Maoists cherished. All these elements exist in the underground films which precede it. *Tout va bien* was rejected by Godard's former audience as pedestrian, and by the small militant faction which still remained as selling out. Probably it was just badly timed. The political fervour of 1968 was dying away, and most people who might have been receptive to it had already reached or passed the theoretical point at which *Tout va bien* arrives. As such, the film perhaps has more impact now, when we are no longer saturated with similar language, than it had in 1972. It seems to have been a very rare case of Godard being behind the times rather than ahead of them, no doubt because it was conceived that way, as an introduction to more 'advanced' work already done, but destined to remain in obscurity.

However, it does contain a direct reflection on the implications of May 1968 – an explicit, although as Margaret Atack has pointed out not a visual, presence – on the conception of a mainstream film. *Tout va bien* represented for Godard a return to the industry after four years of political experimentalism, a return to 'normal' distribution and production, to the necessity to pay for this with box-office returns and hence with a narrative and stars. Discussion of the implications of that return are a major theme in the film. *Tout va bien*'s commercialism is one of the *raisons d'être* of the film; it was not totally essential in 1972 to have stars in order to ensure distribution – and certainly Godard's reputation could have made this unnecessary. *Tout va bien* is an 'anti-commercial' film, devoted from the start to exposing and attacking the commercial system. The attack is carried out, according to the principles set forth in *La Chinoise*, on the two fronts of form and content, although the form is not as revolutionary as the Dziga-Vertov experiments which precede it. It seems to have had the additional aim of compensating for the gradual falling away of a committed militant audience by introducing a 'vulgarisation' of the film-makers' political aims for the general public, using a combination of several of the elements contained in the Dziga-Vertov films. Thus there is the rather intrusive (for a non-politicised audience) political analysis, provided this time by the characters themselves and not, as in *La Chinoise*, by means of direct quotes; there is the development of this analysis as the film progresses, so that the characters at the end are in a position to criticise their earlier attitudes (a means of increasing interest in the political stance); there is a – restricted – use of graphics and titles; and there is, to a greater extent than is perhaps generally realised, recourse to slapstick and to street theatre.[38] All these elements had previously been explored in the militant films, although with greater self-questioning. There is also direct reference to the repercussions of 1968 (the later, factory-based clashes, rather than the too well-known scuffles in the Latin Quarter) to remind the audience that social unrest had already spread outside the limits of isolated incidents.

Its other central theme, the political significance of the everyday environment, directly linked to the thinking of 1968, was to become progressively more important to Godard as his connections with Maoist activism dwindled. 'Se penser historiquement'

[38] Colin McCabe. (1980: 70–1, 76) criticises the 'glorification of violence' at the end of the film. The sequence in question depicts a small group of left-wing students perpetrating a raid on a supermarket, attacking a Communist representative who is selling party literature and departing with trolleys full of goods some of which are thrown to the (mostly indifferent) customers, before violently confronting the riot police called by the management. As in *Weekend* or *La Chinoise*, however, at which the same criticism could be levelled, it seems unnecessary to take this violence at face value, although Godard's ambiguous response when the question is posed to him would seem to justify McCabe's objection ('Even now the terrorists are still for me the inheritors', McCable 1980: 75). The end of *Tout va bien* does not indicate that the group of *gauchistes* achieve much practical success, and the whole episode could reasonably be seen as a kind of 'happening', affording a dramatic presentation of the young militants' rejection of the consumer society, and incidentally revealing the institutional violence of the riot police. Godard's earlier films are filled with flagrantly theatrical violence.

means, as we have seen, not only to consider one's work (as a producer of representations) in its historical setting, but to consider 'private life' in its social context. This idea formed a central part of *Lotte in Italia*, where the lack of political analysis of the militant's home life in the first part is selected as a point of criticism in the second. In *Tout va bien*, some of the more original lines of reflection in the film are to be found in the sequences where Susan/Fonda insists on a political dimension essential to understanding her private relationship. The central characters are intellectuals who feel cut off from 'the revolution', and to some extent, but only to some extent, it is a forced renewal of contact which encourages them to rethink their own production. More important than the class issue, already, however, seems to be the idea, which Susan learns from the striking women, that action which appears to be politico-economic and to be related only to the working environment is very closely linked to the functioning of family life, and not only through the obvious link of prosperity or poverty. The strike represents the opportunity for working women to articulate and affirm their relation to their workplace (including the difficulty of persuading the man that for once it is his partner who is involved in a strike). Godard considered this aspect of the film extremely important, as he indicates in the joint interview which he and Gorin gave in *Politique-Hebdo* (Godard 1985: 375). In his work with Anne-Marie Miéville, including the final formulation of the material filmed for the Dziga-Vertov group's Palestine project, he returns more and more strongly to the idea; the feature film that he made in the late 1970s, *Numéro Deux*, takes place entirely within the protagonists' flat, except for a 'prologue-sequence' which, like that of *Tout va bien*, addresses the conception of the film. Politics are considered only in their impact on an apparently apolitical family. This film opens with an expression of doubt: 'It's a political film ... It's a sex film ... Sex or politics? It could be both together, for once', which is the conjunction which Susan desperately tries to persuade Jacques to accept in *Tout va bien*. For Sandrine in *Numéro Deux*, a strike means nothing. 'It's not the boss,' her husband Pierre explains as he prepares to leave, 'it's the lads. They're on strike', and Sandrine replies, 'I can't see any difference', which is, literally, true. Political action in the workplace leaves her without her husband for the day, just as his work does, while both know that the problems with their sex life are in part due to the irremediable lack of time.

Tout va bien marked the end of an era in Godard's work. His partnership with the Maoist Jean-Pierre Gorin, the member of the Dziga-Vertov group with whom he remained longest in contact, came to an end after their short feature *Letter to Jane*, which acted as a pendant to *Tout va bien*. For the rest of the 1970s he worked essentially in video, although the reflection engaged in during this period also found expression in the highly original *Numéro Deux*. *Numéro Deux* with its explorations of the political implications of the domestic, and its preoccupation with form and what it signifies, is also representative of a current of thinking born of May 1968. Indeed it is more innovative formally than *Tout va bien*, experimenting with the technical possibilities of the small screen to evoke simultaneous images and to present a framed small image within a larger screen. The film's origins lie partly in 1968, partly in the rapid development of video technology. Godard was fascinated by the potential of video, which he considered to be grossly under-exploited. At the time of *Numéro Deux* at least the fascination was connected with a perception of the political implications which could be found in use of simultaneous images – each commenting on the other – a technique which he complained was only used in TV sports programmes, and, occasionally, in news programmes, in ways which were unimaginative at best and at worst manipulative. The technical factor in *Numéro Deux* is introduced from the start, in the prologue sequence which concentrates not on the economic mechanics (as in *Tout va bien*), but on the machinery itself, which Godard is filmed surrounded by and working on. This determinedly materialist approach to the actual, physical *making* of film remained visible in the interstices of many of the highly experimental, although to many hermetic, films of the 'second Godard' of the 1980s; films which, after *Sauve qui peut (la vie)* (1979) and *Passion* (1982), began to concentrate explicitly on the deconstruction of archetypal narratives and an exploration of the ways in which they can be put onto film and articulated with the images, sounds and gestures of contemporary life (*Prénom Carmen*, 1983; *Je vous salue, Marie*, 1985; *Détective*, 1985; *King Lear*, 1987).

There were of course other examples of film-makers whose experiments in form attempted to live up to the theoretical demands of an intellectually experienced 1968; and other directions to the theoretical explorations of *Cahiers* and their like. One of the most interesting areas of re-evaluation is the representation of history in film – not surprisingly in view of the importance given to thinking the contemporary historically, not to speak of the lively current debates which were also exercising the world of historians. It is to this that we shall now turn.

REFERENCES

Braucourt, Guy (1976) '*La Cecilia*', *Ecran 76* 43, janvier: 65–6.

Comolli, Jean-Louis (1967a) 'Une morale de la dépense', *Cahiers du cinéma* 190, mai: 58–9.

Comolli, Jean-Louis (1967b) 'L'Ile, ou l'exemplarité d'un cinéma de combat', *Cahiers du cinéma* 194, octobre: 56–8.

Comolli, Jean-Louis (1969) 'Le Détour par le direct', *I. Cahiers du cinéma* 209, février: 48–53; *II. Cahiers du cinéma* 211, avril: 40–6.

Comolli, Jean-Louis and Narboni J. (1969) 'Cinéma/Idéologie/Critique', *I. Cahiers du cinéma* 216, octobre: 11–16; *II. Cahiers du cinéma* 217, novembre: 7–13.

Comolli, Jean-Louis (1971–72) 'Technique et idéologie', *I. Cahiers du cinéma*, 229, mai–juin: 5–21; *II. Cahiers du cinéma*, 230, juillet: 52–7; *III. Cahiers du cinéma*, 231, août-septembre: 43–9; *IV. Cahiers du cinéma*, 233, novembre: 39–45; *V. Cahiers du cinéma*, 234, décembre–janvier–février: 95–100; *VI. Cahiers du cinéma*, 241, septembre–octobre: 20–4.

Comolli, Jean-Louis (1976a) *La Cecilia: une commune anarchiste au Brésil en 1890*, 'Dossier d'un film': Paris: Dilane.

Comolli, Jean-Louis (1976b) Interview in *Le Monde*, 15 janvier: 12.

Comolli, Jean-Louis (1977) 'Un corps en trop', *Cahiers du cinéma* 278, juillet: 5–16.

Comolli, Jean-Louis (1977) 'On the Practice of Political Film', interview in *Cinétracts* 1, 4, spring/summer: 44–7.

Comolli, Jean-Louis (1980) 'Machines of the Visible', in *The Cinematic Apparatus*, Teresa de Lauretis and Stephen Heath (eds), Basingstoke: Macmillan: 121–41.

Comolli, Jean-Louis (1981–82) Interview in *Jeune cinéma* 139, décembre–janvier: 22–9.

Cornand, André (1976) '*La Cecilia*', *Revue du cinéma/ Image et son* 304, mars: 73–6.

Ecran 78 (1978) 'Ceux qui croyaient à l'art-pour-l'art et ceux qui n'y croyaient pas...', round table, *Ecran 78* 65, janvier: 30–47.

Godard, Jean-Luc (1985) *Jean-Luc Godard par Jean-Luc Godard*, Paris: L'Etoile/Cahiers du cinéma.

Guillemot, Agnès (1990) Interview in *Cahiers du cinéma*, novembre, numéro spécial Godard, 457 (supplément): 60–3

Harvey, Sylvia (1978) *May '68 and Film Culture*, London: British Film Institute.

McCabe, Colin (1980) *Godard: Images, Sounds, Politics*, London: British Film Institute.

Magny, Joel (1990) '*Tout va bien*', *Cahiers du cinéma*, novembre, numéro spécial Godard, 457 (supplément): 121–2.

Moullet, Luc (1990) 'Suivez le guide', *Cahiers du cinéma*, novembre, numéro spécial Godard, 457 (supplément): 104–11.

Passek, Jean-Loup (ed.) (1987) *Dictionnaire du cinéma français*, Paris: Larousse.

6
The representation of history

'Il faut se penser historiquement'. The ultimate lesson of *Tout va bien*, originating in the theories of Brecht, lay behind the work not only of Godard but of other directors, such as Alain Tanner, Gérard Guérin or René Allio, who were searching in the aftermath of 1968 for a suitable method of rendering a politically relevant account of everyday life. The basic Marxist concept of 'history', the wider context of social and cultural change in which it is necessary to understand one's present experience, was an essential tool for a whole current of cinematic thinking. It is therefore not surprising that history in its more casually accepted sense, and its cinematic representation, should also undergo reconsideration in the 1970s.

Debate on the links between cinema and history had two main strands; the first, which does not particularly concern us here, concerned the relationship of documentary footage and archive material to the events and periods that they represent (see *Cahiers du cinéma* 1975; Comolli 1977; Gervais 1970), and had its roots in the practical concerns of historians and history teachers, although the insistent questioning of documentary representations of the present and of the recent past – not least the events of May – fed into and invigorated the debate. The second strand concerned the historical feature film. How, and why, should the cinema represent the historical past, and what historical past should it represent? The what, the how and the why are three parts of the same question, of course, and the decisions taken are closely linked; we will attempt to look at each part, briefly, in general terms, and then to consider their solutions in the work of René Allio (*Les Camisards; Moi, Pierre Rivière...*) and Franck Cassenti (*L'Affiche rouge*). Jean-Louis Comolli's *La Cecilia*, treated in an earlier chapter, is also relevant here.

The historical film was not a common phenomenon in the immediate aftermath of 1968, at least not in France. At the appearance of *Les Camisards*, in 1971, François Regnault observed that it 'belongs to a genre which we have gone without, with one or two rare exceptions, for a long time' (Regnault 1972: 71).[1] The references for comparison at the time come not from France but from Italy, and the same is true even in 1975; *Cahiers*' article on the possible representations of history in the cinema (Kané 1974–75) refers to two films by Italian directors (Rossellini's *La Prise de pouvoir de Louis XIV*, a television film, and Pasolini's *Fiore delle 1001 notte*, which cannot strictly be called a historical film) and one French one – Renoir's *Marseillaise*, made in 1938! To observe the full flowering of the genre, it is necessary to direct our attention to the second part of the decade, roughly from 1974, when the historical past suddenly became a prominent subject in the French cinema,[2] and the object of a serious attempt at re-evaluation.

Firstly, on the level of what is represented. The subjects chosen are no longer the traditional highspots of history. On the contrary, the films favour individuals, or groups of individuals. As Jill Forbes has said regarding *Lacombe Lucien*, these films 'valorise history as an individual and not a collective experience' (Forbes 1992: 244); this is true, but the narration is generated, in almost every case, from the relation between the individual and the collective experience, a relation which is in some way exemplary. *Cahiers* perceived this in *Lacombe Lucien*: 'Lacombe is a Frenchman under the Occupation, a guy with a concrete relation to Nazism, to the country, to the local power-structure, etc. And

---

[1] 'appartient à un genre dont on se passe, à quelques rares exceptions, depuis longtemps'. The text was written some time before its publication in *Cahiers*, and destined for the release of the film.

[2] On the pre-twentieth century past: *Je suis Pierre Rivière* (Christine Lipinska, 1975), *Que la fête commence* (Bertrand Tavernier, 1975), *La Cecilia* (Jean-Louis Comolli, 1976), *Moi, Pierre Rivière…* (René Allio, 1976), *Le Juge et l'assassin* (Bertrand Tavernier, 1976). On the early twentieth century: *Stavisky* (Alain Resnais, 1974), *Souvenirs d'en France* (André Téchiné, 1974), *Une fille unique* (Philippe Nahoun, 1976), *Violette Nozière* (Claude Chabrol, 1978). On the Second World War and the Resistance, after *Le Chagrin et la pitié* (Marcel Ophüls, 1971, a documentary montage which called into question the dominant representation of collaboration and resistance), *La Brigade* (René Gilson, 1974), *Les Guichets du Louvre* (Michel Mitrani, 1974), *Lacombe Lucien* (Louis Malle, 1974), *L'Affiche rouge* (Franck Cassenti, 1976), *Nous étions un seul homme* (Philippe Valois, 1978). Not an exhaustive list, it may give some impression of the extent to which history invaded the cinema after 1974. Post-1945 history was a different proposition: the Algerian War, for example, was covered by a great silence.

we shouldn't ignore this way of personifying history, embodying it in a character or group of characters who at any given moment represent the essence of an exceptional relationship with power' (Foucault 1974: 14).[3]

The individuals are characterised by rupture with the society of their period, through revolt, crime or simple obliviousness (of which Lucien is an example). Thus Allio (*Les Camisards*) and Comolli *(La Cecilia)* portray groups in revolt who do not succeed in creating a revolution; while several films take as their subject the career of a criminal (Pierre Rivière, in two films, Joseph Vacher in *Le Juge et l'assassin*, Violette Nozière or Stavisky). Even the important sub-group of films which deal with the Second World War collect a number of untraditional central figures. Gilson *(La Brigade)* and Cassenti *(L'Affiche rouge)* centre on groups of resistants marginalised as a result of their nationality; *Lacombe Lucien* presents an almost inadmissible figure, a collaborator who is not a double-dyed villain,[4] while the portrayal of co-habitation (it cannot be called collaboration) in the under-rated *Nous étions un seul homme* (Philippe Valois, 1978) is several hundred miles – apparently literally – from the march of history as we know it.

The displacement from centre to periphery also operates geographically. Paris gives place to the provinces, and the city (even provincial) to the rural back-country. The revolt of *Les Camisards* is not only against the repression exercised by an official religion, but also the protest of the rural population against the oppression of the urban aristocratic culture. The relation between a politicised urban class structure in formation and a countryside only slowly integrating such new ideas is one of the themes of *Le Juge et l'assassin*; the ahistorical nature of the rural population explains the career of Lacombe Lucien and the relationship of the two protagonists of *Nous étions un seul homme* where the events of the war seems so distant that they are

[3] 'Lacombe, c'est un Français sous l'occupation, un mec qui a un rapport concret au nazisme, à la campagne, au pouvoir local, etc. Et nous ne devons pas ignorer cette manière de personnifier l'histoire, de l'incarner dans un personnage, ou un ensemble de personnages qui condensent, à un moment donné, un rapport privilégié au pouvoir.' Interviewer (Pascal Bonitzer and Serge Toubiana are named) is quoted.

[4] A move had been made in this direction with *Hiroshima mon amour*; however the importance of *Le Chagrin et la pitié* in obliging the French nation to face the reality of 'everyday collaboration' is immeasurable.

scarcely comprehensible as relating to daily life.[5] Such remote settings imply a different relationship to the events of history; they are integrated slowly, but their repercussions can be both profound and unforeseeable, as several of these chronicles of rural disaffection make clear. Rural revolt can be seen as deeply rooted, which might explain the attraction of the subject three or more years after the explosion of 1968 had died away.

The subject-matter of history has thus been displaced from the centre to the margins. The revolutions of the history books are ignored in favour of small and forgotten movements, heroes give place to anti-heroes, and the central stage of history to remoter regions where news penetrates slowly and may be given another sense. The move from centre to margins is itself sufficient for us to link this tendency in the cinema to post-'68 developments; by 1974 the discourse of revolution itself had begun to fragment and move from centre to margins, from Paris to the provinces. A number of minority groups were taking up the watchword of 'prise de parole' which was no longer a slogan for revolt bandied around the streets in a mass voice. At the same time, the individual in revolt against society and treated by the latter as criminal and insane also made his or her appearance in films with a contemporary setting, and in this context the trope predated its treatment in history. Examples would be Alain Tanner's *Charles mort ou vif* and *La Salamandre*, or *Pierre et Paul* by René Allio, who was about to become a pioneer of the historical movement. A historical and theoretical foundation for this analogy was sought in the work and around the name of Michel Foucault, whose *Histoire de la folie*, in 1961, had posited the creation by society of a type of the social outcast whose identity might fluctuate but who would always, for one reason or another, be shut away. The renewed interest in historical criminal cases, analysed in the context of the surrounding society, certainly owes something to Foucault, who took an active part in debates on these issues and occasionally offered support and documentation to films which interested him. We may also suppose that the prevalence of films re-examining cases from the nineteenth and early twentieth centuries reflects a desire to touch

[5] The film's very rare mention of the Nazi persecution of the gypsies serves, however, as a denial of rural escapism.

on questions which in a contemporary context would be impossibly sensitive (Prédal 1977: 25).[6]

The choice of subject-matter, therefore, can be seen to stem in part from its relevance to contemporary reality in the wake of 1968. The history of minor revolutions and experiments in alternative societies is apparently probed in order to shed some light – or at least provide a new angle – on 1968 and its aftermath. The relation of the historical criminal to contemporary reality is more complex. The presentation of these cases invariably places emphasis on the relation of the anti-social individual to the socio-economic code: the study of the criminal is indissociable from that of the society which condemns him for his crime. Thus the study can reveal unexpected contradictions in the structure of society, and the motives for 'criminal' behaviour are related to their sources in the complex and contradictory values of what is considered 'normal', a process that calls into question the whole foundation of social values. There are obvious similarities between contemporary, May-inspired films such as *Pierre et Paul* or *Charles* and this form of procedure, although the distance afforded by the temporal gap reduced the subversive force of the historical 'criminal' film.

Apart from the possible application of historical subject matter to current events and problems, however, there is implicit in this trend a need to reflect upon the definition of history itself. This is achieved firstly by giving a privileged position to those whom the history books forget, or proposing a re-evaluation of popular myths such as the Resistance movement. The latter trend was ambiguous. A cogent argument (put forward in *Cahiers du cinéma* by no less an authority than Michel Foucault: see Foucault 1974) held that these representations contributed (not necessarily intentionally on the film-makers' part) to effacing the popular memory of the Resistance with its empowering implications for ordinary people, and to rehabilitating the collaborationist bourgeoisie who had supported Giscard d'Estaing in 1974.

---

[6] 'Nombreux sont ... les jeunes réalisateurs qui tentent de poser dans le passé des problèmes que le manque de recul ne permet pas toujours de présenter clairement dans la réalité complexe du présent'. There are, however, one or two examples of analysis of criminal motivation in a contemporary setting, notably *La Machine* (Paul Vecchiali, 1977). A polemic against the death penalty perhaps provided a relatively 'safe' topic to serve as a pretext for such work.

These films also call into question the traditional notion of history, however, through the revelatory power of their supposedly marginal subject-matter. This is particularly true when the narrative includes, usually in a marginal position, historical events regarded as major. A film like *Stavisky*, not considered particularly radical nor indeed exactly marginal in its concerns, illustrates clearly how precise concentration on one individual story can nonetheless open the film in many directions. *Le Juge et l'assassin* demands a re-evaluation not only of the Dreyfus affair but of late nineteenth-century French society in general. In *Moi, Pierre Rivière...*, the events represented seem to be entirely parochial, but the influence of a wider society is inevitable, and Allio's film exposes the significance of the most apparently insignificant details of rural life.

The work of the *Annales* school of history was, of course, extremely relevant to this new departure in cinema. It is probably also at the source of the third way in which the films in question attempted to re-evaluate history; that is, through an interrogation of the nature of the historical document, and, more particularly, of the reconstruction, the representation, of history. In some cases, at least, films manage to call into question not only the traditional matter of history, but the manner of its telling. We move now, then, from the Why? to the How? of the new historical film.

There is no one answer to this question; films of the 1970s which use their historical setting to effect some form of analysis or social comment are extremely numerous and extremely varied. By no means all film-makers couched their historical inquiry in an innovative form. This could on occasion lead to ambiguities (as in the case of *Lacombe Lucien*) but it was not always seen as a disadvantage. *Jeune cinéma*, comparing Gilson's *La Brigade* with *L'Affiche rouge*, observed that, although 'for Gilson, the idea was to put forward a new vision of the Resistance: it's a film at first degree, as it were' while 'Cassenti foregrounds problems of representation and the questioning of the form becomes the main subject of the film', and although '[Cassenti's] skill consists ... in showing that it is the elaborating of an appropriate investigative method on which the unveiling of reality will depend', it is Gilson's film that is the more successful: 'In a word, the representational problems of the actors in 1976 rather stifle the questions which the Resistance members were asking in 1944, they offer only a brilliant reflection of them while *La Brigade* allows for the beginning of a real intellectual exploration free of any stereotypes' (Prédal 1977: 27–8).[7]

Nonetheless, our intention here is to consider three films where the historical reflection is accompanied by an attempt to use the resources of sound and image to further that reflection. Within the body of film theory represented by *Cahiers du cinéma*, the problem of the representation of the historical past was conceived as specific, at least from the appearance of *Les Camisards* in 1971(see Aumont 1972; Regnault 1972).

Cahiers proposed the concept of the *historical signifier*; that is, the elements of the film which denote its setting in a period of the past, specific or not. The absolute necessity of a historical signifier raises a series of questions concerning authenticity: whether it is necessary, how it can be established, and what its function is in the reception of the film by the audience. This question is of paramount importance to any definition of the aims of a historical film, and *Cahiers* establishes a relation between the historical signifier and Brecht's theory of *Verfremdungseffekt*.

On the level of cinematic practice, *Jeune cinéma* noted in 1977 that among the exponents of the new historical cinema precise accuracy was neither attained nor even desired: 'all the young French film-makers are openly declaring their right to anachronism.' They quote René Gilson's refusal of a 'superficial picturesqueness that would "charm" the spectator, that is distract him [sic] from the vital point: political reflection' (Prédal 1977: 28).[8] Nonetheless, a certain degree of accuracy was needed if only to avoid distracting the spectator by too obvious a discrepancy between representation and reality.

---

[7] 'pour Gilson, l'idée était de proposer une nouvelle vision sur la Résistance: c'est un film, en quelque sorte, au premier degré'... 'Cassenti met ... au premier plan les problèmes de représentation et l'interrogation sur la forme devient le sujet principal du film' ... 'l'habileté [de Cassenti] consiste ... à montrer que c'est précisément de la mise au point d'une méthode d'investigation appropriée que dépendra le dévoilement de la réalité' ... 'En somme, les problèmes de représentation des comédiens de 1976 étouffent un peu les questions qui pouvaient se poser les résistants de 44 dont ils n'offrent que le brillant reflet alors que *La Brigade* permet d'amorcer une véritable réflexion intellectuelle justement dégagée de tout stéréotype.'

[8] 'tous les jeunes cinéastes français revendiquent ouvertement le droit à l'anachronisme' ... 'pittoresque superficiel qui allait "séduire" le spectateur, c'est-à-dire le détourner de l'essentiel: la réflexion politique'.

Pascal Kané's article 'L'Effet d'étrangeté' (Kané 1974–75) provides the most detailed exploration of the implications of the historical signifier. The starting point is the assumption that it has one inevitable function, however it is used, which is to strike the audience as unfamiliar in the sense that the audience cannot supply sufficient information about the world that is represented to supplement what is given.[9] This has two, inevitable, effects, not explicitly stated by Kané but underlying all of what follows. Firstly, the film-maker has the authority to impose an analysis which the audience will probably be unable to contest; secondly and more importantly, the audience, confronted with a representation of the world which is necessarily fragmentary, will tend to supply the lack with reference to its own *familiar* experience. Thus, almost automatically, the representation within the film will be brought into comparison with that experience, which is related to two main systems of reference: firstly, the present-day, secondly, whatever notions the audience may have previously held concerning the period represented in the film.

Kané postulates three possible ways in which this confrontation of unfamiliar and familiar may take place (Kané 1974–75: 79),[10] only one of which implies an active interaction and exchange. Firstly, there is an aggressive use of authenticity, which Kané locates in Rossellini's film about Louis XIV. This method deliberately overloads the film with external indications of period, allowing next to no connections between what the spectators see and their own life experiences, and considerably outweighing any vague information they may have on the period in question. The point of the exercise is to alienate the spectator, in the sense that we are compelled to total detachment and watch events rather as behavioural scientists learn about an unknown species.

The second approach, which Kané illustrates with reference to *Il Fiore*,[11] relates neither to any present-day experience of the

---

[9] Kané accepts that there will be degrees of unfamiliarity, but a basic tenet of this article is that the effect comes into play even if the period depicted is known to the audience (although this particular case is not considered in any detail).

[10] 'nous éliminons d'emblée [les feuilletons d'époque] où l'altérité radicale du sujet historique est immédiatement recouverte (où, si l'on veut, le "sujet" n'est pas l'histoire), ou est simplement niée dans une mascarade de bals costumés'.

[11] *Il Fiore* never claimed to be a reconstruction of history. Kané's summary betrays a strange wish to ignore the nature and even the existence of the source text, not to mention possible visual referents. But this is not the place …

audience, nor to any recognisably authentic historical source:

> absolute strangeness of the practices, the discourses, but also the
> bodies, the places: a cinema fascinated by 'the Other', a pure enjoy-
> ment of the heterogeneous, without any reference point or historical,
> sexual, economic or even architectural anchor for the story (a
> characteristic example is the proper names, which are totally foreign
> to our onomastic space). History is no more than a particular variant
> of mythic discourse. (Kané 1974–75: 80)[12]

The only possible reference for the audience is one of mythic
relationships.

It is only with the third possibility that any exchange between
audience and film is possible. Kané evokes here Brecht's theory of
the 'gestus social' ('the expression through gestures and facial
mimics of the social relations existing between people in a given
era' (Kané 1974–75: 82)[13]). The use of the 'gestus social' in the
historical film, as explained by Kané, depends on a dialectic
between familiarity and unfamiliarity, the gestures may be familiar
but their meaning unfamiliar, and the audience recognises them
and *at the same time* is struck by their unfamiliarity. The example
from *La Marseillaise* of Louis XIV eating tomatoes, alone, during
the siege of the Tuileries details three unfamiliar significations
attached to the familiar gesture, all of which are revealing. There
is first the contrast of the everyday action and the illustrious
historical figure performing it; secondly the contrast between the
banal action and the violent events taking place elsewhere of
which the tomato-eater seems unaware; thirdly the contrast
between the familiarity of the action to the audience and the
evident signs of its unfamiliarity to the king. Each of these contrasts
creates surprise in the audience, which in turn generates questioning and leads to conclusions (human as well as political factors
determine the action of a king, the king is alarmingly remote from
the events of his reign to say the least, everyday things such as

---

[12] 'étrangeté absolue des pratiques, des discours, mais aussi des corps, des
lieux: cinéma fasciné par "l'Autre", pure jouissance de l'hétérogène, et absence de
toute butée, de tout référent historique, sexuel, économique et même architectural
du récit (exemple caractéristique, les noms propres, totalement étrangers à notre
espace onomastique). L'Histoire n'est plus alors qu'un cas particulier du discours
mythique'.

[13] 'l'expression par les gestes et les jeux de physionomie des rapports sociaux
existant entre les hommes d'une époque déterminée'.

tomatoes were extraordinary luxuries in 1789 and certainly not available to everyone). All these conclusions the audience can draw for itself, and they will therefore have more force than mere given information.

The Brechtian procedure which according to Kané constitutes the *raison d'être* of a historical cinema, thus depends on an active confrontation between familiarity and unfamiliarity: 'On the one hand, to make daily life opaque through showing a banal fact as extraordinary and fascinating; on the other, to make History accessible and exemplary by looking behind our misleading knowledge and clichés and seeking out what speaks to us today in History and can guide our analyses and our actions' (Kané 1974–75: 83).[14]

Kané makes no reference to recent French historical films. It seems that in 1975, form in the French historical cinema was still at a low priority. *Les Camisards* is an exception, with regard to which the debate on the use of the historical referent was first launched, but it was not a typical case, nor was it considered by *Cahiers* to be exemplary, and until 1975 it had had few emulators. The vogue for the historical cinema was identified with a 'mode rétro', not confined to France; films like *La Brigade*, *Lacombe Lucien* or *Stavisky* represented for the formally oriented *Cahiers* a reason to enquire into the failure rather than the success of the French historical cinema (Kané 1974–75: 83).[15] Films which are experimental in the Brechtian sense remain a minority, but we will consider here three which make clear efforts to reflect both on the materials of their production and on history and its mechanisms.

The work of René Allio is exemplary. In the 1970s he made two rural historical films – *Les Camisards* in 1970–71, and *Moi, Pierre Rivière...* in 1976 – and two 'contemporary' urban films: *Pierre et*

---

[14] 'D'un côté, opacifier la vie quotidienne en rendant insolite et fascinant un fait banal; de l'autre, rendre l'Histoire accessible, exemplaire, en recherchant derrière les savoirs trompeurs, les représentations figées, ce qui, aujourd'hui dans l'Histoire nous interpelle, peut guider nos analyses et nos actions'.

[15] 'tout ce cinéma qu'on dit aujourd'hui 'rétro' [...] on peut définir par le détournement qu'il opère de la scène historique en un champ d'investissement "érotique" ou "fantasmatique" dont le piquant [...] n'est que l'inscription, sur le mode principalement fétichiste, de cette étrangeté, débarrassée de toute contrainte d'authenticité par rapport à son référent réel, comme de toute production d'une espace de lecture critique'

Paul (1969) and *Rude journée pour la reine* (1973). Brecht was a constant and very conscious referent in both genres, and indeed even Allio's contemporary films can be treated as historical documents. (*Pierre et Paul* contains an extended reflection on the relation of recent history to contemporary reality through a son's reaction to records of his father's life, both familiar and unfamiliar to him: while *Rude journée* relates its protagonist's dilemma partly in reference to a historical fantasy which allows, or entraps, her into a transcendence of her environment and most of all her class.)

The history of *Les Camisards* took place in 1702; the group were Protestant peasantry in revolt against the religious repression which followed the revocation of the Edict of Nantes. The film concentrates on one small band, from its formation as a permanent entity to its final decimation at the hands of the army. Four of the participants – the most individually distinguishable – escape to join another leader and continue the struggle.

The film establishes from the start two opposing groups of characters, the nobles and the Camisard peasants. Although individuals are of course distinguished, it is the division into groups that stands out first, and Allio, in his introduction to the film for *Avant-scène* (Allio 1972a: 9), recognised that the central character is not any individual, but the group of Camisards: 'this new "collective" character'.

In *Les Camisards* the treatment of the historical signifier is complex, both regarding Allio's treatment of the *objects* of history (costumes, props) and even the relation of the scenario to history or to fiction. A glance at the *Avant-scène* screenplay indicates immediately how important the historical documentation of the film was considered. In contrast to the magazine's normal practice of preceding the screenplay with one critical article, *Les Camisards* is introduced by eleven pages of documentation, seven of which are purely historical; there is a two-page extract from Ladurie's book *Paysans du Languedoc*, and another from an introduction to the Camisard journals; there is a year-by-year chronology of the revolt of the Camisards (which however omits the few months with which the film is concerned); finally there is an introduction to the film by Allio which at least purports to be historically accurate. The fact that *Avant-scène* did not provide anything like this amount of documentation for *Moi, Pierre Rivière...* or for *L'Affiche rouge*, both of which it published, suggests that its presence is due to Allio, and that attestations of authenticity were very important to him.

It seems that the majority of the individuals in the film, however, are fictional. There are exceptions, such as Abraham Mazel or Cavalier, but their relation to their historical counterparts is tenuous. There was a Camisard leader named Laporte, but he is not the Gédéon Laporte of the film. The character of Jacques Combassous, who takes on the function of narrator, is, and is not, the Bonbonnoux whose journals are a major source of documentation on the period. The other characters around whom a semblance of personal narrative is built are almost certainly fictional as individuals. At the level of the group, however, historical fact is adhered to; there were similar groups of Camisards in revolt in the Cévennes between August and October 1702. This relation of fiction to reality rejoins the idea that a historical representation should bring into play the forces of history, as distinct from the importance of individuals; Allio's use of the 'gestus social' works to confirm – and even to over-confirm – this.

Details of historical accuracy are not usually a priority to the spectator of a film: however, there are elements in this text itself which announce it as a historical document. The use of Combassous' voice is an important example. The character Jacques Combassous does appear in the film; however, long before his appearance, the sound-track accompanies the filming of certain events with the account of them supposedly taken from Combassous' journal. The language is quite consistent with what we might expect of contemporary documents, as which it is received. (*Cahiers* notes that it is a 'pastiche of the language of Bonbonnoux' "Journal"' (Regnault 1972: 66n).) The use of this 'text', invented though it is, connotes historical reconstruction. The manner of filming incidents tends to confirm this. Very small importance – in comparison to the traditional fiction film – is given to dialogues within the group. This, and the near-absence of individual close-ups,[16] reasserts the primacy of the group as a force over the individuals in it, and also precludes personal involvement of the spectator while increasing the sense of radical temporal separation – we do not know what these people said. For explanation of the action, the spectator is

---

[16] Sequences of close-ups, either separate shots or included in long travelling shots across the group, are relatively frequent, however.

as often as not reliant on Combassous, and his text is the only indication in the film of the passing of time and of the events connecting individual incidents. During the 'temps morts' between incidents the image is reduced to an illustrative role, travelling across mountain scenery or showing images of the group at rest or moving on which are not precisely situated within the narrative. The text, with its apparent historicity, becomes all the more important.

In both text and image, Allio was very aware of the need to establish some form of dynamic relation between the past and the present. He observed in *Avant-scène* that '[history] in *Les Camisards*, with the costumes, the objects and the social customs, takes on such defined forms they may slightly hide the correspondences with the present day; you have to reveal their meaning yourself' (Allio 1972a: 9).[17] The work involved in the unveiling of the sense is, of course, precisely what will render the film interesting to formalist critics; we must now consider Allio's visual inscription of the dialectic between familiarity and unfamiliarity.

The vital concept here is the differentiation of the two groups. He explains in *Avant-scène* – this point was taken up again by *Cahiers* – that the costumes and the language of the nobility were conceived according to different rules from those of the Camisards. The costumes of the nobles were conceived and constructed with a view to precise authenticity, but of a certain type; all these costumes had been created as homogeneous wholes, and some had previously served in the theatre.[18] As regards historical detail, they are no doubt correct, and they correspond to the *idea* which an audience may have of the costumes of the early eighteenth century. The reference, for an audience, is to vague historical expectations drawn from images of the court of Louis XIV in children's history books or from the theatre of Molière and Marivaux; thus the costumes of the nobility in the film function, as Allio states, to produce 'a show … a theatricalisation of the whole person' (Allio 1972a: 9).[19] The same applies to their language,

---

[17] '[l'histoire] prend dans *Les Camisards*, avec les costumes, les objets et les moeurs, des formes si définies qu'elles peuvent masquer un peu les correspondances avec notre temps; il faut dévoiler soi-même leur sens.'

[18] Allio worked in the theatre before entering cinema; his co-scriptwriter for *Les Camisards* was an avant-garde director, Jean Jourdheuil, whose work he admired.

[19] 'une parade … une théâtralisation de toute la personne.'

radically unfamiliar to twentieth-century ears except, again, in the particular context of the theatre. Allio insists that it is in fact historically accurate: 'You may think when you hear it that it's 'stagey'; in fact it's not theatrical at all, it's the way the nobility spoke, but we're used to hearing it in Marivaux and Molière' (Allio 1972a: 10),[20] but it is to the referent 'theatre' that a twentieth-century audience will turn. The effect of historical unfamiliarity in the scenes of the nobility is therefore to de-realise the characters. Individual characteristics, in no way relating to the unfamiliar or the historical, augment the effect; François de la Fage and Catherine de Vergnas correspond exactly, in the physique of the actors, their narrative role and their language, to the *jeune premier* and ingénue roles of a comedy of the period, and Capitaine Poul, the swaggering soldier, is also a theatrical stock character.

The approach to the Camisards is quite different. Historical accuracy is no longer even a criterion, the limit is set at historical probability – the general effect is acceptably eighteenth century. The principal aim when making the costumes, according to Allio, was that they should look comfortable on the wearers, and they were put together from heterogeneous elements, 'some of which were definitely modern'. The costumes do indeed look 'worn', as Allio intended, and even in some cases acceptably wearable today. Anachronism of costume, however, is not particularly noticeable; the language and apparent social relations (the 'gestus', literally) are a different matter.

Cahiers observes that the language of the Camisards 'apart from the biblical metaphors and imprecations ... is the everyday language of the 20th century' (Aumont 1972: 66).[21] This is mitigated by the rarity of intimate conversations among the group, and in the discourse of the captains, even where the language is familiar, the *tone* remains reminiscent of their subsidiary role as preachers. The voice of Combassous, whose language although clear has all the signs of a text of the period, also ensures that the Camisards remain identifiably historical. Nonetheless their conversations are far from being as alien as those of the nobility, and

[20] 'On pourrait penser quand on l'entend qu'elle fait "théâtre"; en fait, elle n'est pas théâtrale du tout, c'est celle que parlaient les nobles, mais que nous avons l'habitude d'entendre dans Marivaux, dans Molière'.

[21] 'aux métaphores et imprécations bibliques près ... est le langage courant du XXe siècle'.

on the few occasions when their private conversation is presented there is little distance between them and the audience.

Certainly true accuracy would have been an extreme choice, since the historical Camisards would have spoken Occitan among themselves. Allio had considered this but rejected it: 'I wanted whatever Occitans saw in *Les Camisards* to be visible to Bretons and Alsatians too' (Allio 1972b: 24).[22] Thus the guiding factor was identified as relation to the audience; the aim was to create a direct link between eighteenth-century protestants and twentieth-century left-wing regional movements. Spectators are expected to turn to their own experience to interpret that of the Camisards.

This becomes even more significant with regard to the social relations which become apparent through language and all the gestures of inter-relation. The mode of behaviour among the nobles is highly artificial and expresses a hierarchy and etiquette which would appear old-fashioned even to the most conservative spectator. The social behaviour of the Camisards has two strands. That which is expressed through the language and gestures of religion bears a strong charge of the unfamiliar; the normal social expression, however, is much nearer to the post-'68 French left-wing. The group has a very loose hierarchy, and authority comes from knowing the right course of action (Laporte, Cavalier) or inspired expression (Mazel): the same qualities lifted Cohn-Bendit to prominence. Social relations are easy and welcoming; new arrivals are integrated promptly and pleasurably. There is a measure of sexual freedom and a relation to the natural world which corresponds very closely with late 1960s ideals. It is, in fact, easy for a contemporary audience to identify with the Camisards at the level of attitudes: even the unfamiliar elements correspond to what the audience recognises as desirable. The unfamiliar religious dimension, although understood to be common to all the group, is expressed in extreme form only by a minority of leaders.

The 'group' (class) division which the film's narrative demands is thus greatly enhanced. The nobility are at worst ridiculous, at best give the impression of being trapped in their roles. (Any vaguely sympathetic member of this group is shown as drawn to the Camisards on at least one occasion.) The

---

[22] 'ce que je voulais, c'est que ce que les Occitans voient dans *Les Camisards*, les Bretons ou les Alsaciens le voient aussi'.

Camisards on the other hand are close to modern experience. This was of course central to Allio's intention, but it came in for considerable criticism, particularly from *Cahiers*.

Cahiers' reproach is that the enormous difference in audience reaction and relation to the two groups means that all questioning is blocked. Faced with 'intimate tenderness (with as an extra the "Left Bank" or hippy connotations already mentioned) on one side, grotesque mockery (the big guns of the alienation effect) on the other' (Aumont 1972: 68),[23] the audience tends to annul all connection between the two. The forces which act on one are not the same as those which act on the other; everything opposes the two groups, and there can be no possibility that the relations between one and the other can be in any way modified, or even that one can act on the other except by annihilation: 'alternation is substituted for struggle here'.

Putting this in the terms of *Cahiers'* later theories, the confrontation of familiarity and unfamiliarity here notionally raises no questions and therefore reveals nothing. The conflict between the strange ways of the nobility and the recognisable language and attitudes of the Camisards is absorbed by the theatrical reference; that is the nobility are established in the minds of the audience as caricatures, sinister in themselves by virtue of the power of life and death that they wield, but not requiring any explanation of their existence in terms of social forces, because they are accepted as products of the theatre.

This is undeniably valid to some degree. However the strong difference in familiarity between the two opposed groups has other, more positive results. The importance of the religious element, while not ignored, is reduced; the unfamiliar language and gestures of religious fervour are outweighed by the continuous, and greater, unfamiliarity of *all* the behaviour of noble society, both within and outside a religious context. As a result, the conflict is presented in other terms. Firstly, as a class confrontation – the Camisards are agricultural workers, small craftsmen or foot-soldiers who have deserted, and their origin is made clear before they take to the hills. The first sequence in the village church, where the priest calls the roll of his parishioners as if in school,

---

[23] 'intimisme attendri (avec en supplément les connotations "rive gauche" ou hippies déjà relevées) d'un côté, rigolade ubuesque (les gros sabots de la distanciation) de l'autre'.

establishes the population *as a whole* (the Camisards are not yet identifiable) as minors in the eyes of the ecclesiastical establishment.

The Camisards are thus given a class identity which is linked to institutional powerlessness and, literally, a *patriarchal* order. Attributing attitudes perhaps abusively twentieth-century to them then leads the audience to feel solidarity with them which transcends the audience's own origins and avoids the clichés of the 'working-class'. It is effective, but *Cahiers'* historical disapproval is nonetheless comprehensible. The attitudes of the liberal intelligentsia of the twentieth century are attributed to the country people of the eighteenth on very thin evidence, even if the audience is thereupon required to confront its familiar ways of thinking with an unfamiliar context. Although the existence of a rigid hierarchy also seems familiar it is impossible to ignore how different that hierarchy as portrayed is, and that in itself might encourage the spectators to rethink their own position.

Apart from a class conflict, the film also presents conflict between the city and the country, Paris and the provinces. This too is to a great extent created by the 'theatricalisation' of the nobility. Allio notes that the costumes of the nobles 'are not "worn" ... They haven't really taken on the shape of the body: it's the body which takes on the shape of the costume' (Allio 1972c: 9).[24] The ill-defined 'place' of the nobility is designed also to 'take on the shape of the costumes'. Identifiable only as house or garden, the décor is reduced to a minimum; the camera concentrates on the human beings, who take up a lot of space with their *costumes de parade*, and occasionally on objects such as a laden table. By contrast the 'place' of the Camisards is abundantly described; their camps on rocky hillsides, the fields in which they work, the valleys and woods they tramp through and the pools they bathe in, are shown at length. The humans become mere figures in a landscape; they are sometimes entirely absent, when the passing of time is illustrated by a shot of the hills, and when they are in the picture, they are shown in interaction with their surroundings. Their costumes are suited both by their colour and by their evident convenience to their surroundings, and thus help to

---

[24] [Ce costumes-là], ils ne sont pas "portés". ... ils n'ont pas vraiment pris la forme du corps: c'est le corps qui prend la forme du costume.'

establish an idyllic relationship with nature; they belong to the place. When nobles venture into the landscape, their elaborate costume and unfamiliar manners become inappropriate to the point of ridicule. The culture of the nobility is alien not only to the country people's lifestyle, but to the place itself.

This dichotomy however admits of ambiguity. The Baron de Vergnas, when not entertaining, dresses in a neater version of the Camisards' clothes, and his gestures and manner betray unease with the language and style of the court. Vergnas has nothing in common with the Camisards in terms of class, but he shares with them religious and regional loyalties.

Vergnas refutes the presumption that the two camps cannot act upon each other. His costume, his gestures, his language, all indicate divided loyalties, lying in the conflict between his class and his origin and religion.[25] The contradiction is already being resolved in favour of the dictates of class. He has renounced his Protestantism and entertains his noble visitors in his house; his daughter is entirely integrated into the gestus of the nobility. However, the division is still active in Vergnas. When he accepts the Camisards' invitation to take communion with them, he stands out little in terms of costume or gestures, but he is clearly uneasy both here and among the nobles.

Vergnas bears the signs of internal struggle and development much more clearly than Combassous, the character singled out by *Cahiers* as the exception to the general stasis, although he moves away from and not towards the 'working class'. His meeting with the Camisards is a real moment of choice, in which we do not feel that the outcome is inevitable, but he commits himself unequivocally to the side of the King and the aristocracy. Undoubtedly, this character does reveal the historical contradictions to which he is subject. Specifically, he presents a situation where class and other loyalties (religious and regional) conflict; Allio's conclusion seems to be that the forces of class interest are stronger, but that there is the possibility of self-identification on other terms.

---

[25] Religion is related to the city–country divide in the film; the majority of the local population relate 'naturally' to the Protestants, even when converted through apathy. Protestantism serves as a sign of local identity and a rallying point, and its actual language and forms of thought are rather devalued. Allio was unable to ignore the religious determinant, but he has altered its probable historical significance.

Cahiers claimed that 'filming history means filming popular struggle, class struggle. But it means filming it in order to produce *knowledge*, of a specific kind which is different from simple perceptual knowledge ... *Les Camisards* is a passive reflection of contradictions analysed in the abstract, caught in the vice of omnivalent metaphor and references for references' sake; it replaces that knowledge with an effect of recognition which it has itself created the basis for ... About the Camisards and their particular struggle, and the real forces which were at work in it, we will learn nothing new' (Aumont 1972: 71).[26] It is true that the film takes the class division as read (a similar reproach could be levelled at *Coup pour coup* – with which *Cahiers* suggests a comparison). Vergnas, however, provides an interesting model of the interaction of class with other identities. The contemporary relevance of this as 'identity politics' – not yet so-called – came more and more to the fore within the left, is obvious. Allio intended the film to relate to regional issues; the rather ill-defined discourse of Protestantism may stand for other ideological causes. Vergnas and Combassous (the upper and the lower middle-class respectively) both undergo a moment of choice as to whether or not to join the Camisards, and neither result is inevitable (although Combassous shows little sign of conflicting loyalties; his main deterrent is his taste for a quiet life). The revolution is still in the hands of the workers, but the forces which work on their supporters are not entirely class-determined.

By 1976 and *Moi, Pierre Rivière...* (or, to give it its full title, which may also serve as synopsis, *Moi, Pierre Rivière, ayant égorgé ma mère, ma sœur et mon frère...*), matters had been greatly complicated. The film's referents and its aims are multiple. There is the text, written by Pierre Rivière in 1835 to explain his case, published with commentaries, by Foucault and others, in the course of the 1970s, and read in voice-over on the film's sound-track, of which it is by far the greatest part. Behind the text, there

---

[26] 'filmer l'histoire, c'est filmer les luttes populaires, la lutte des classes. Mais c'est la filmer pour en produire une *connaissance*, sur un mode spécifique distinct de la simple connaissance sensible ... Reflet passif de contradictions analysées abstraitement, pris dans le tourniquet de la métaphore omnivalente et du référent pour le référent, *Les Camisards* substitue à cette connaissance un effet de reconnaissance dont il forge lui-même les données ... Des Camisards, de la spécificité de leur lutte, des forces réelles qui y étaient à l'oeuvre, on ne saura rien de plus.'

is the event. Foucault suggests in fact that act and text be regarded as two parts of a whole: 'while undertaking to kill half his family, he imagined the writing of a text which was neither a confession nor a defence, but an element of the crime' (*Avant-scène* 1977: 6).[27] The existence of this extraordinary document allowed the film to operate the analysis of a 'fait divers' on the assumption that: '*The "fait divers" is no more than what a murder* like the one we are dealing with *is reduced to by the press and the justice system* ... we will therefore attempt to show what in the life and the behaviour of the main protagonists *exceeds this reduction*' (Jourdheuil 1976: 46).[28]

The film's second referent is Foucault; both its methods ('what we must appropriate is not so much the results of Foucault's work as his genealogico-paradoxical approach' (Jourdheuil 1976: 47)[29]) and its subject, society considered through the treatment meted out to the 'anti-social individual', criminal or insane ('*crime makes the institutions talk, they talk about it and about themselves*' (Toubiana 1976: 47)[30]) are drawn from his work. The presentation of the 'fait divers pensé historiquement' is interpreted in relation to work on the similarities and the differences between social and anti-social discourse, and the way in which the first receives and reads the second. This could be applied to the rejection and imprisonment of inconvenient subversives such as Charles (*mort ou vif*) or Pierre (*et Paul*), but Pierre Rivière is no revolutionary. The apparatus of justice is uncertain how to cope with him simply because he does not fit into any established category. Its response, 'administrative incarceration', reflects this: 'if Pierre is a criminal, he should be sentenced to death; if he's mad, to the asylum; but life imprisonment doesn't correspond to anything' (Bonitzer 1976: 49).[31] The 'déraison raisonnante' which Foucault identified

[27] 'en entreprenant de tuer la moitié de sa famille, il [a] conçu la rédaction d'un texte qui n'était ni aveu, ni défense, mais plutôt élément du crime'.

[28] '*Le fait divers n'est rien d'autre que ce à quoi un meurtre* comme celui qui nous occupe *est réduit par la presse, la justice* ... nous nous attacherons donc à montrer dans la vie et le comportement des principaux protagonistes *ce qui excède la réduction*.' His emphasis.

[29] 'ce que nous devons nous approprier c'est moins les résultats des travaux de Foucault que sa démarche généalogico-paradoxale'.

[30] '*le crime fait parler les appareils, qui en parlent, parlent d'eux-mêmes* '.

[31] 'si Pierre est un criminel, il fallait la mort; s'il est un fou, l'asile; mais la prison à vie ne correspond à rien'.

in the seventeenth and eighteenth centuries, but which was no longer officially accepted by the nineteenth, is the only appropriate category available. As in the case of the *révoltés*, therefore, there will be a desperate attempt to prove insanity in order to justify the verdict.

The film presents history through the context of the murder, and through the discourse of power opposed to its antithesis – the articulate criminal. It is also an attempt to re-present a neglected social group: 'the wish to give a true image of peasant life' as Allio said (*Avant-scène* 1977: 6).[32] The 'image juste', if such it is, arises out of a curious relation of images to text. The images of *Pierre Rivière* have practically no narrative function. A series of very short sequences, for the most part filmed in long-shot, their relation to the incidents described in the text is tangential, and apart from Pierre himself, we scarcely ever see the features of the protagonists. The dialogue (as opposed to the voice-over text) is also minimal.

The images, in fact, are non-specific, even iconic, definable only in broad historical terms – early nineteenth-century, but in many cases they could belong to the eighteenth or even the seventeenth as easily. It is by their conjunction with the voice-over that they are given a particular sense, which allows us to name the protagonists, the place, the year. At the same time the words of the voice-over – a text, not conceived for visualisation – often recount events generally and rapidly. The courtship of Pierre's parents, which covers several months, takes place, in the text, in the space of a few sentences. The images accompanying these sentences are as follows: 1) a rural market-place; 2) the young couple sitting together on a bank, in idyllic harmony; 3) a woman putting flowers on a grave; 4) a brief scene between the couple and the woman's parents. Given the length and complexity of the period evoked by the text, these images are obviously totally inadequate, mere illustrations – 'juste une image'.

The conjunction of, and tension between, image and text, creates a much closer approximation to an 'image juste'. The outside forces, economic and social, which shape the life of the Rivière family are fully present in Rivière's own text, but the non-specific nature of the images facilitates the understanding of the

---

[32] 'l'envie de donner une image juste de la vie paysanne'.

general which frames the particular. Thus the constant disputes over property and land are illustrated almost always by 'impersonal' images which become theatrical representations of the tensions stemming from property rights. Towards the end of the film, the image shows Pierre, recognisable but in long-shot, crossing a field as the text states: 'Monday it couldn't be, because I had to go to the ploughing at Cavaillon's'. 'It' designates the projected murder. The structure of rural society, shared labour, and Pierre's situation as a farm-boy, determine his existence so strongly that even the most violently anti-social action cannot be permitted to interfere with them, and the tension between the particular action and the general situation is illustrated by the contrast between the image – which shows no disturbance of normal routine – and the hidden violence of the text.

The extraordinary success of this film in at once recreating and analysing its little piece of history stems more from the opposition of general and particular than from that of strangeness and familiarity. For the average cinema audience, the unfamiliarity probably relates more to a geographical and social than to a historical referent. The scenes in court do not establish the nineteenth-century state apparatus as particularly remote or strange. The figures of the rural hierarchy are a little dated, but probably familiar from contemporary novels, while the language of the judge and his secretary, or the various medical experts called in to pronounce on Pierre's case, would not sound out of place in a local court report today.[33] On the other hand, the audience has next to no access to the psychology of the protagonists (with the exception of Pierre himself, but that access is based on an objective, critical reception of his text), and the gestus of the Normandy countryfolk is probably relatively unfamiliar to the urban middle-class 'average' audience for a film of this type in France. Allio's intention was to represent a familiar rural reality, and to that end he made the film in the region in which it was set, using local people as actors and as participants:

[33] I think we must assume that this represents a deliberate choice on Allio's part. As a contrast one could consider the first part of Bill Douglas' Comrades (1986). Douglas, like Allio, is concerned with more than mere reconstruction; in subject the film is comparable to Les Camisards, in period to Pierre Rivière. Here the nineteenth-century bourgeoisie are far further from familiar experience, approaching the caricature used for the Camisards nobles.

'there was already one thing which our future colleagues shared with us, the wish to give a true image of peasant life, so rarely shown in the cinema (and they knew that very well)'

The opposition of the urban and the rural, already present in *Les Camisards*, has thus here become the driving force behind the film, synonymous with class and not parallel with it. The conception of the project rests on the assumption that the difference between the mode of expression (the 'gestus social') of the past and the present within each milieu is much smaller than that which divides the two, and just as there is little that is startling in the words of the officials, there is little that is fundamentally 'historical' in the acts and images of the countryside. The historical referent is limited to the superficial – costumes (but the costumes are not elaborate) or farming methods – while the motivations, although possibly unfamiliar to the urban intelligentsia, had not lost their relevance in rural society by the 1970s. 'The whole drama of Rivière is a drama of Justice, the Code Civil, the Law, the Land, marriage, property ... And peasant life still goes on within that same tragedy. And so what's important is to have today's peasants act out this old drama which is also the story of their lives' (Foucault 1976: 53).[34]

The rural drama may seem unfamiliar, but it is again the urban world that is represented theatrically; it appears only within the ceremonial of the legal system, and the use of professional actors, recognisable in some cases, for all the bourgeois characters,[35] opposes them to the local non-professionals who play the *paysans*. Intentionally or not, the actors 'act', to a greater or lesser extent, with theatrical mannerisms. The urban, bourgeois element is thus denoted as artificial in *Pierre Rivière* as in *Les Camisards*; but, this time, an urban audience is finally deprived of any 'place' in the film.

[34] 'Tout le drame de Rivière, c'est un drame du Droit, un drame du Code, de la Loi, de la Terre, du mariage, des biens ... Or, c'est toujours à l'intérieur de cette tragédie-là que se meut le monde paysan. Et ce qui est important donc, c'est de faire jouer à des paysans actuels ce vieux drame qui est en même temps celui de leur vie.'

[35] This includes, for example, the parish priest, so I have chosen to use the 'class' rather than the geographical definition, but *Pierre Rivière*, even more than *Les Camisards*, tends to equate the two and it would be possible to read into 'bourgeois' its original meaning of 'town-dweller'. I have avoided translation of the word 'paysan', which has no equivalent in English as the reality it represents does not.

Pierre Rivière is an attempt to appropriate a cinematic language – cinema being an essentially urban code – and find an adequate expression in it of rural society. It is in this sense that Foucault read the film, and in this function that he saw its importance:

> I think that it's politically important to give *paysans* the chance to act this *paysan* text. Hence also the importance of having actors from outside to represent the legal world, judiciary, the lawyers ... all these people who are city people and, at bottom, are outside the very direct line of communication between *paysans* of the 19th and of the 20th century, something Allio managed to incarnate and, *up to a point*, to have his rural actors incarnate (Foucault 1976: 53).[36]

The 'up to a point' recognises the limits of this 'prise de parole'; the subject remains entirely Allio's, as does the film's conception, and if some of the forces which structure rural life in the nineteenth as in the twentieth century are presented, there is not much room for contemporary application of the analysis.

Nonetheless the rural system is more central to the film than the crime of Pierre Rivière. The event is de-realised by its presentation – the bodies of the victims, identified by the voice of the coroner and by their names in sub-titles at the beginning of the film, seem like dolls, and there is a discrepancy between the horrific textual descriptions and the intact bodies on the screen which denotes the incident as 'mere' narration. The murders themselves are off-frame, practically non-existent in the film, so brief is the sequence. As Foucault observed with regard to Rivière's text: 'a really extraordinary crime, but relayed by a discourse so much more extraordinary still that in the end the crime no longer exists' (Foucault 1976: 52).[37] The 'extraordinary discourse', in which the combination of reason and unreason, familiarity and unfamiliarity, is shown as posing an insoluble problem to the judges, is supported by the play of images (and a few intercalations

[36] 'Je crois que c'est politiquement important de donner aux paysans la possibilité de jouer ce texte paysan. D'où aussi l'importance des acteurs extérieurs pour représenter le monde de la loi, les juristes, les avocats ... tous ces gens qui sont des gens de la ville et qui sont, au fond, extérieurs à cette communication très directe entre le paysan du XIXe siècle et celui du XXe siècle, qu'Allio a su réaliser et, *jusqu'à un certain point*, a laissé réaliser à ses acteurs paysans.'

[37] 'un crime vraiment extraordinaire, mais qui a été relancé par un discours tellement plus extraordinaire encore, que le crime finit par ne plus exister.'

of other testimonies), all of which further reduce the importance
of the crime itself in favour of its context – personal, socio-
economic or imaginary. Rivière's text already narrates these
elements (the perceived humiliation of his father, the endless
litigation, the source of his decision in 'stories about sailors and
soldiers') rather than the crime itself; the film in turn provides a
context in which to insert the text. Through the 'universal' image
the particular becomes general. Pierre's references to his imaginary world are confronted with the factors which could have
forged his imagination: popular engravings depicting 'stories
about sailors and soldiers' or presenting new machines of a kind
that Pierre dreams of inventing. Allio's film in no way attempts to
solve the mysteries contained in Pierre Rivière's text, but it
'elucidates' it in a very similar way to that in which the text
'elucidates' the crime, by requiring us to see it in a wider,
historical context, to 'think the text historically'. As Serge Le
Péron suggests, however, this does not necessarily decrease the
text's opacity: 'in trying to make too much clear you make
everything mysterious, in leaping in front of every enigma there's
a risk that in solving it you will uncover another next to it, and
soon become attached to that one' (Le Péron 1976b: 58).[38]

One enigma which the film brings to the fore is that of the
relation of Pierre Rivière to a world in which he seems both
entirely integrated and an outsider. The reasons for his crime lie
entirely within rural society: in the long 'legal drama' which
estranges his parents, in a system of values which gives the
husband power (if limited power) over the wife's belongings, but
more insidiously has male dignity depend on authority over
women, seen as the 'natural' state of affairs. When Pierre sees his
mother's behaviour as contrary to these norms – 'it's the women
in charge now – Judiths against Holofernes' – he prefers to
question the state of society rather than questioning his values –
all is no longer as it once naturally was and still should be. Thus
the act which sets him outside the social order is, paradoxically,
committed in the name of that order.

Pierre's crime is socially reactionary, stemming from over-
identification with his own social structure, but he appears as an

[38] 'à vouloir trop élucider on rend tout mystérieux, à se projeter au-devant de
toute énigme, on risque en l'éclaircissant d'en dévoiler une autre, toute proche, à
laquelle on s'attache bientôt.'

outsider in the rural context. It is the testimonies of his neighbours, *paysans*, which label him 'bizarre', 'an idiot', 'crazy', 'cruel';
the schoolteacher, on the other hand, speaks for his intelligence
and his 'very gentle character'. He is more literate than his
entourage, and he strongly desires education, for which he looks
to bourgeois society: 'observing the talk which masters and
servants have together'. He dreams of distinguishing himself by
his inventions because 'I had much more esteem for myself than
others'. The image accentuates Pierre's solitude; he is almost
always framed alone, and very frequently he watches the previous
or the subsequent scene. Pierre is a spectator to the life of his
milieu, and almost every scene is filmed from the point of view of
a watcher (Le Péron 1976b: 56),[39] even when Pierre is not actually
shown hidden in a corner to observe. Other signs indicate his
detachment from the codes of peasant life. There are regular
accounts of subversion ('détournement') of the apparatus of the
farm. Thus Pierre 'slices the heads off cabbages'; he appropriates
the farm horse for escapades or cruel games. A scythe is used to
terrify the local children, and a billhook eventually serves the
ultimate asocial purpose of murder weapon.

On the one hand, then, Pierre is firmly integrated into the
world (the gestus, the discourse) of the peasantry, but on the
other hand he despises that world and misuses its language and
its objects. 'He hasn't developed in harmony with the village, but
has grown up beside it or against it. He belongs there even though
he's incomprehensible to the villagers' (Toubiana 1976: 48).[40] To
the audience, the dialectic of familiarity and unfamiliarity becomes
extremely complex. Pierre has great control of his language, and
some of his aspirations are comprehensible enough. Over the
question of Pierre's mental state, we find ourselves as incompetent
to judge as the court of the nineteenth century. It is as hard to
determine whether Pierre's text, and his act, is 'social' – determined by and in the same sense as the dominant values around
him – or 'anti-social' – in reaction against those values; and the

[39] 'Le cadrage est celui de la conversation, ... du témoignage, du rapport
humain, de la petite propriété et du petit nombre'. Le Peron sees this as an
appropriate scale for the world represented, but the film is scarcely 'intimiste' and
the images *never* directly engage the spectator; it implies a close observer, a role
which Pierre almost constantly fills, much more than an interlocutor.

[40] 'Ce n'est pas en harmonie avec [le village] qu'il s'est développé, c'est à côté ou
contre lui qu'il a grandi. Il est des leurs tout en étant pour eux méconnaissable.'

question is complicated by the positive value which the audience will probably assign to some of Pierre's more 'anti-social' traits such as his wish for education. The practices which would imply normality are therefore uncertain; abnormal behaviour comprises some reactions that seem acceptable and reasonable to twentieth-century urban society, and others as alien to us as they are to the village. Is Pierre a victim of his 'excess of knowledge, excess of violence and imagination' (Toubiana) and thus oppressed by the restrictions of his milieu, or is he alienated and embroiled in the myths of society to the extent that he is willing to annihilate all that threatens to disprove them? Is he, perhaps, an individual caught in the contradictions of much broader developments, a 'victim' of his historical circumstances at the cusp of a revolution which is not only industrial but social and which is just beginning to touch the apparently ageless assumptions of rural Normandy (the shock of social change being, after all, relevant and even in a sense familiar to French society of the 1960s and 1970s)? All that the film can tell us is, on the one hand, that Pierre Rivière's relation to society is fundamental to any understanding of his action or his text; on the other hand, that the nature of that relation remains opaque.

Pierre Rivière thus addresses the 'pensée historique' firstly in an attempt to create a dynamic understanding by opposing the particular (the anecdote) to the general, secondly in its revelation of the particular problems which beset such understanding without adequate provision of shared discourse. The society of *Pierre Rivière* cannot easily be assimilated to an urban norm, yet it is being judged – by the audience or by the courts – according to one, and the result is disturbing to any belief in universal social values.

The eighteenth century and the nineteenth century, in *Les Camisards* and *Moi, Pierre Rivière…* respectively, are treated with reference to a contemporary reality. It is the echo which the films find in the audience's own experience, or the way in which they force us to acknowledge the insufficiencies of our experience, which gives them force; strict authenticity is finally of minor importance. The real Camisards may have spoken Occitan, and their revolt may have been principally religious, but their relevance to 1971, for Allio, lies essentially in the regional, popular nature of their movement. *Pierre Rivière*, which betrays considerably more uncertainty and ambiguity in its portrayal of conflicting values, contents itself with glances rather than gazes at the history it represents and in so doing creates an uneasy, inaccessible world which highlights most of all the audience's own incomprehension. When the events portrayed are still a part of living memory, however, the situation is different. In considering Franck Cassenti's *L'Affiche rouge* (1976) we will see that the attempt to re-present the history of the Resistance in its concordances with 1976 implies specific problems relating both to the conception and to the reception of the film.

Michel Foucault said – regretfully – in an interview with *Cahiers* in 1974 that the existence of films such as *Le Chagrin et la pitié* and *Lacombe Lucien* was making it impossible to envisage making a film perpetuating the heroism of the Resistance (Foucault 1974: 8). *L'Affiche rouge* can most profitably be seen as an attempt to address this very question; its subject is not merely the Resistance, but how the facts relating to the Resistance can be imbued with a positive symbolic value. In this film we are effectively invited to participate in the transformation of history into legend, a legend which – while manipulating historical accuracy – may itself become a historical agent with positive significance.

L'Affiche rouge is a cinematic representation of the arrest and trial of the Groupe Manouchian, a detachment of Resistants composed mainly of immigrants from Eastern Europe and the Mediterranean. The arrests took place in 1944, and the Germans publicised the event in the hope of discrediting the Resistance by calling on French xenophobia, hence the 'Affiche Rouge', the red poster that gives the film its title. These are the facts, which were being drawn to public attention in 1976 by the publication of two books on the subject in the previous two years.[41]

Cassenti was a member of the PCF, and this *in itself* led to the film being attacked in publications hostile to the Party, particularly *Cahiers du cinéma* (Fargier 1976; Le Péron 1976a). The general availability of the facts, with which Cassenti was alleged to have taken liberties at least by omission, was one of the foundations for complaints, as, quite reasonably, was the strange absence from the film of any of the surviving witnesses to events

---

[41] One book was written by Mélinée Manouchian (1974), another by Philippe Ganier Raymond (1975). A number of survivors from the group, including Mélinée, appeared on a television programme about the Resistance in the summer of 1976.

although the point of departure of the story is a theatrical reconstruction based on interviews with the survivors. Since audiences with an interest in such matters would almost certainly have at least watched the 1976 TV programme, this omission on Cassenti's part does seem somewhat suspect, although it is in part compensated for by Mélinée Manouchian's public declaration of approval for the finished work.

I do not propose to discuss in detail *Cahiers*' criticisms of the film, but rather refer the reader to the articles cited which are both thorough and entertaining. The essential points: that Cassenti avoided context, that he concentrated on episodes in the group's existence when it was least active, and that he glossed over conflicts within the group especially when they reflected badly on the PCF, all have some justification if the film is to be taken as an accurate representation of history. The accusation that the film avoids showing the group in any action which might seem contrary to the *ideology* of the PCF (that is, directed against the German working class) merits a brief mention, however, since it rejoins *Cahiers*' reservations concerning *Les Camisards* and the role of familiarity or unfamiliarity in relating audience to film. In fact, the role of the 'historical signifier' was one that preoccupied Cassenti, as the introductory dialogue to the film makes clear:

'Don't forget that this all happened just over thirty years ago. Most of us weren't born.'
'Thirty years isn't that long ago…'
'… We know next to nothing about them.'
'It's simple, they were men and women like us.'
'No, not like us.'[42]

This dialogue, attributable to the fictional actors, also represents the situation of a potential audience. The events are, in fact, temporally far enough removed to be unfamiliar, but not so far that the audience will expect any great differences of attitude between the protagonists and themselves. There are obvious problems with the function of the familiar/unfamiliar dialectic in

---

[42] 'N'oublie pas que tout cela s'est passé il y a un peu plus de trente ans. La plupart d'entre nous n'étaient pas nés.'
'Trente ans ce n'est pas si lointain…'
'… Nous ne savons presque rien sur eux.'
'C'est simple, c'étaient des hommes et des femmes comme nous.'
'Non, pas comme nous.'

this film. For an audience around thirty years old, ex-68ard and left-wing, the Occupation, unfamiliar, risks being understood through an experience of opposition to a State apparatus and an authoritarian political structure associated, ironically, with General de Gaulle. This form of experience identified attacks on oppression with attacks on the hierarchy. Showing the Resistance in action against the ordinary German soldier would, indeed, shock this kind of perception – which the PCF could hardly disavow – and the 'not like us' of the introductory dialogue would risk being interpreted not in the sense (which most of the film tends to give it) of 'superior to us, more heroic', but of 'fighting a different battle', radically separate and irrelevant, or worse, unprincipled. The tensions between the Left of the 1940s and the Left of the 1960s are, in any case, a well-known phenomenon which in France was most problematic in the direct orbit of the PCF; 1956 and indeed the Prague Spring of August 1968 had their part to play in that. Cassenti was faced with a challenge in attempting to transmit the ideals of the Resistance convincingly to meet those of a new generation who suspected him and the origins of his discourse from the very start.

Allio too used tactics of omission and adaptation to give the Camisards historical relevance, and in all fairness to *Cahiers* it should be said that they exposed the historical trick in both cases. However, they admit Allio's right to manipulate history to a certain extent in the name of contemporary relevance, deploring only the over-simplification of the result; in the case of Cassenti the misrepresentation itself is attacked as a misinterpretation of the precise battle being fought by the resistants. In other words, Allio is attacked insofar as his simplification may lead to misinterpretation of the play of present forces, while Cassenti is accused of misrepresenting the past – in the name, of course, of a political programme for the present which *Cahiers* does not accept.

Such criticism, perhaps justified in itself, however misses the fundamental interest of Cassenti's film: that is, the way in which it enquires into the representation of history rather than its own accurate or inaccurate reconstruction. In that enquiry the very traits that *Cahiers* criticises take on a rather different role.

L'Affiche rouge hinges on the decision by a group of actors from the Théâtre du Soleil to mount a theatrical representation of the fate of the Groupe Manouchian; the film interweaves the preparation of this performance with sequences evoking cinematically events of the 1940s. The facts about the group are certainly confused and arrive sporadically. What becomes clear first is the resonance of the as-yet undescribed events: from the first sentence of the sound-track, 'N'oublie pas que tout cela s'est passé il y a un peu plus de trente ans', not so far from the opening of a fairy-story, the legendary aspect of the group's achievements is insisted on. The rather mysterious title increases this impression: 'You want to do a play about the Affiche Rouge?' asks one woman in the first sequence after the titles. The theatrical method tends to favour the high emotional points of the 1944 events, which further places the resistants in the realm of heroic legend. The spectator without historical background is however informed slowly, and without chronological order, leading to *Cahiers*' reproach that the film lacked historical context. A little historical knowledge (which was however as we have mentioned available at the time) is certainly desirable to allow the full force of the introductory references to function, and also to understand the significance of the choices that must be made with regard to the representation. The choice of episodes to be dramatised is frequently made in response to anecdotes told by the 'survivors' (actors playing the survivors, as we have mentioned). These anecdotes are obviously not subject to chronology, neither do they latch on to what would be automatically considered historically significant; they are the centres of individual memory.

Where the film finds its strength is as an essay on the role of memory in the creation of history – both the personal memories of those involved and the folk-memories which may make of Manouchian a legend. What the actors do seek to do (and all the conversations between actors and survivors in the 1970s sequences make this clear) is to represent the Groupe Manouchian *as it is remembered*. The chronological tension of the first conversation thus takes on further meaning: the kind of legendary oral history which seems to call upon an unlocatable, distant past is here captured at the moment of creation, when it is still a matter of direct, immediate, contemporary experience; the story must, in order to fulfil the aims of the theatre group, be located at once infinitely far off (almost *outside* history) and near. In this context the insistence (vilified by *Cahiers*) on the importance of the actors' physical resemblance to their characters also makes perfect sense. The workings of historical forces, vital to any analysis of the reality of the *event*, have little impact on the reality of memory; their revelation is an intellectual exercise. By contrast, an exact physical resemblance will evoke a memory even when every historical, social and even ideological circumstance works against it, and this contradiction is inscribed in the film; a young motor-cyclist is greeted fervently by the mother of one of the group because of his appearance *alone*. She knows nothing of his circumstances and he knows nothing of hers, he is politically indifferent and has no connection with the Group or with the play, although he too is struck by his own resemblance to the photograph of her son.

The disproportionate importance of the trial and death of the group, and of moments of relaxation and intimacy, which *Cahiers* considered disempowering to the resistance movement are to some extent validated in this context. Fargier attacks the stereo-typical nature of the representation of the derailment: 'It doesn't represent *one* precise act of war included in a complex whole, it presents a *sign* cut off from its context and made unreal ... Sabotaging a train is shown as a natural, obvious action for the Resistance' (Fargier 1976: 14).[43] In a historical analysis of the group, this would indeed be an abuse, but it is a precise notation in an analysis of their existence *in memory*, and it is presented to the audience without ambiguity, as a representation, a 'sign', indeed, of Resistance. The memory of the 'acts of war' of the Groupe Manouchian is thus merged and also dilated in the much greater whole which is the Resistance movement, apart from the assassination of Ritter, where the status of the victim indivi-dualises the action. Even in the personal memories of survivors this is probably true, and it is given expression on the poster by the categorisation of acts as '*attentats*' or '*déraillements*' – repre-sented in the film by one '*attentat*' (the most illustrious, the one which *would* be remembered) and one derailment.

Intimate memories, where the protagonists exist only in their individual identity, are not susceptible to generalisation, and the personal incidents selected all relate the dead to the living individual who bears their memory in the present. Thus Olga, the

---

[43] 'Il ne représente pas *un* acte de guerre précis inséré dans un ensemble complexe, il exhibe un *signe* coupé de son contexte, déréalisé ... Le sabotage d'un train est donné comme un acte naturel, évident de la Résistance'.

only woman in the group, survived and, 'represented' in the pre-theatrical preparations by her daughter, is shown at the moment when she reveals that she is pregnant, when she later decides to send her daughter away out of danger, and at her execution (before which she wrote to the daughter). Certainly, such scenes relate more to the personal memories of the survivors than they do to folk-memory, but the dynamic of the film is precisely folk-memory in the process of formation, a process which is material-ised by the work of the actors. A personal anecdote – such as Alfonso's reply to his interrogators – is re-created, framed in its theatrical setting, to become the property of all the audience, the legend.

The importance of the time after the group's arrest stems partly from the emotional charge it contains for the survivors, but most importantly from the existence of documents which have perpetuated it more precisely and more poignantly. The prison letters ensure that this particular stage of the Group's existence has been preserved precisely while the undocumented years of clandestinity have to some extent receded and merged together. The Affiche itself, already public property, constituting a founda-tion on which the legend can build, represents the ultimate example of this function of the document, *against* its original intention. It has become almost synonymous with the Group: the actors are asked, 'Vous voulez faire une pièce de théâtre sur l'Affiche Rouge?' and not 'sur le Groupe Manouchian?'. The question is significant: before the translation by the actors (and by Cassenti) of the survivors' personal memories into a public document, the Affiche Rouge is presented as all that is known about the group, the only way in which it is remembered.[44]

The film's 'epic' quality, then, comes not from a critical reading of the story of Manouchian, but from a reflection on the function of theatre and through theatre of film and of popular representations of history. The play, the finished representation, concentrates only on the moments of emotional drama, and asks

---

[44] The film assumes that the translation of negative document into positive legend is unproblematic; the possibility that there might still exist a neo-Fascist construction of memory from the same document is considered non-existent or rather not considered at all. Assuming a homogeneous reception of the construction is perhaps a weakness in the film, and a serious result of the lack of historical analysis: 'good' and 'bad' are never linked to material causes.

practically no questions about the history behind the story, although the introductory dialogue half-promises that it will. However, the 'spectacle' (filmic reconstruction and street-theatre alike) develops before our eyes, documenting the process of translation of personal memories into the elements of a nascent legend, and then into a *mise-en-scène*. Ultimately the incidents are converted into the stylised popular form of the *commedia dell'arte*. This represents the final point of the transformation, when the personal has been totally absorbed by the folk-memory, and physical resemblance is no longer a factor. The individual characters have become universal mythic figures – the Fool, the Dame, the Devil. The procedure shows the gradual disappearance of historical analysis into mythical representation; but it also exposes and analyses that disappearance, while posing the possibility that it may, itself, have active historical significance.

It might seem that, as *Cahiers* suggested, Cassenti is merely indulging in myth-making on his own account, but in favour of the PCF. It might well have been in his interests to do so. The introduction to the trial sequence, however, calls the whole process into question. The group's trial is introduced by a Goebbels-figure, who has two functions: he is the historic Goebbels (transposed, in the language of folk-memory, to an ambiguous and sinister puppet-figure), but he is also the *metteur-en-scène* who translates, on his own terms, the historical event of the trial into memory, legend and folk-theatre: 'a spectacle, which will enter the history of tragedy', with descriptions of the protagonists which transform them too into pantomime devils. 'I, Goebbels, the *metteur-en-scène* of the Third Reich' is in fact engaging in exactly the same process, although with a very different purpose, as are the actors of the Cartoucherie, and through them Cassenti. His spectacle also is entitled *L'Affiche rouge*. The process of creation of a historical legend through representation is thus exposed to criticism: the mechanics of transformation are in themselves neutral, as effective for Nazi as for Communist propaganda. *L'Affiche rouge* (Cassenti's) illustrates the process of creating history as *mise-en-scène*. In so doing it makes use of the results to establish the Groupe Manouchian as a legend which does benefit the PCF, potentially, but it also shows the dangers of such a vision of history. It is at the end of *L'Affiche rouge* that the process of historical analysis needs to start. The film inscribes that need. The woman who enquires into the actors' project at the beginning of the film asks if they are working on 'history [or 'story', that of Manouchian – her inter-locutor has just used the word] with a small h or History with a capital H, because you know, in History with a capital H there's not much room for immigrants'. Cassenti has illustrated the process of creating a place for this group of immigrants in history with a capital H, in the History-myth; the process is simple, but in the end, although there is a place for *these* immigrants, there is still none for 'immigrants'. This kind of history does not allow for abstractions, groups, social forces. Here is where *Cahiers*' quite justified critique begins, but they omit the film's own incorpor-ated self-criticism.

All the above films contributed to an exploration of what can be achieved by representing the past, and the ways in which the past can be read and comprehended by the present. The majority of historical films explore the latter point in one way or another, aiming at least to establish a relation between past and present. *Pierre Rivière*, exceptionally, concentrates on the *difference* between the two, postulating the absolute necessity of recognising difference in order to read the real implications which the discourse of the past has for the present, (or that of the country for that of the town). The outsider, who fits in neither place, is here the elucidating factor; through the questions which arise around Pierre – Why does this society condemn him? Why does his own society condemn him? What are his motivations? – what emerges is the insufficiency of our understanding of history, of cultural difference, of the real forces behind any action. As such it is the most desperate call to action of all the films presented: 'donner la parole' is not enough unless we are capable of hearing what is said, and hearing it right. A new interpretation of history is necessary, but by no means achieved yet; and discourses of alterity must be not only heard but also understood and not merely assimilated. Cassenti's film establishes the need for a re-appraisal of a historical language too easily assumed into myth – and in this context the Théâtre de Soleil's own film of their seminal representation of the French Revolution, *1789* (1974), is at least a valuable document, as well as indicating the audience which such interrogations of the myths of history had in the early 1970s. Allio in *Les Camisards*, and Comolli in *La Cecilia*, went some way towards providing such a re-appraisal, although the overwhelming reappearance of history-as-spectacle in the cinema of the 1980s and 1990s in France more or less overwhelmed these tentative moves towards a more adventurous approach.

REFERENCES

Allio, René (1972a) 'Continuité dans le changement', *Avant-scène cinéma*, février: 9–10.

Allio, René (1972b) Interview in *Positif* 138, mai: 19–28.

Aumont, Jacques (1972) 'Comment on écrit l'histoire?', *Cahiers du cinéma* 238–9, mai–juin: 64–71.

Avant-scène (1977) Dossier *Moi Pierre Rivière*, *Avant-scène* 183, mars.

Bonitzer, Pascal (1976) 'Les Puissances du faux', *Cahiers du cinéma* 271, novembre: 48–9.

Cahiers du cinéma (1975) Dossier 'Cinéma et histoire II', *Cahiers du cinéma* 257, mai–juin: 22–34.

Comolli, Jean-Louis (1977) 'Le Passé filmé', *Cahiers du cinéma* 277, juin: 5–14.

Fargier, Jean-Paul (1976) 'Histoires d'U', *Cahiers du cinéma* 272, décembre: 5–18.

Foucault, Michel (1974) 'Le Mode rétro', interview in *Cahiers du cinéma* 250, juillet–août: 5–15.

Foucault, Michel (1976) Interview with Pascal Kané, *Cahiers du cinéma* 271, novembre: 52–3.

Gauthier, Guy (1993) *Les Chemins de René Allio*, Paris: Cerf.

Gervais, Ginette (1970) 'Le Cinéma donne vie à l'histoire', *Jeune cinéma* 43, janvier: 20–5.

Jourdheuil, J. (1976) 'Le Quotidien, l'historique et le tragique', *Cahiers du cinéma* 271, novembre: 46–7.

Kané, Pascal (1974–75) 'L'Effet d'étrangeté', *Cahiers du cinéma* 254–5, décembre–janvier: 77–83.

Le Péron, Serge (1976a) 'Système de l'Affiche', *Cahiers du cinéma* 270, septembre–octobre: 53–7.

Le Péron, Serge (1976b) 'L'Ecrit et le cru', *Cahiers du cinéma* 271, novembre: 56–8.

Manouchian, Mélinée (1974) *Manouchian*, Paris: EFR.

Prédal, René (1977) 'L'Histoire dans quelques films français récents', *Jeune cinéma* 103, juin: 25–30.

Raymond, Philippe Ganier (1975) *L'Affiche rouge*, Paris: Fayard.

Regnault, François (1972) 'Les Camisards et le film d'histoire', *Cahiers du cinéma* 238–9, mai–juin: 62–74.

Toubiana, Serge (1976) 'Celui qui en sait trop', *Cahiers du cinéma* 271, novembre: 47–8.

7

Two directors: William Klein and Alain Tanner

As a conclusion to this survey of the traces of 1968 on the French cinema of the following decade, it seems appropriate to consider two film-makers whose work encapsulates many of the currents and issues which have previously been discussed, and who may be said to be exemplary in terms of their responses to the demands of the time. In August 1968, the Avignon festival, whose special statute permitted films to be shown there without the *visa de censure*, presented the *avant-première* of a film still waiting for the Ministère de la Culture to establish whether it would ever be released at all. The film-maker, William Klein, had been led by the length of the list of alterations required by the Ministry to fear that he never would be granted a visa, and thus he presented the film, *Mister Freedom*, at Avignon to ensure that it would at least get a viewing somewhere. In fact, the choice was not inappropriate, for *Mister Freedom* is a film made very much in the vein of experimental theatre. Its subject-matter, and its general irreverence especially towards de Gaulle, together perhaps with the incorporation of sequences of the May events, led the French censors to treat it as subversive.

Klein was already well established in the world of French cinema by 1968, although his origins were neither cinematic nor French. He is an American, of New York Jewish stock, a fact which he has claimed as an influence on the work he produces (Klein 1977: 20); he first came to Paris as a graphic artist and a pupil of Fernand Léger, although he soon turned to photography, and it was in this medium that he made his name. His strikingly dynamic photographs were published in albums each devoted to a great city (New York 1956, Rome 1958, Moscow 1964, Tokyo 1964); he also worked extensively in the world of fashion. His outlook on this latter appears to have been distinctly unconventional, and his first full-length feature film, *Qui êtes-vous, Polly Magoo?* (1966) was a detached and critical spectacle-parody on the subject. The

theme of *Polly Magoo*, a critique of the consumer society, was
shared with another future revolutionary of 1968, Jean-Luc Godard,
but the spectacular and colourful treatment was the antithesis of
Godard's starkness. Like Godard, however, Klein is concerned
with producing a construct based on reality rather than a
reproduction of reality – both, in other words, bring a measure of
theatre into their approach to the cinema.

   Polly Magoo and the earlier short *Broadway by Light* (1959)
extended the preoccupations and themes which he treated as a
photographer: fashion modelling and the dynamics of the city
respectively. Working with Fernand Léger was also undoubtedly
influential; Léger was much concerned with the social function of
art, and he worked in a formalist idiom (he had long had links with
Cubism) which had always had important links with performance.
Léger himself made films; his second cinematic experiment, *La
Fille au coeur préfabriqué*, made in New York during the war as an
episode of a compilation film called *Dreams that Money Can Buy*
(1947), is described in the *Larousse dictionnaire du cinéma français* as 'a love story about animated dolls'. The similarities with
Klein's themes are obvious. 'Animated dolls' constitute all the
protagonists of *Mister Freedom*, while the characters in *Le Couple
Témoin* (1977), although human, are dehumanised both by their
social environment and by their particular situation in the film.
For most of the film they appear as 'human automatons', overridden by the gadgets that surround them, 'au coeur préfabriqué'.[1] As for 'dreams that money can buy', the growing power
of consumerism constitutes the major theme of *Polly Magoo* and
Le Couple Témoin, and a subsidiary one of *Mister Freedom*.

   Klein's cinematic identity was thus being formed well before 1968
– indeed even before he became seriously involved with cinema.

   Mister Freedom was presented to the censors in the aftermath
of May and contained sequences shot during the events. Its
subject, too, seems to bear clear and direct relation to them.
Mister Freedom, a character not dissimilar to Superman, is
despatched by the Freedom Corporation to France, to investigate
the Corporation's loss of influence there through the agency, and
to the profit, of Moujik Man. Freedom offers the French leader,

----

[1] A 'mannequin' is of course also the term for a fashion model, a woman
reduced (professionally) to the status of a doll to hang clothes on. It is the identity
of the woman behind the doll that forms the subject of *Qui êtes-vous Polly Magoo?*

Super French Man, his assistance in fighting Moujik Man, but is scornfully turned down. He finds that France contains a strong 'Anti-Freedom' movement, motivated not only by Moujik Man, but by another adversary, Red China Man. He becomes embroiled with double agents, and finally loses so much ground that, in the wake of a popular uprising against him, he is driven to the use of *l'arme absolue*, after which, in the middle of the resulting wasteland, he admits his ultimate defeat.

The film was widely taken to be a reference to, and 'explanation' of, May. Klein always denied this, and the circumstances of its making render a direct relationship based on hindsight, at least, impossible. At the time of the May events, the film was at the montage stage. All that remained to be shot were a few sequences relating to the final uprising. Klein started filming in the street as early as 1 May, although film taken later was incorporated (Klein 1978). The film came before the censors too soon after May for any much later timing than this (attested to by Klein in 1978) to be credible. Despite its appearance after May, therefore, *Mister Freedom* was made before the events, although it came too late to gain a reputation as a precursor on the lines of *La Chinoise*.

In what follows we shall be most interested in the ways in which Klein responded to his experience in 1968, and in relating the themes which he developed in his subsequent work to the currents of the progressive French cinema of the time as a whole. In this context he does seem to have developed to some degree as an 'anti-Godard' (Held 1967): enough parallels can be drawn between the two to make the comparison instructive, and we will return to it at the end of this analysis.

Klein was, at least at first glance, very much less prolific than Godard. Against Godard's thirteen films between 1968 and 1980, Klein made seven, including *Mister Freedom*, and of these all but two (*Mister Freedom* and *Le Couple Témoin*) are documentaries. *Eldridge Cleaver* and *Le Festival pan-africain* both appeared in 1969, as indeed did *Mister Freedom*, once the last problems with the censors had been ironed out. *Muhammad Ali: The Greatest*, in 1974, was at once a continuation of his examination of American black consciousness and a follow-up to a much earlier film (*Cassius le Grand*, made in 1964, footage from which in fact forms the adapted first part of *Muhammad Ali*). His second fictional feature film of the 1970s, *Le Couple Témoin*, appeared in 1977; it was originally conceived as an episode of a much larger project, but eventually it was a very low-budget film.

Klein's film of the May events, *Grands soirs et petits matins*, appeared in 1978. Klein had been extremely active throughout May, not within the Etats-Généraux, which irritated him, but as part of a group which he had set up to shoot footage when required, and which called itself Cinéma Sorbonne. The group had been integrated into the general organisation, which delegated particular groups to particular circumstances. It was assigned the Sorbonne meetings and infrastructure. This organisation did not long survive the period of action and, as a result, Klein in 1978 was still in possession of the footage he had shot and which he had partly edited into a four-hour film 'which I didn't try to distribute, but which exists' (Klein 1977: 18). This footage, edited into an average-length feature film, proved to be one of the most interesting versions produced of the events. In 1980, Klein directed *The Little Richard Story*, a return to the documentary and to his interest in the black American hero.

We will concentrate essentially on the 'French' films: *Mister Freedom*, *Le Couple Témoin* and *Grands soirs et petits matins*.[2] *Mister Freedom* is a film contemporary with the May events, and therefore an expression of Klein's preoccupations at the time but not really a precursor of the 1970s. Klein in fact suggested that despite the nominal French setting it too was really a film about America.

> For me as an American, making *Loin du Viêt-nam* or *Mister Freedom* was a very political act and also a chance to shed clear light on the American system ... In any case, *Mister Freedom* is a very American film, purely American, even though I made it in France. It's not France that I'm representing, not even the reactions of the French, it's people's Americanisation. (Klein 1968: 14, 19)[3]

---

[2] The films about black consciousness must be considered as American, released first in the USA and aimed at the American audience, although they were received with interest in France and some of the funding for *Muhammad Ali* at least was of French origin.

[3] 'Pour moi américain, faire *Loin du Viêt-nam* ou *Mister Freedom*, c'est un acte très politisé, et aussi l'occasion d'exposer en clair le système américain ... De toute façon, *Mister Freedom* est un film très américain, purement américain, même si je l'ai tourné en France. Ce n'est pas la France que je mets en scène, ni même les réactions des Français, mais l'américanisation des gens'.

He notes that the film's relevance was recognised by many countries: 'what's odd is that the Cubans who bought the film thought it was about the Cuban situation, and the Greeks think it's a film about Greece', and he claims to have been totally unaware that the unrest in France was so close to coming to a head: 'I certainly wasn't expecting the French political awakening, in different circumstances besides, to reach such proportions, and people who think that it's a film made since May explaining May are obviously wrong' (Klein 1968: 19).[4]

Nonetheless France is the nominal setting, and various particularly French symbols – the Phrygian cap, the Marseillaise, and most importantly the tricolour which forms so insistent a recurring colour-scheme[5] – constantly remind us of this. There are more telling references. The enormous inflatable puppet who is Super-French-Man resembles de Gaulle both in appearance and characteristics – insistence on etiquette, obsession with national independence, and entire authority over ministers represented by noisy but controllable ranks of pinball machines. The reference to the disaffection of youth with the 'Freedom culture' which provides a common concern for Mister Freedom and Moujik Man when the two meet, takes up the Marxist/Leninist/Maoist phenomenon which Godard had already made known. 'I'm just as fed up about it as you ... they're kids ... Red China Man has been stirring them up' complains Moujik Man. The FAF ('Français Anti-Freedom') quote Chinese proverbs during their councils of war, and reject Moujik Man because he is of no practical help, thus re-echoing in a more broadly caricatured image the tics of Godard's mini-cell. However, there is one important difference from the perception of indigenous French radicals: in the final showdown, Super-French-Man, approached for aid by Mister Freedom, responds with a dismissive 'Merde' and is thus portrayed as himself an insurgent. Here Klein shows that the film does indeed

---

[4] 'Ce qui est curieux, c'est que les Cubains qui ont acheté le film le considèrent comme un film sur la situation cubaine, que les Grecs trouvent que c'est un film sur la Grèce. Je ne m'attendais certes pas à ce que la prise de conscience des français, dans une situation du reste différente, prenne une telle ampleur, et les gens qui croiraient que c'est un film fait depuis mai, qui explique mai, se trompent évidemment'.

[5] As it does in so much of Godard's work, before and after May. A constant reminder of the setting, its ambiguity – since the colours are also those of the American flag – is more pronounced or at least more obvious in Klein's work. It also, of course, theatricalises the setting.

correspond to a concern with Americanisation rather than an attentive examination of French contestatory politics in 1967. The phrase which caused the major part of the trouble with the censors – 'To the dictatorship of the people, of Freedom, of Moujik Man, of Red China Man, I prefer my own' – illustrates quite well the general satire to which Klein was exposing all parties to the conflict and his international outlook. The 'coincidence' of the outbreak of the May events in his opinion worked against the film: 'the film's basis was distorted and it was badly timed' (Klein 1970: 65).[6] If he had made it after May, he said, he might have set it elsewhere to avoid so precisely national an interpretation of his more broadly applicable schema. He said in 1969 that his great interest was to make films about America – from a counter-cultural perspective, obviously – and that he did not consider himself fully integrated into either French life or the French cinema: 'I had always avoided making French films because, even though I've lived here almost twenty years, I don't feel that I could film the French as I would like to, there are things which you can't feel and can't grasp when you weren't brought up in the country. And then I've never considered myself as truly part of France, but always as an exile, an "outsider" – except for a few weeks last May and June, for the first time' (Klein 1968: 19).[7] He was to reiterate this last point in many subsequent interviews.

There are further ramifications to the argument that *Mister Freedom* is not a 'French' film. The mode of its making, and its various themes, fit the preoccupations and aims of the French cinema of the time and the directions which it would, for a while at least, pursue. Apart from the question of Americanisation and the consumer society (related, here, by the representation of the Freedom embassy in Paris as a giant supermarket), the relation of form to political content in this film is very important.

Mister Freedom is made up of caricatures, with the comic strip as an explicit reference. The various characters' names and natures

---

[6] 'les données du film se trouvaient faussées et il est mal tombé'.

[7] 'Je me suis toujours gardé de faire des film français parce que, même si je vis ici depuis près de vingt ans, je n'ai pas l'impression de pouvoir filmer les Français comme je voudrais: il y a des choses qu'on ne peut pas sentir ni saisir quand on n'a pas été élevé dans le pays. Et puis, je ne me suis jamais considéré comme faisant partie de la France, mais toujours comme exilé, "outsider" – sauf pendant quelques semaines en mai–juin dernier, pour la première fois.'

bear more relation to the American than the French comic-strip tradition, but the *bande dessinée* (BD) is nonetheless a *French* cultural phenomenon. French reviewers had no difficulty in relating the film to specifically French traditions: behind the BD, but visually very prominent, lay the grotesque figures of distorted authority of Jarry's *Ubu roi*, and behind them again the *guignol*.

Klein's reflections on the current debate on the desirable form for political cinema are, in these circumstances, very interesting. His previous project had been a contribution to *Loin du Viêt-nam*, which seems to have influenced him in two ways in preparing the scenario of *Mister Freedom*. Firstly, he felt that the 'documentary' method – of which *Loin du Viêt-nam* was still an example – had problems attracting an audience: 'we knew very well that a documentary would be condemned to be seen only by those people who could be bothered to go to the Mutualité to listen to four hours of speeches and applaud afterwards, and that wasn't the aim' (1968: 14). This problem was currently exercising the minds of the militant groups, to whom the danger of preaching only to the converted was the most urgent issue, and similar arguments occurred in the debates over the validity of popular political thrillers and avant-garde form. Klein seems not to have been tempted by conventional fictional cinema; neither, despite his undoubted political commitment, does he speak of a search for a 'revolutionary form' in so many words. Yet the problem of appropriate form is very real to him, and he seeks an answer at the meeting of popular and of artistic culture, of America and France.

In the case of *Mister Freedom*, he justifies his choices through an appeal to efficiency: the documentary, a form which he himself favours ('Personally, I adore the documentary, and I think in a sense that it's all there is', 1968: 14), led to a restricted audience; and general exposure to television news broadcasts has led to its 'realism' losing a great deal of its impact: 'It [news footage of a woman attacked by the American police] made not an ounce of difference to anyone. It became a spectacle, a huge psychodrama without any real political content' (Klein 1969a: 29).[8] On the other hand, he was most impressed, in Joris Ivens' contribution to *Loin*

---

[8] 'Cela ne faisait ni chaud ni froid à personne. Cela devenait un spectacle, un immense psychodrame sans contenu politique réel'.

du Viêt-nam, by an episode showing Vietnamese peasants and soldiers flocking to watch a piece of very schematised satirical theatre. Dissatisfaction with documentary, and this proof of the efficacy of *guignol*, led to his choice of the form for *Mister Freedom*. Godard and others had already experimented with it, but the couching of the new politics in a form based on popular culture was perhaps exemplified in *Mister Freedom* as in no other French (or even perhaps European) film. The idea, although advanced by Dziga-Vertov, produced no more than a flirtation among his followers in 1970: although use of the theatre was common, direct reference to even one truly popular tradition was rare, and the crossing of traditional popular and subverted mass culture seems to be unique. In an interview with *Image et son* (Klein 1969b), Klein puts great emphasis on this point, to which he attributes the effectiveness of the film. The origins of the method lie partly in Klein's perception of the political situation: 'There's a puppet show aspect to the way Americans conceive of politics and war which everyone accepts and which is frightening' (Klein 1968: 14),[9] partly in *Loin du Viêt-nam*, and partly in the influence of Léger and the idiom of the artistic 'underground'; although Klein's comment in *Image et son* (Klein 1969b, 84)[10] – 'I think that what is renewing cinema is things which come from outside it: from theatre, from television, from carnival, from mime etc.' – indicates that he was aware of related experiments taking hold after 1968. We rediscover theatre in, for example, the work of Straub, Comolli, Cassenti, Rivette, not to mention many more fleeting appearances, while television technology will become an important element of Godard's work, and the reference to 'carnaval' reflects the spirit of festival expressed not only in other films inspired by '68, but also in the events themselves, and relates to ideas of overturning of hierarchies and the mingling of many voices described by Bakhtin. In fact, the examples that Klein selects, taken from high and low, 'popular' and 'mass' culture, are themselves a carnavalesque mixture of inspiration entering the new cinema.

The post-'68 discussions of film form, however, seem not to have noticed the experiment of *Mister Freedom*. The Marxist-

---

[9] 'Dans la façon des Américains de concevoir la politique, de faire la guerre, il y a un jeu de guignol que tout le monde accepte et qui est effrayant'.

[10] 'Je crois que tout ce qui renouvelle le cinéma, ce sont des choses venues de l'extérieur: le théâtre, la télévision, le carnaval, les mimodrames, etc.'

Leninist groups, apparently, took exception to being caricatured (as they had taken exception to *La Chinoise*): 'In their opinion [Red China Man] was a caricature. And you must caricature the enemy but not your friends. But the starting point of the film was carnival-puppets and if all the characters weren't carnivalesque it would have been cheating' (Klein 1969b: 80).[11] And while *La Chinoise* could not be ignored, despite objections, William Klein was not Jean-Luc Godard, and thus *Mister Freedom* remained isolated. Despite Klein's claim (Klein 1970: 65)[12] that 'I thought that documentary was boring everybody', he returned to it for the films on Eldridge Cleaver and Muhammad Ali. His attitude to documentary, however, excludes any pretence at objectivity: 'I don't think that documentary has ever been realist and I have never tried to be objective. I've always loaded the dice' (Klein 1970: 66).[13] In his next feature film, *Le Couple Témoin*, Klein returns to the stylisation of *Mister Freedom*, but he has abandoned the references to comic-strips and to guignol and concentrates on a 'designer' appearance appropriate to the content.

Le Couple Témoin, made in 1977, no longer addresses the politics of international relations and state power, although it does contain an examination of political pronouncements through the character of the Minister. Its precursors are the vaguely anti-consumerist comedies which had existed in France and elsewhere even before 1968. It is slightly futuristic, and premises a government experiment to determine statistically the ideal living conditions for the young urban couple of the 1970s. Claudine and Jean-Michel, the 'couple témoin', chosen because they are '66 per cent average', are installed in their hyper-modern flat and subjected to various reaction tests by a team of *psycho-sociologues*, the whole experiment being simultaneously presented live on TV through cameras hidden in the couple's flat. The satire which had begun to date might profitably be revived in a Europe transfixed by reality-TV…

---

[11] 'A leur avis [Red China Man] était une caricature. Et on doit caricaturer l'ennemi mais pas les amis. Or, la donnée du départ de ce film c'est le carnaval-guignol et si tous les personnages n'étaient pas carnavalesques ça aurait été truqué'.

[12] 'je pensais que le documentaire emmerdait tout le monde'.

[13] 'Je crois que le documentaire n'a jamais été réaliste et je n'ai jamais essayé, moi, d'être objectif … j'ai toujours pipé les dés'.

Claudine and Jean-Michel soon begin to express signs of revolt which, we are told, reduce their 'averageness quotient'. At the same time, the controlling government department gradually reveals itself to be fictitious, the TV chat show staff which provide the frame narrative are no more than ventriloquists' dummies, and control, such as it is, is exercised by the psychologists whose sanity is more than questionable. The film ends with a group of children posing as terrorists invading the flat, actively encouraged by the couple and appreciated silently by the psychologists in an upper room. Although the tone is light the premise is paranoid: no revolt is independent. When the control room computer finally flashes up 'Experiment Over', Claudine and Jean-Michel having declined to leave with the children (for where?) are left standing in the rain on an unfinished housing estate with no indication of where they can go from here.

Le Couple Témoin is not as rigorously constructed as *Mister Freedom*, and many of its targets were hardly original. But its contestatory spirit, its vigour and its determined stylisation were becoming rare in the French cinema by 1977. Claudine and Jean-Michel are in an unsophisticated way exposed to a *prise de conscience*; their wide-eyed wonder at the array of gadgets presented to them at the beginning of the film is converted into ever-greater irritation until at last they break into angry parody of the patriotic song they obligingly delivered during an official dinner party, and they begin to worry about their social definition. In taking part in this experiment they have after all lost earnings, and why will Claudine have lost so much less than Jean-Michel? When the children appear and the couple unconditionally take their part, they lose all respect for the objects around them, which as the children point out are not theirs (but would it have made so much difference if they *had* been theirs)?

But there is nowhere for the couple to go beyond their moment of joyous anarchy. The children depart with affectionate but definitive farewells, the experiment is closed, and all that remains to Claudine and Jean-Michel are the striped clothes like prison uniforms which are the sign of their participation in the experiment.

It is tempting to see in this ending a jaundiced comment on the forlorn hopes of the early part of the decade. Klein was evasive: 'If you think it's serious, it's serious. You can also decide that it isn't serious' (Klein 1977: 22),[14] adding that he inclines to the latter opinion. Nonetheless the film needs to be considered in conjunction not only with Klein's more general comments in the late 1970s on the aspects of the previous decade which he considered significant, but also with *Grands soirs et petits matins*, which appeared the following year, anniversary *oblige*, and which constitutes a direct reflection on the turmoil of ten years previously.

Klein was intensely and actively involved in the events, and for the first time considered himself integrated into French life ('in May, I was surprised and very moved to find that the notion of foreigner/French and even foreigner among the French no longer existed' (Klein 1978: 41)[15]); but, at the same time, he lived the events without ever engaging with any political faction, any group or any ideology: 'Even in my militant period, I was never prepared to raise my fist, to sing the Internationale or to belong to a group' (Klein 1985: 43),[16] despite telling *Cinema 70*: 'I consider a political film to be ineffective if it is produced outside a political movement and distributed outside a political party' (Klein 1970: 64).[17] A tension between inside and outside, then, is clearly visible both in *Le Couple Témoin* and in the editing of the May footage.

The first point of comparison is that both are marked by pessimism. The title *Grands soirs et petits matins* given to the 1968 footage evokes anticlimax. The wave of revolutionary intoxication is followed by the realisation that nothing much has changed and that the participants have to cope as best they can with the morning after. Much the same could be said of Claudine and Jean-Michel's situation after their *défoulement* with the children. *Le Couple Témoin* ends on a damp building-site, *Grands soirs* in the deserted, water-splashed corridors of the Sorbonne. (*Mister Freedom* also ends with devastation, albeit more dramatic and less realistic.) It was a truism by 1977 that 1968 had failed to achieve

---

[14] 'Si on trouve que c'est sérieux, c'est sérieux. On peut aussi trouver que ce n'est pas sérieux'.

[15] 'en mai, j'étais surpris et très ému de constater que la notion étranger-français et même étranger entre français n'existait plus'.

[16] 'Même dans ma période militante, je n'ai jamais accepté de lever le poing, de chanter l'Internationale ou d'appartenir à un groupe'.

[17] 'Je trouve inefficace un film politique produit en dehors d'un mouvement politique et distribué en dehors d'un parti politique'.

its aims, but the sense of failure is heightened here by the lack of definition of those aims in the first place. This is very clear also in *Le Couple Témoin*, where everyone's aspirations are formulated in the most woolly of terms. Claudine, asked by the Minister what she would do in his position, responds with a list of negatives – no more work, no more prisons, no more rich, no more poor, no more governments: 'and we'd be, like, happy'. We would apparently be on the way to no man's land. The Minister is no more precise, however, in his own promises. The children have no obvious aims other than to amuse themselves and to be allotted three minutes on TV – once they have them, they have no idea what to say in them, a situation which illustrates exactly a famous Sorbonne *graffito*. The psychologists are perhaps the most coherent revolutionaries – we become progressively more convinced that their aim from the start is to subvert the experiment and induce dissatisfaction in their guinea-pigs – but they are merely negative and, dissatisfaction obtained, they leave the unfortunate couple unaided and alone. They are aware that they are in a false position – the phrase 'the perversion of the social sciences', which they use to describe their work, was current in 1968 – but they are unable to resolve it, and apparently despise their 'average' victims. The reasons for their strike or work to rule during the ministerial visit are never made clear. Claudine and Jean-Michel, convinced of the worthlessness of what they have left behind, have nothing at all to put in its place, and not even companion-ship and support in the mud. Incidentally this does not prevent some very telling things being said in the course of the film, but they are only said, never acted upon or carried through.

In *Grands soirs et petits matins*, naturally, a great many plans are made, much of what is said is positive, and some of it is precise. However, we are left with an overall sense of imprecision, largely due to the number of different projects and aims that the film presents. This theme, however, develops gradually. To begin with, the principal subject is the organisation of the events themselves, deployment of available speakers and helpers, and discussion of the feasibility of 'l'option de la rue'. However, even this exhilaration is damped, at the end of Part I of the film, with a television picture of Pompidou announcing that 'this demon-stration [that of the Right] was able to proceed in perfect order' in stark contrast with the eager anticipation of revolution (*The*

Revolution, '*le Grand Soir*') which had been taking place earlier.

From about halfway through Part I of the film, the emphasis changes from the means to the end: the theme is summed up by the speaker in the Sorbonne, at the beginning of the second part, who claims: 'from this crisis which France is experiencing a new era may emerge'. The camera shows us various groups or single speakers evoking desired changes, sometimes through speeches from a platform, sometimes in informal conversation, sometimes simply through displaying banners or chanting slogans. Their aims range from the setting-up of 'autogestion' (a discussion in the Sorbonne café) and the nationalisation of Citroën (banners during a rally) to the reform of the 'grandes écoles' (speaker) and the furthering of the interests of Breton peasants and small shopkeepers: even the frustrated wish of a café waiter to go to night school. Cohn-Bendit speaks of 'revolutionary order ... the possibility of restarting production for the profit of the working class' but clearly not all the groups of people who are shown discussing the possible consequences of what is going on would either use this language or entirely endorse this aim.

The last part of the film (second half of Part II) returns again to shots of demonstrations, after a sequence where four different leaders of the movement explain their positions. Until the end (the last shot of damp corridors) the revolutionary momentum seems to be kept up, but somehow the dank ending is not surprising. The active, immediate energy of the beginning of the film disperses into a confusion of discourses, not conflicting but at the same time not co-ordinated. The final footage of the demonstrations is similarly uncoordinated. Some of it is recognisable from the first part of the film, but it is no longer set against discussions which define it as planned and corresponding to a need for direct action. In fact, *Grands soirs et petits matins* presents 1968 as not so much losing momentum (there is no footage of the subsequent return to normality) as losing direction.

At the same time, however, and also by the same means, the film does give a clear picture of the precarious unity of different interests that was so important for Klein. Although both *Le Couple Témoin* and *Grands Soirs* end pessimistically, pessimism is by no means the principal content of either film. The majority of *Grands soirs et petits matins* concentrates on action and optimism, and *Le Couple Témoin*, besides being consistently very funny, moves, until the final shot, towards rather than away from a revolt that we long for more with every new disaster. Klein's position seems to be that of the Minister in *Le Couple Témoin* (fortuitously: I do not wish to suggest that he wanted to make this rather fatuous politician a mouthpiece for 'the truth'): 'I am a pessimist but one who is always hopeful'. Neither film presents change as impossible, but both point to fundamental problems in the formulation of a coherent project. The lack of clear goals should be linked to a more general problem, that of language.

This may seem an inescapable commonplace when referring to 1968 – what language is appropriate to expressing revolution in terms of street discourse, of the cinema, etc? The question had a definite and precise meaning for Klein, even before the problem of his own cinematic language came to be raised. Commenting both on *Grands Soirs* and *Le Couple Témoin*, he has linked the films explicitly to the *language* of 1968: 'I think that the subject of my film [*Grand soirs*] is almost the fantastic fever of words which exploded at that moment' (Klein 1978: 41).[18]

To refer to 1968 as a 'fever of words' may seem reductive on the part of a director who has acknowledged the profound effect exercised on him by the ideas expressed during May. (Klein 1977: 18).[19] It nonetheless corresponds to the representation of the events which *Grands Soirs* provides. Throughout the film the emphasis is on talk; not merely the platform speakers which many of the short militant films reproduced, but planning meetings to which Klein had access in his 'official' capacity, and even more tellingly informal conversations recorded among the crowds on the Boulevard Saint Michel or listening to the speakers. Klein has placed a great deal of emphasis on reproducing different kinds of discourse: in the first few minutes the film moves from a political discussion, to a march where language becomes chants and placards, to a radio speech by de Gaulle (and the mocking 'De Gaulle au poteau' which greets it), to the violence of the first demonstrations – itself a kind of language – to street conversa-

18 'Je crois que le sujet de mon film [*Grands Soirs*] est presque le fantastique délire verbal qui a jailli à ce moment'.

19 'Il est arrivé que, en mai 68, quand tout le monde mettait en question le cinéma, moi je l'ai mis en question réellement en ce qui me concernait' ['It happened that, in May 1968, when everybody was calling cinema into question, I really called it into question in my own case.'].

tions, reaction to them, and then to a speaker addressing a noisy crowd. There is relatively little footage of the action itself, just enough to provide a reference for those already familiar with it; and even when filming a demonstration, Klein's camera explores the crowd and homes in on particular faces – as indeed it does while recording the speeches both of the activist leaders and of de Gaulle. The emphasis is on the variety of individual experience and even more on the language used to express that experience, from the political phraseology of the speakers: 'restarting production for the benefit of the working-class' to the street-corner philosophers: 'the CGT has always been disgusting'.

This language is a 'fever' to the extent that the numerous intersecting discussions finally lead to a lack of conclusion (it is no coincidence that the last speech reproduced in the film refers to the difficulty of communication between organisers and militants). The combined effect of all the different modes of expression, however, is positive in the immediate, however confused it may be, and if Klein recorded this 'fantastic' confusion, it was because he perceived it at the time as both valuable and important. Ten years later, he observes how a large proportion of the language of May had been forgotten, or, worse, recuperated. This reflection underlies both films. 'If I made the film about May, it was also because people had forgotten some of the themes of May, and a certain language too', he said to *Jeune cinéma* (1977: 20).[20] A similar concern lies behind *Le Couple Témoin*: 'la qualité de la vie', he observes, was a 'May phrase' taken over by the government and robbed of its original sense as he understood it. The appropriation of the rhetoric of revolution by consumer-oriented progress is the foundation of the wry satire in *Le Couple Témoin*, from the psychologists' attempt to quantify 'the happiness threshold' to the discourse of the Minister, the most unrepentant abuser of revolutionary concepts.

The Minister throughout speaks to and through the media, even when he is theoretically enjoying a meal at the couple's flat: in any case every private event in the couple's flat is mediatised. Anything the Minister says is thus for the benefit of the electorate, and we are not surprised to hear him formulate vaguely reformist

---

[20] 'Si j'ai fait le film sur mai, je l'ai fait aussi parce que les gens avaient oublié certains thèmes de mai, et un certain langage également'.

phrases which go no further than the broadest banalities – as Claudine utters Utopian banalities. He speaks of the need to 'reconcile man [sic] and the City' (as did the Situationists): in order to achieve this, 'we must shake up received ideas'. A little later he speaks of 'Man, supra-logic' (and this time catches himself and corrects his gender-specificity) and appropriates the rhetoric of a human environment based on unquantifiable values. The irony of this in the dehumanised and mechanised environment of the *appartement témoin* would be apparent, but in any case he is stopped short by Claudine's interruption: 'This is all very well but apparently you can bend spoons too', and, all rhetoric forgotten, the Minister bows to the requirements of reality-TV and show-business.

The 'qualité de la vie 77' is the principal target of Klein's satire but other 'May phrases' can be found scattered through the film, emptied of their original meaning and with no effective substitute: spare words, as it were, to be picked up and refurbished by the spectator if he or she so wishes. Not all the contestatory phrases are as lost in their new context as those in the Minister's speech: some are still valid comments on the action, although they are not presented as such. Words are just words, presented as typical of what might be said in a given situation; no action in the film occurs as a direct result of anything said, not does any idea expressed serve to modify the opinion or attitudes of another character. However there are many sharp criticisms not only of the caricature-world of the film, but of the society in which the viewer is locked. One obvious example is the psychologists' conversations regarding their role or lack of it; but there are other, more transient figures who briefly and inexplicably adopt the phrases of May. The dummy television broadcast at one point initiates a panel discussion of the 'experiment' which includes a *contestataire* who points out that totalitarian societies have always chosen to represent themselves in a couple. At this point we already know that everyone in the TV show is no more than a puppet in the hands of the psychologists and that this man is a mere stereotype like everyone else on the set; we can therefore take him or leave him. He provides a reminder that by 1977 the activists of May had become TV pundits representing just another viewpoint which always needed its spokesperson; on the other hand, the idea is worth a moment's thought – without taking it as revealed revolutionary truth – if the audience is inclined to pick it up as it passes. Since no character is presented as a clear source of valid interpretation, even a puppet may have a point: the audience has to look for what it can find and react individually to every new idea. A mannequin may be no more ridiculous than a vapid politician or a couple of crazy scientists – who are, of course, manipulating the puppets, although we understand that the latter are emitting the truisms that their roles demand rather than expressing the point of view of their animators.

If the audience does choose to hear this comment, it opens up another field of interpretation to the rest of the film. The same thing occurs elsewhere, for example when the couple, just before the experiment's end and the incursion of the children, begin to talk about the economic difference between them (up to this point we have considered them only as consumers of goods, without considering at all that they need the resources to do so and therefore have other social roles: this too is a sharp reflection of game-show conventions). At another point the couple are unexpectedly showered with cabbages by farmers protesting at the glorification of their lifestyle. The scene is funny but ... why not? During the meal with the minister there is even one state-ment which has some power and narrative effect. It is attributed to a New York Jew – thus suggesting that the film-maker feels some solidarity with this particular voice of lucidity: Jean-Michel is told that his passivity may 'lead him to Auschwitz'. The reference jars the audience, and it is made to strike Jean-Michel: a kind of complicity briefly develops between him and the Jewish doctor. Later, the doctor requests that he sing for the audience, Jean-Michel, rather than submitting, returns the request, and the doctor in his turn submits. The audience reads the layers of irony which are for once attributed to the characters and not supplied at their expense.

Finally there is the intervention of the children, mostly characterised as anarchic, ludic and ultimately pointless; during the fraternisation which occurs between invaders and invaded, however, rejection of consumer gadgetry is summed up, finally and intelligently, by the question of who owns the television set. The couple have no control over what comes out of it, and do not understand its mechanism, thus they have no control over it at all, so how can they regard it as theirs? The question is left unanswered and indeed defused since *nothing* in the flat can belong to the couple, but the question, a serious one, is there for the taking.

Language in *Le Couple Témoin* is thus deprived of all narrative function other than to characterise or stereotype the speakers: but the meaning which it is emptied of in the film may still act on the spectator. Clichés in fact provide a good deal of the film's humour given the incongruous circumstances in which they are uttered, but they are more than a mere series of gags: those incongruous circumstances force some reconsideration of the words themselves. In 1969 Klein told *Image et Son* that he hoped that the film's audience would laugh or grow angry the next time they heard one of Mister Freedom's formulae uttered by a real politician. (Klein 1969b: 82). The same aim evidently applies to the commonplaces in *Le Couple Témoin*, and it is not even a function confined to spoken language. The contents of the flat are similarly translated into visual or tangible clichés. Claudine and Jean-Michel are offered the choice between various styles of furniture, among them 'traditional' or 'ecologist', the words have a referent but it is the merest bow to surface appearance. The change in surface that they evoke, besides, is incongruous in the bare, white-walled futuristic *appartement témoin*. They are signs which signify nothing. The couple move in boxes of books – the complete works of Zola and Balzac and a set of reproductions of great paintings – similarly as a representation of 'culture' devoid of content.

Not everything in the film is a cliché, but all is similarly emptied of narrative significance, and telling words must be noticed by the audience as they pass. Similarly in *Grands soirs et petits matins*, everything said is the centre of attention, it all relates to the 'revolution' which is the subject of the film, but it is so varied, and at times self-contradictory, that the audience must listen carefully to the 'fever of words' in order to pick out what we choose to consider most significant. It is more than likely that the choice will be different for every spectator. The film's success perhaps rests in that directed confusion which places the audience in a position very close to what must have been the actual experience of many participants, at least of those whose choice of discourse had not already been irrevocably made.

A word should now be said about the language of film itself, which is much more active in controlling our response than the words spoken, certainly in the case of *Le Couple Témoin* but also I think in *Grands Soirs*.

The two films represent the two different conceptions that Klein uses in his film-making. *Grands Soirs* is a documentary, *Le Couple Témoin*, like *Mister Freedom*, an extremely stylised comedy. As in *Mister Freedom*, the characters in *Le Couple Témoin* seem to have certain characteristics of dolls or automatons; the influence of the comic strip is less obvious, but there are elements of slapstick and popular theatre; the set is extremely stylised, little more than blank white walls dotted with mysterious numbers, and a few pieces of token furniture. Although we may retrospectively relate this 'poverty' of location to the film's very low budget, it does not appear as a handicap during the viewing. The relationships between the living couple and the mock-scientific figures and diagrams which surround them is handled with a variety of camera angles which constantly combine the two – we are reminded of Léger's machine-men – and turn shots into abstract compositions, where incomprehensible numbers and arrows combine with a careful arrangement of forms and a restricted formal colour scheme.

Le Couple Témoin, then, reflects Klein's love of stylisation; it is a film which owes much to painting and also to the theatre. *Mise-en-scène* and camera position combine to make of Claudine and Jean-Michel human beings who participate in the nature of diagrams and of robots. Occasional scenes shot in double-speed, that long-established trick of film comedy, also contribute to this effect. Chris Marker commented that in Klein's films human beings are also signs: 'the creature of flesh and blood that nevertheless still retains a graphic function … [so that] … the letter becomes man, man becomes a sign, and the personage becomes – in its double sense – a character' (Marker 1977–78: 490). One portion of the characters in *Le Couple Témoin* does, as we have already noted, prove to consist of dummies. In the documentary *Grands soirs*, on the other hand, much of Klein's filmic effort is directed towards emphasising the human, as opposed to the play of larger forces; in demonstrations the camera soon abandons wide general shots to home in on the crowd, wandering among them (sometimes moving in the opposite direction to the marchers) and focussing on individual faces. A similar procedure accompanies the filming of speeches; although the camera may remain on the speaker for a while, it soon veers away to explore the crowd of listeners, combining very fast movement with sudden attention to anonymous individuals.

In the middle section of the first part, which is given up to the internal organisation meetings in the Sorbonne, there is insistence on the minor, as well as on the major, action. Meetings convene to plan the deployment of demonstrations, but also to prepare sandwiches. In the Bureau de Liaison of the Comité d'action lycéenne (CAL), the operatives take phone calls alternately from a sister organisation elsewhere to learn the extent of the strike, and from a mother wanting to know when her offspring will get home.

We have already noted the importance in the film of informal street-corner discussions. Klein has in several cases incorporated incidents which remind us of the actual conditions of filming these people: a man is accused of performing for the camera, a group objects to the process of filming. Such moments create a keen sense of immediacy – while ensuring that the myth of cinéma-vérité is exploded – and the importance given throughout to the individual, the anonymous and the 'private', if such a word can be used of action that takes place entirely on streets and in meeting rooms, gives the film an aura of authenticity. This 'parti pris', however, is not at the expense of the political. Although it does not promulgate one particular line, the film never strays from the presentation of the events as a revolutionary force. The insistence on the 'minor' paradoxically strengthens this impression, for every individual is shown in political action. The street groups are discussing the impact of the events and the participants' hopes of future developments; the individual faces focussed on are, of course, selected from a crowd in directed motion, and at any moment they are liable to utter the current chant, or even to begin the Internationale. Even those making sandwiches or taking a nap in a quiet corner are doing these ordinary things in extraordinary circumstances and for an extraordinary reason. Significantly, as the film draws to an end, the emphasis changes. The camera no longer searches the crowds for individuals intent on their action, but instead concentrates on the well-known faces of the leaders of the movement as they make their speeches, or circles high above scenes of demonstrations where violence is the dominant motif. Close-ups show confusion or distress, people covering their faces with handkerchiefs after a tear-gas attack, or moving aimlessly around the site of the demonstration.

In general, Klein illustrates May 1968 by concentrating on the individual action of many, unnamed, participants. The force of this approach is the picture it gives of May as a popular movement. It also highlights the inevitable interrelation of the personal and the political, a favoured theme of the post-'68 Godard, it will be remembered. The telephone conversations in the CAL office are reminiscent in their treatment of the sequence in the strikers' office in *Tout va bien* where a woman has to convince her husband that she is needed with her colleagues. However, Klein is presenting the idea from the opposite end; while Godard's films tend to concentrate on proving that the personal is also political, Klein here is demonstrating that the political (May '68) is also personal, and all the more strongly political for that.

The 'intimate' style also means that Klein in presenting '68 is entering the action itself. Throughout *Grands soirs*, it is clear that he is more concerned with subjective experience than, for example, with providing an accurate historical record of the development of events. Although there is some temporal progression, the shots of meetings and demonstrations are on the whole not dated, while a spectator who takes the film as a historical record might, for example, assume that violence only became important in the demonstrations at the very end of the period. On the other hand, the method of filming creates a sense of involvement. Although Klein has spoken of the impact which written titles can have in a film: 'Things written on the screen ... arouse much greater attention in the spectator' (Klein 1970: 66)[21] he here avoids them almost totally, using instead placards, posters and graffiti, which provide a written commentary without the intrusion of an authorial voice. Neither is there a voice-over commentary explaining what is going on; the spectator has to find his or her own way, although where a location is necessary Klein usually finds a way to provide it, in the form of a banner or through a speech. The identity of speakers, except in the penultimate sequence, is not given; an 'ahistorical' omission which perhaps, if anything, enhances the importance of the words spoken and of observed reactions to them. The lack of an external source of interpretation

---

[21] 'Les choses écrites sur l'écran ... suscitent une attention beaucoup plus grande du spectateur'.

works, again, towards a greater immediacy of what is presented, as does the incessant, erratic camera movement (erratic in direction but rarely in quality: there are a few shaky 'hand-held' shots, but not many), which skims, extremely fast, across seas of unfocussed faces in order finally to focus on one. At other times the camera wanders, moving from a face to a hand holding a placard to the placard itself. All these movements, preferred to cuts, approximate quite nearly to the behaviour of the eye in a situation where everything seems important, and the choice of what to concentrate on is uncertain. Klein was very much aware of the unsatisfactory nature of any documentary: 'Documentary films are always incomplete, there are always aspects which we miss' (1970: 65);[22] the use of fast camera movements is one way of indicating that there exists a great deal on which the camera could pause, but does not; it emphasises the selectivity of the filming exercise even in one location; and the fragmentary nature of the film's evidence is obvious. The speed of movement also gives considerable dynamism, not always identified with the revolutionary dynamism that moves the crowd – the camera sometimes moves 'against the tide', creating some confusion and a certain sense of dilettantism, as if the film-maker were curious rather than involved.

Between *Le Couple Témoin* and *Grands soirs* there exists very little unity of style. While in *Le Couple Témoin* the emphasis is primarily on *mise-en-scène* and editing, with a final result at the limit of stylisation, *Grands soirs* concentrates on the camera's exploration of real space and the capturing of fragments of 'lived reality' which take on a general significance. Much of the film resembles an album of photographs in which we are shown not merely the photographs themselves, but also the process of selecting them out of the chaos of the surrounding reality, a description also applied to Klein's photographic work (Bergala 1981: xiv).[23] In *Le Couple Témoin*, on the other hand, the chaos of reality might not exist. The film is constructed in isolation from it; the

[22] 'Les films documentaires sont toujours incomplets, il y a toujours des éléments qui nous échappent'.
[23] Bergala describes Klein's work as referring to 'le moment où le réel sort du chaos et de l'insignifiance pour faire bonne figure, pour prendre sens et forme' ['the moment when reality emerges from insignificance and chaos and becomes presentable, taking meaning and form'].

world which the camera enters is already a coherent sign system. Klein himself has referred in interview to the contradictions in his extremely varied work, (Klein 1975: 58) but 1968 is a constant presence in all he chose to do in the 1970s. In the nine years between *Mister Freedom* and *Le Couple Témoin* he restricted himself to documentary, taking very seriously the rejection of commercial structures and distribution: 'I didn't want to produce cinematic objects as a director in a certain context any more, I didn't want to make any more fiction films, I didn't want to make art any more' (Klein 1977: 18);[24] and for a while he sought to make films linked to a specific political cause. During this period, however, Klein's reflections on the political cinema indicate that he considered the most important factor to be the way in which the film was received: 'I think that a film is not political in itself, it's political by its use; and the most politically inspiring film in the world, if it's only distributed on the Champs-Elysée, won't inspire anything at all' (Klein 1971: 60).[25] The reception of *Eldridge Cleaver* in America epitomised the political use of a film (every showing became the starting point of a debate, Klein notes in the interview quoted above). However, even in 1971 he expresses doubts about the efficiency of 'alternative production' and a preference for 'playing the system' where possible: 'I think above all that we do it badly … In the long term it's unhealthy and it's not viable, and I think that cinema groups who want to provide counter-information … should be able to use the contradictions of the system better, as they say, in order to finance themselves' (1971: 59–60).[26]

By 1977–78, when *Le Couple Témoin* and *Grands soirs* appeared (the moment when Klein returned to France), his initial rejection of his 'other mode' (that is, the stylised fiction film) has given place to a new enthusiasm. Reading his interviews concerning the style of *Mister Freedom* and his belief in the renewal of cinema

[24] 'je ne voulais plus produire comme réalisateur dans un certain contexte des objets cinématographiques, je ne voulais plus faire des films de fiction, je ne voulais plus faire de l'art.'

[25] 'Je pense qu'un film n'est pas politique en soi, il est politique dans son emploi; et le film le plus mobilisant du monde, distribué seulement aux Champs-Elysées, ne mobiliserait rien du tout'.

[26] 'Je pense surtout qu'on se débrouille mal … A la longue, c'est malsain et pas viable, et je pense que les groupes de cinéma qui veulent fournir une contre-information … devraient pouvoir mieux employer les contradictions du système, comme on dit, pour s'autofinancer.'

through outside factors, it is perhaps surprising that he drew away from it at all. In *Jeune cinéma* in 1977 he observes that 'I refused art out of masochism – in any case out of stupid idealism, but also masochism ... and after lots of experiments I've come to the point where I can see no reason to deny yourself something which after all you enjoy' (Klein 1977: 19).[27] Looking back to the mid-1970s a little later, he observes: 'there was a period in my life when artistic experiment and the need for personal expression seemed derisory when weighed against certain causes for the benefit of which I wanted to efface myself. In one or two of my films I may have made propaganda for what I thought was worth it. Fine. But I don't think I'd do that today' (Klein 1985: 43).[28]

By 1977 then Klein had rethought his post-'68 stylistic choices (although after 1977 he returned to the documentary mode), but he had by no means discarded the themes of May; neither had he returned to an unquestioning acceptance of the dominant modes of production. He saw *Grands soirs* as an alternative to Lawaetz' 'official' version, which he rejected (Klein 1978: 41). Documentary or stylised fiction alike were used to produce unconventional work contesting any form of received discourse.

It should not be forgotten that Klein's career also included continuous work on advertising films; in his interview with *Révolution* in 1985 he claimed to have made 150 of them. He even claimed to have attempted to subvert this genre, but also admitted that he sometimes found this side of his work a burden: 'personally, I do find it rather wearisome to have to earn my crust with stuff I don't care about. Making one advertising film, fine. It can be fun but, in the end, it does get boring' (Klein 1983: 5).[29] The complaints of Jacques/Montand in *Tout va bien* draw extremely close to this, and Klein made commercials for DIM stockings just

---

[27] 'je refusais l'art par masochisme – en tout cas par idéalisme béat, mais par masochisme aussi ... Et après un tas d'expériences j'en suis arrivé à ne plus voir de raisons de se refuser à faire ce qui tout de même vous fait plaisir.'

[28] 'à une époque de ma vie, les recherches esthétiques et le besoin d'expression personnelle m'ont parus dérisoires à côté de certaines causes au profit desquelles je voulais m'effacer. Dans un ou deux de mes films, j'ai pu faire de la propagande pour ce qui me semblait en valoir la peine. Bon. Mais je ne pense pas que je le ferais aujourd'hui.'

[29] 'personnellement, je trouve en effet assez pénible de devoir toujours gagner ma croûte avec des trucs qui ne me concernent pas. Faire un film publicitaire, bien. Ca peut être amusant mais, à la longue, c'est quand même ennuyeux.'

as does Jacques. There is no way of telling if this *might* be deliberate, of course, but the coincidence returns us finally to the presentation of Klein as 'anti-Godard' referred to briefly at the beginning of the chapter. Neither film-maker ever refers to the other,[30] but many of their preoccupations, both of form and content, are similar. Both examined the implications of a consumer culture before 1968. Both contributed to Chris Marker's collective film *Loin du Viêt-nam* in 1967. Both were profoundly marked by their activities in 1968 (when both played an active role in the filming of the events) and both, in its aftermath, turned to an examination of the black movement in America: Godard, in *One + One* and *One A.M./P.M.* (1972); Klein, in his documentaries on Eldridge Cleaver and on the Pan-African festival. Both were preoccupied by the need for an appropriate form for true political films, although Klein, unlike Godard, avoided a specific political line, and their conclusions seemed antithetical (Klein moved away from stylisation, Godard explored it). Both found inspiration in the schematisation and stylisation of the 'avant-garde' theatre and comic strips, both experiment with the use of letters and graphic signs on the screen, and both find in the personalising of politics or the inverse a fundamental theme. The terms of comparison suggested by J.F. Held (Held 1967: 32).[31] should be nuanced somewhat in the post-1968 context. Certainly, Godard approaches his post-'68 films from a politically involved perspective, yet Klein's approach to the events themselves, as seen in *Grands soirs*, is paradoxically much closer and more involving than Godard's. *Grands soirs* could almost be said to 'vibrate in unison [with 68] ... without understanding it at all' – or, at least, without attempting to interpret; Godard's film tracts do specifically interpret what they show.

William Klein is something of an anomaly in French cinema. Not really French, not really, or at least not exclusively, a film-maker, all his important work in this field is grouped in the late 1960s and

[30] In Godard's case, the silence is, to the best of my knowledge, total (unless the *Tout va bien* episode can indeed be counted); Klein was once approached in a telephone opinion poll with the question 'Aimez-vous Godard?' but replied only 'Je ne suis pas très fort à ce jeu.'

[31] 'C'est une sorte d'anti-Godard; là où l'homme aux lunettes noires, moraliste, vibre à l'unisson de nos désarrois sans rien y comprendre, génial et bête ... Klein garde l'oeil froid, il analyse, il dissèque. Rien n'est moins futile.'.

the 1970s. The events of 1968 took on the added significance of providing the closest link he had ever felt with a country where he had already filmed as a detached observer, and yet, paradoxically, detached him from French cinema (in the sense of films made for a French audience) during most of the 1970s. The second example we have chosen of a film-maker deeply committed to and influenced by 1968 shares some of Klein's detachment. Alain Tanner, a Swiss whose cinematic career had begun in England, observed 1968 from an even more detached viewpoint than Klein, since he was sent to Paris as a reporter for Swiss television, and so while living the experience of May he was simultaneously engaged in analysing it. Tanner (unlike his compatriot Godard) both lived and worked in Switzerland in 1968, and the movement found little or no echo there; the result was a possible objectivity, but also a sense of frustration. A successful movement for change in France could have few implications in Switzerland, where the native conservatism is a factor on which Tanner has frequently remarked, and therefore he was debarred from full participation in the movement by its irrelevance to his own future. On the other hand, his position in Paris was not quite that of a foreign correspondent. Even if the Parisian students could not directly affect conditions in Switzerland, their revolt was expressed in a common language, if the movement should succeed it would spread into the very borders of Switzerland, and the whole discourse of discontent which May '68 expressed with regard to France was equally, if not more, applicable in the neighbouring country. Tanner thus approached '68 as a spectator, but a spectator hoping, in the possibly very near future, to assume a role in the action. This passionate non-involvement appears in his report of the events, *Le Pouvoir est dans la rue*, while the text of *Charles mort ou vif*, and the interviews which Tanner gave at the time, betray a will to project the energy and the force for change of May 1968 onto a society where they seem non-existent. Thus *Charles* is set in a 'near future', in which student revolt is a reality in Switzerland; Tanner identifies with 1968 not because he feels at one with the French (as Klein did), but because he senses at once the possibility and the impossibility of similar movement in Switzerland. May is a constant, often explicit, theme in Tanner's work throughout the 1970s, but it is always a Swiss version of May, channelled through his Swiss protagonists when fictional unrest is not invented for Switzerland.

Alain Tanner, film-maker, is a product of May '68, belonging to the generation which Serge Daney identified as that of the population of his films: 'Tanner for his part ... films only one generation, but in many situations, the generation which, having been born in '68, will soon be ten years old' (*Cahiers du cinéma* 1977: 48).[32] This has little to do with his chronological age; he was nearly forty at the time of the events. His function, his age and his nationality were all factors which at once marginalised him and affected his reaction in vital ways. He noted in an interview in 1970 that for his contemporaries, the outbreak of revolt was not so much a revelation as a reminder (for Tanner, a thoroughly welcome one): 'For my generation which was no longer the same age as the students, May revived lots of things. Even for people who had buried their libertarian sentiments. I too had repressed things which came back to the surface' (Tanner 1970: 60).[33] His formative years had been the 1950s: 'I'm not a product of the 60s but the 50s ... At that time there was a coincidence between a questioning of official culture and oneself on the one hand and the arrival of the image on the other. It was the early days of television, which was a source of image production' (Dimitriu 1985: 11).[34]

1968 marked neither the beginning of Tanner's political consciousness, nor of his engagement with the image-spectacle. Throughout the 1950s and 1960s he had worked on the margins of cinema, and in television. For the latter he had been extremely productive, making 'forty or so current affairs films' between 1964 and 1969 (*Avant-scène* 1970: 37).[35] His first practical experience of the cinema, in London in the late 1950s, had brought him into

[32] 'Tanner, lui, ... ne filme qu'une génération, mais sur plusieurs scènes, la génération qui, d'être né en 1968, aura bientôt dix ans'. The reference is to *Jonas qui aura 25 ans dans l'an 2000*, which, more than any other of Tanner's films, and perhaps more than any other film, constitutes a résumé of the position of that generation ten years after.

[33] ' Pour ma génération qui n'a pas l'âge des étudiants, mai a réveillé un tas de choses. Même chez des gens qui avaient enterré des sentiments libertaires. Moi aussi j'avais enfoui des choses qui sont remontées à la surface'.

[34] 'Moi je ne viens pas des années 60 mais des années 50 ... A ce moment-là il y avait une conjonction entre une mise en cause de la culture officielle et de soi-même d'une part et l'arrivée de l'image de l'autre. C'était le début de la télévision, qui était une source de production de l'image.'

[35] Tanner wrote this career outline himself; the dismissive formula thus presumably reflects his attitude to his TV work in 1970. Further details of the 'quarantaine de films' can be found in Dimitriu 1985: 22–7.

contact with the British Free Cinema. It was in London that he made his first film, a documentary short;[36] in 1969, he had made four films not destined for television, all documentaries – only one was feature length. By 1968, then, he already had an established career. However, May '68 was to deflect that career dramatically.

For Tanner, as for Godard, it marked a major change of direction, but whereas the latter left the commercial cinema to turn towards television and experimental documentary, Tanner was inspired to write his first fictional scenario, and to turn his attention towards commercial production. The scenario for *Charles mort ou vif* was written in June, and the events 'certainly influenced' it (Tanner 1974a: 50).[37] In the same year, with four other Swiss film-makers, he founded the Groupe 5 to facilitate the production of fictional feature films.

Mainstream cinema could reasonably hope for social influence in Switzerland to a much greater extent than in France. The foundation of the Groupe 5 represented the first serious attempt to establish a Swiss cinema. Although not all the five directors were as politically motivated as Tanner, they shared a commitment to social relevance, and had no intention of simply aping the product of the major distributors. Their production was thus 'alternative' both in presenting a Swiss audience with films based in Swiss life and Swiss culture, and in producing films where social and artistic considerations would override the straightforwardly commercial. The first of these factors meant that a low-budget Swiss film had probably a greater chance of being widely shown in Switzerland than an equivalent French film would have in France. The cinema offered Tanner a genuine possibility of introducing new ideas and forms of discourse to a wide public, who might be receptive to them since the film by its very existence represented a break with tradition. Thus it was entirely logical to translate the creative energy acquired from the experience of May into a feature film; and following on the success of this first experiment, to dedicate himself almost entirely to the cinema throughout the 1970s.[38]

---

[36] *Nice Time* (1957), in collaboration with Claude Goretta.

[37] 'les événements ont eu une influence certaine sur mon scénario écrit en juin.'

[38] Tanner made four television programmes in 1969, subsequent to *Charles mort ou vif*, and two in 1970. He did not work for television again until 1978, when he produced a half-hour programme reflecting on the difference between cinema and television (see Dimitriu 1985: 129–32).

In the ten years following 1968, Tanner made five films which show a clear, if complex, progression from film to film, and form, as a group, a reflection on 1968 and its implications. *Jonas*, in 1976, seems to bring this reflection to a logical conclusion; Tanner himself considered this film as a synthesis of his work to date, after which 'I need to go elsewhere' (*Cahiers du cinéma* 1977: 41).[39] However, the themes do not suddenly disappear. *Messidor*, in 1979, also concludes some of the strands which run through the preceding work, as well as reworking questions raised by *Jonas*. Throughout the 1980s and beyond, Tanner's films continued to subject Swiss society to a disciplined and often merciless scrutiny. *La Femme de Rose Hill* (1989), more than twenty years later, carries some echoes of *Charles mort ou vif*, although the optimism and the sense of an unrepressed revolt which survives when the protagonist is silenced have disappeared.

The films of the 1970s, however, even when they end in failure to all appearances, keep alive the hope that somehow, somewhere, someone will succeed in effecting a change for the better. *Charles mort ou vif* (1969) ends with the internment of Charles, but he is not the only vehicle of revolt in the film, and the others are unrepressed and undeterred. *La Salamandre* (1971) resolves nothing, for better or worse; Rosemonde ('la salamandre') is free, but where she will go or what she will do is impossible even to guess. *Retour d'Afrique* (1973), like *Jonas* (1976), ends with the birth of a new generation; the decision to have a child, in both films, implies the preservation of the alternative ideals of its parents ('We're going to spring a child on them', 'On va leur faire un enfant dans le dos!' says Vincent in *Retour d'Afrique*, and Jonas is conceived in much the same spirit). Only *Le Milieu du monde* (1974) leaves its society closed in on itself.

All five films represent a search for political cinematic expression; more precisely, for a way to express the need to re-form the socio-political structure of Switzerland. I have selected here for discussion the three that bear the most obvious and direct relationship to May 1968: *Charles mort ou vif*, *Retour d'Afrique* and *Jonas*, but the other two are conceived under the same influence and represent stages in the same research and efforts to come to terms with similar problems and themes.

[39] 'il me faut aller ailleurs'.

The fact that all the films take place in Switzerland means that the role of May '68 is ambiguous: the events are hardly ever referred to directly, even in the two films in which they or their effects are the most evident, *Charles* (at the beginning of the series), and *Jonas* (at the end). Although all the interviews which Tanner gave regarding the latter film give an important place to the reference point of 1968 (*Cahiers du cinéma* 1977: 42; Tanner 1977: 46), for six out of the eight people who form the centre of the film – according to *Cahiers* all part of that 'generation born in 68' – the reference is no reference at all.[40] In *Charles mort ou vif* it is disguised. There are references to student action, but in Switzerland, not in Paris, and we have already mentioned that *Charles* is set in a 'near future'; the actions of the Légitime Défense group are not a historical reference but a foretaste of what may be. Within the characters' frame of reference there is no place for May 1968. Within that of the film-maker and the audience, however, it is intensely present. Imprecise references and broad hints abound; there are references to the month of May: 'Il est de retour, le joli mois de mai', hums a detective tracking the student Marianne through a snowstorm; the hippy Paul whom Marianne tries to draw out of his passivity quotes: 'In May, do what you will. Popular saying' ('En mai, fais ce qu'il te plaît. Dicton populaire'). Marianne's method of educating Paul through a series of political/poetic catchphrases produces a 'coherent' text which runs through the film, not attached to any one author, deriving obviously from 1968 graffiti. This 'free text' provides a close formal link between the film and the events.

1968, then, enters *Charles* and *Jonas* less as a precise reference than as a structuring force. It is integrated through subversive content and through the form which that content takes. The matter of form is fundamental when discussing Alain Tanner. His films are immediately readable on the straightforward level of narrative – in contrast to the formalist experiments of a Godard or Straub/Huillet – but further investigation does always prove that the narrative form is not straightforward at all. In reading Tanner's comments on all his films, it becomes clear that their

[40] Only Max the journalist and Marco the history teacher can refer to it as an event in their lives – and then only marginally. The others, even if their attitudes are what would have been generally considered in France as 'post-'68', have developed independently and in relation specifically to the culture of Switzerland.

production was governed by a continual tension between form and content. Thus in reflecting on *La Salamandre* Tanner insists principally on the significance of the characters and of their dialogue. *Retour d'Afrique* on the contrary was conceived as a formal exercise, investigating 'for example ... the signification, the implications of a tracking-shot, that is more generally of the tool called cinema' (Tanner 1973b: 25).[41] and the story has a secondary role. The two terms of this oscillation were identified by Tanner in the same interview as 'intuitive' and 'reflexive' cinema; he claims to have, at the same time, two opposing attitudes faced with the narrative base of a film: 'to keep the form of the story, and at the same time to work on it, dismember it, take it apart to see how it works'.[42] All his films have elements which move in both directions, although the degree to which the narrative is coherent or fragmented varies.

Some of Tanner's films superficially resemble those of the Nouveau Naturel. The places in which the protagonists live and work are very important in defining them, but Tanner avoids the temptation to insist visually on their environment. This choice is certainly made for reasons significantly different from those which underlie naturalism; Tanner is not so much interested in evoking the real poverty of the environment as in reducing the power of distraction which is contained in a 'rich' image: 'I always try to simplify the image as much as possible to make it say as little as possible' (Tanner 1971: 114).[43] Nonetheless his austerity does not lead to schematic settings: rooms, flats, factories in Tanner's films are no more than ordinarily bare, and his choice of a simple image rejoins the restricted interiors of naturalism.

Rosemonde in *La Salamandre* corresponds exactly to the typical protagonist of the Nouveau Naturel; 23 years old, casual worker in various shops and factories, unsettled, politically unaware but ever-changing in response to new experiences. The Marie of *Jonas* is of the same type; Adriana (*Le Milieu du monde*) also fits the general description, while if Mathieu (*Jonas*) is in a

[41] 'par exemple ... la signification, les implications d'un travelling, c'est-à-dire plus largement de l'outil cinéma'.

[42] 'garder la forme du récit, et en même temps la travailler, la dépiauter, la mettre en morceaux pour voir comment elle fonctionne.'

[43] 'J'essaie toujours de simplifier le plus possible cette image pour lui faire dire le moins possible.'

slightly different category by virtue of his age and definitive politicisation, there are still the common factors of class and precarious social position. Even when the protagonists seem more nearly middle-class, Tanner deprives their surroundings of any particular attraction, and their work is a source of frustration and rarely a seat of power. Real life, for all Tanner's protagonists, takes place elsewhere. Thus Marco the teacher of *Jonas* carries on in a slightly shabby classroom a job whose boredom he tries as best he can to alleviate by unconventional methods, but in which he has very limited success. His pupils are amused but not necessarily convinced by his classes, and his attempts to subvert his work end in dismissal, as surely – if not as dramatically – as they do for Marie. Charles, the managing director, sees his workplace simply as somewhere in which he is ill at ease. Vincent and Françoise in *Retour d'Afrique* actually move in the course of the film from middle-class to working-class milieu, and the move is presented as reducing rather than increasing their frustrations.

The relation of these protagonists to their environment is invariably one of revolt, sometimes taking the form of total rupture (Charles, Rosemonde, Vincent and Françoise), sometimes of subversion of their own activities (Marco, Marie, Madeleine in *Jonas* – but all three make the break eventually – and, perhaps, the various journalists – Pierre and Paul in *La Salamandre*, Max in *Jonas*). All Tanner's films follow a pattern of 'soft revolt' in the sense that in no case is violence a necessary step or even seriously considered. In *Charles mort ou vif* the option is briefly raised. Marianne's revolt is not entirely non-violent, and it is identified as a response to another kind of violence which is being exercised on her:

> *Paul*: You're a member of this thing called 'Légitime Défense'?
> *Marianne*: Yes
> *Paul*: Funny name.
> *Marianne*: Why?
> *Paul*: It's more you who are doing the attacking.
> *Marianne*: People our age … whether they accept or refuse the world that's been made for them, are under attack from all sides, whatever they do in order to enter that world or, on the other hand, not to enter it. (*Avant-scène* 1970: 23)[44]

---

[44] *Paul*: Vous faites partie de ce machin qu'on appelle 'Légitime Défense'?
Marianne: Oui.

This exchange may seem to constitute a justification of violence, in that Marianne is an entirely positive character, not only aware herself from the start of the film of her position and where she is going but also responsible for raising the awareness of both Paul and her father: she is also the instigator of the 'free text'. However, when real violence is used by a repressive system against Charles, he decides not to defend himself, and persuades Paul also not to oppose resistance which it is fairly clear will in any event be ineffective: 'it's better', in Charles' opinion, to accept the inevitable, and the film seems to endorse him in the last title: 'He Laughs Loudest Who Laughs Last'. Following *Charles mort ou vif*, the protagonists in Tanner's films are entirely peaceful in their revolt until *Messidor* in 1979, where the violence is ultimately pointless and leads to disaster.

The Tannerian revolt seeks to avoid acts of violence directed against real or imagined oppressors: the barricades and battles of 1968 are definitely not what Tanner believed to be the real face of the events. The films are concerned with changing mentalities, and on this level revolts are both sudden and total. The characters concerned subject their own lives to traumatic change, which is sometimes portrayed as causing a form of self-inflicted violence, hence Charles' drinking bouts: rupture is also given a physical reality through the destruction of objects – Charles' car, for example.

Tanner's characters and situations, even their revolt against their situation, approximate often to those favoured by naturalism. The treatment of the attempted revolt, however, in every case goes beyond the simple representation that naturalism would imply and embarks on an analytical investigation of action, its causes and consequences and the possible points of view available from which to read it. The films have also been classed as utopian in outlook (Serceau 1983a: 124), but this too is oversimple when we consider their complex relation to reality.

Paul: C'est un drôle de nom
Marianne: Pourquoi?
Paul: C'est plutôt vous qui attaquez.
Marianne: Les gens de notre âge, … qu'ils acceptent ou qu'ils refusent le monde qu'on leur a fait, sont agressés de toutes parts, quoiqu'ils fassent pour entrer dans ce monde ou, au contraire, pour ne pas y entrer. .

It seems all but inevitable that a film such as *Jonas* should be classed as utopian. It concerns a group of eight people converging on an ideal alternative farming venture in the depths of the Swiss countryside. Their harmony is not as perfect as might be considered desirable, but this very fact seems to qualify their community as utopian (that is, impossible). The same could be said of *Charles mort ou vif*, although the experiment is on a smaller scale, and even of *Retour d'Afrique*, with the ideal community reduced to the ideal couple-in-society. However, when compared to clearly defined utopian films such as *L'An 01* and *Bof!*, Tanner's films stand out. Firstly, the experiments they present do not appear as impossible per se. The functioning of the community of *Jonas* – or the *ménage* of Paul, Adeline and Charles – stands up to the most rigorous scrutiny; the groups are constructed within social constraints and taking account of them. Secondly, they are not entirely perfect. Within these ideal communities, there are still tensions: Charles' post-alcohol inertia irritates Paul; Marguerite is ill-disposed towards Mathieu's interest in alternative education. In both of these conflicts, the indispensable but unworkable collaboration of dreamer and worker, the ideal and the practical, is the cause. Sexual tensions also exist; a relationship between Charles and Adeline proves impossible despite the apparent desire of all parties, including Paul, to promote it.

Thirdly – and here one may compare the films with other accounts of short-lived communities, such as *La Cecilia* or *Qu'est-ce que tu veux Julie?* – failure is not definitive. The community of *Jonas* lives on; although the children return to school, and Mathieu to his previous employment, the group identity is reaffirmed by Mathieu's song in the final sequence; he lists the eight characters who, as a group, he feels are supporting him and in some way contributing to his life. The eventual reasons for the failure of the community of Charles, Paul and Adeline are in no way inherent within it. Charles' discovery is a misfortune, even if the organisation of the social structure is too efficient for him to remain for ever in hiding. There seems to be no structural reason why these experiments should not survive; they are thoroughly anchored in surrounding reality, and the tensions within them may make them bend but not break. Michel Serceau puts Tanner 'at the crossroads of all Utopias without really developing one and never totally identifying himself with any of them' (Serceau 1983b:

108)[45] – not, perhaps, developing any experiment in the sense of the perfection, the self-contained stability, implied in the idea of a Utopia, but nonetheless allowing the possibility of *relative* improvement subjected to analysis and interrogation within the film itself. The mistakes incorporated never seem inevitable. To quote Charles Dé, 'You know, an exemplary failure is certainly more difficult than an exemplary success'. Tanner's utopian experiments are 'exemplary failures' which open up possibilities for an improved attempt. As Michel Serceau says regarding *Jonas* (1983b: 115): 'Quite as much as he's asking a question, isn't Tanner laying a bet on the year 2000?'

The dichotomies which underlie Tanner's work (naturalism, distanciation; coherence or fragmentation of the story) are present in each film. The narratives are firmly anchored in a reality regarding which Tanner allows no illusions, eludes no problems, but they function on the level of the exemplary fable. 'It's certain that no Swiss business magnate ever left his factory like the hero of my film', Tanner observed about *Charles* (*Avant-scène* 1970: 9n).[46] All the films present a coherent 'story', developing chronologically the situations and relations of the characters, but all comprise elements which escape that chronological structure, often elements of the verbal text of the film which seem designed to be received separately from the narrative and which have a function outside it. Thus the quotations which structure the latter part of *Charles*, or those which occur in the conversations of *Retour d'Afrique*; thus the voice-over of *La Salamandre*, with its utterances in the past historic which sound like phrases from a badly written novel. In the filmic language itself the tension between naturalism and detachment operates between the *mise-en-scène* – almost invariably 'naturalist', voluntarily unspectacular, and giving priority to long sequences and camera movement which allow the relations between the elements of a scene to be established gradually – and the montage which is accentuated; a change of sequence is more often than not a sharp change of subject, and continuity is purposely ignored. Tanner has said:

---

[45] 'au carrefour de toutes les utopies sans en développer réellement aucune et sans se confondre complètement avec aucune.'

[46] 'Il est sûr qu'aucun industriel suisse n'a jamais quitté son usine comme le héros de mon film'.

The reality one films is not Reality, it's something absolutely remade and reconstructed, which one can sometimes make similar to reality or not. It's a matter of choice. I think that there are anchor-points in the film which are indeed in naturalism because the spectators can get their bearings there, because all cinema is based on the *effect of reality* … Naturalism is … something which I totally reject otherwise. (Tanner 1977: 52)[47]

Tanner thus rejoins the great debate between 'form' and 'content' in the post-'68 cinema. The champions of the political virtues of formal experiment generally held a negative opinion of the 'Nouveau Naturel', ranking it as a move to refresh a traditional cinema rather than to revolutionise the art. When Tanner mentions the controversy in interviews he is always unconditionally on the side of form. Thus in his introduction to *Le Milieu du monde* he wrote: 'The content is entirely in the form [...] It seems obvious today that the work has to be done on the language' (Boujut 1974: 13–14)[48] and, speaking about *Jonas*:

The cinema is an art, and definitely nothing else, it's not propaganda, which is definitely a different thing. Putting images and sounds together is an essentially artistic form of work. From the moment when you give way to compromises because you think you'll reach more people, you're getting into propaganda, and what language do you use when you get into propaganda? You start to use the dominant discourse [...] *The truth of a film, its purpose is in that object which is the film, it is nowhere else, and if that object tells me something else, I regret it.* (Tanner 1977: 49–50)[49]

---

[47] 'La réalité que l'on filme n'est pas LA réalité, c'est un truc totalement refait et recomposé, que l'on peut parfois faire ressembler à la réalité ou pas. C'est une question de choix. Je pense qu'il y a des points d'ancrage du film qui sont effectivement dans le naturalisme parce que les spectateurs s'y retrouvent, parce que tout le cinéma est fondé sur *l'effet de réel* … Le naturalisme est … quelque chose que je repousse complètement par ailleurs.'

[48] 'Le contenu est tout entier dans la forme [...] Il apparaît aujourd'hui évident que le travail doit se faire sur le langage'.

[49] '*Le cinéma est un art, et strictement rien d'autre*, ce n'est pas de la propagande, laquelle est strictement autre chose. Mettre ensemble des images et des sons, c'est un travail de nature essentiellement artistique. A partir du moment où vous vous laissez aller à un compromis parce que vous pensez toucher plus de monde, vous entrez dans la propagande, et quel langage utilisez-vous si vous entrez dans la propagande? Vous commencez à utiliser le discours dominant [...] *La vérité d'un film, sa finalité est dans l'objet qu'est ce film, elle n'est pas ailleurs, et si cet objet-là me dit le contraire, je le regrette.*'

He accepts that this may deter part of his potential audience: 'I believe very deeply that the content of the film is in its form, one must really try to *work on the form*. I don't think that it's disrespect to the audience to say that if even if some leave us on the way, it's still reasonable to ask for a little bit of work, and to offer them a dialogue' (1977: 53).[50] Tanner, like Godard, Straub/ Huillet, Allio, has quoted the influence of Brecht on his work, but his approach, once again, seems contradictory:

> I am very much influenced by Brecht. *I do not want to make Brechtian cinema.* The whole approach to cinema which I try to have comes from that source: theories of alienation, the relationship between audience and stage, audience and screen, etc ... The voice-over is indeed a very important means of creating that slight step backwards, completely breaking the narration or identification with a character. I'm not a disciple of Brecht, but this approach ... corresponds exactly to what I want to do. *We have to try to find the way to do it in the cinema*, something which has been very little done after all. (Tanner 1974a: 51)[51]

These extensive quotes make clear the extent to which Tanner's aims differ from those of the naturalists. Certainly, Tanner once distanced himself from the impersonal aspect of formalism: 'I don't like ice and I want to give the audience the chance of a tactile, almost a sentimental, relationship with the characters', he said in 1973 (Tanner 1973a: 107).[52] He distinguishes between films on this subject. *Retour d'Afrique* and *Le Milieu du monde* he describes as formal essays; the other pole of his work, however, he refers to not as naturalism but variously as 'my little Genevan

---

[59] 'Je crois très profondément que le contenu d'un film est dans sa forme, il faut essayer vraiment de *travailler sur la forme*. Je ne pense pas que c'est mépriser le spectateur que de dire que si certains nous abandonnent en cours de route, c'est tout de même valable de leur demander un petit travail, de leur offrir un dialogue.'

[51] 'Je suis très influencé par Brecht. *Je ne veux pas faire du Brecht au cinéma.* Toute l'approche que j'essaye d'avoir au cinéma découle directement de là: des théories de la distanciation, des rapports public-scène, public-écran, etc. ... La voix-off est un moyen très important justement pour créer ce recul, briser complète-ment la narration ou l'identification du personnage. Je ne suis pas un disciple de Brecht, mais cette approche ... correspond exactement à ce que j'ai envie de faire. *Il faut essayer de trouver le moyen de le faire au cinéma*, ce qui finalement a été très peu fait.' My emphasis.

[52] 'Je n'aime pas la glace et je veux laisser au spectateur la possibilité d'un rapport du bout des doigts, presque sentimental, avec les personnages'.

theatre' (Tanner 1977: 46)[53] and 'a little "café-théâtre" side' (*Cahiers du cinéma* 1977: 41).[54] *Jonas* represented the synthesis of the two poles. Tanner never elaborates on the question of theatricality. Although he claimed Rivette's *L'Amour fou* as an influence, in his own 1970s films the theatre is very rarely an explicit reference.

Charles mort ou vif immediately introduced Tanner to an international audience, and was particularly well received in France, where it was unanimously hailed as the film which everyone had been waiting for, the first to really claim the inheritance of May. 'The Swiss mountains have given birth to a child of May. He is very beautiful. He will be a prophet' (Jean Collet, *Télérama*). '*Charles mort ou vif* is up to this day the most intelligent film which the spirit of May has inspired' (Jean-Louis Bory, *Nouvel Observateur*). 'This film was born of the very special conjunction of a revolution: May '68, the best film-maker currently exercising: Alain Tanner and an extraordinary actor [François Simon]' (Mireille Amiel, *Cinéma 70*). 'One of the most characteristic works of the May spirit' (André Cornand, *Revue du cinéma/Image et son*). 'The only fiction film to clearly confront the burning issues of today' (Jean Delmas, *Jeune cinéma*) (*Avant-scène* 1970: 38–9). And finally: 'It is from Switzerland that, while we're still waiting for it in France, the finest cinematic child of the month of May 1968 has arrived' (Philippe Haudiquet, *Avant-scène* 1970: 9).[55] The film was generally identified as belonging to May '68 before it belonged to Switzerland, and the particular importance of the conjunction is ignored; only Marcel Martin, in *Les Lettres françaises*, seems to have noted the real significance which May might hold for a country in which nothing had happened.

    Charles mort ou vif tells the story of a middle-aged managing

---

[53] 'mon petit théâtre genévois'.

[54] 'un petit côté "café-théâtre"'.

[55] Collet: 'La montagne suisse a accouché d'un enfant de mai. Il est très beau. Ce sera un prophète'; Bory: '*Charles mort ou vif* est, jusqu'à ce jour, le film le plus intelligent qu'ait inspiré l'esprit de mai'; Amiel: 'Ce film est né de la rencontre privilégié d'une révolution: mai 68, du meilleur réalisateur actuel: Alain Tanner et d'un acteur prodigieux'; Cornand: 'L'une des oeuvres les plus caractéristiques de l'esprit de mai'; Delmas: 'Parmi les films de fiction, le seul qui nettement affronte le brûlant d'aujourd'hui'; Haudiquet: 'c'est de Suisse que nous parvient, alors qu'on ne cesse de l'attendre en France, le plus bel enfant cinématographique du mois de mai 1968'.

director, who, following a TV interview which obliges him to look back over his life, begins to realise the frustrations which he has repressed for many years. He leaves his firm and his home, and moves first into a hotel and then into the home of a young couple whom he meets in a café. The couple, Paul and Adeline, are trying to live an 'alternative' lifestyle. They welcome Charles (or Carlo, as he becomes), and he settles down in apparent symbiosis with them. Meanwhile, Charles' son Pierre, a conservative young man eager to take over the family business, sends out a detective in search of his father. The daughter, Marianne, a militant student, is in contact with Charles; the detective finds him by dint of following her, and Pierre sends an ambulance to transport his father to the Flickmann hospital. That is the bare bones of the story, and already some unusual elements are detectable. This 'révolté' is neither young, nor working-class, nor in a situation of instability. On the contrary he enjoys all the advantages of a secure position in a secure country: 'I will tell you that I have a villa, a family, a dog, stacks of insurance policies, two cars, and a chalet in the mountains, with a Swiss flag in the garden', he says during the TV interview, amending the list finally: 'no, there isn't a flag, but there might as well be'. Charles, Tanner told *Télérama* (Tanner 1970: 60),[56] is 'a bit symbolic of Switzerland'; he is absolutely non-marginal, 'in the middle of the world'. The conclusion is clear: it is not only the under-privileged or the powerless who need to revolt in order to express themselves; even those central to the power structure are in fact powerless to change it. Charles from the start is fully aware of this; he explains to the reporter his gradual shelving of vague youthful discontent, without anger, as if recounting the inevitable.

In his two television interviews Charles develops from vague unease to an acute consciousness of dissatisfaction. The role of the spoken text is here established as essential; the image, reduced entirely to the protagonists in uninteresting décors, is secondary. The only strong visual impression which remains is that of Charles himself, rarely off-screen and often in close-up; like the fictional television programme, the film is a portrait of this man. But, while the implications of the title of the TV programme, 'Les gens sont comme ça' ('People are like that'), are that the

---

[56] 'un peu symbolique de la Suisse'.

subject can be seized and defined at this chance moment, the film precisely denies this; Charles is changing. The face in the image reflects this change – and, at the same time, the protagonist himself becomes aware that his face reflects change, since key scenes in the process of his *prise de conscience* have him studying his face, in the bathroom mirror or on a TV screen. An essential stage in the change in Charles, in fact, is a gradual arrival at self-consciousness, both of his image and of his own history. As a result of the TV programme, Charles is forced to consider himself in his own environment – 'se penser historiquement'. Tanner had experienced the strong effect that this can have when as a TV director he was responsible for making programmes of essentially the same nature.[57]

Charles becomes aware of himself in history as he becomes aware of himself-as-language. As his account of himself gets more detailed, the image changes from a close-up to a long-shot of Charles and the reporter in the garden; the image-Charles becomes less clear as the text-Charles becomes complicated. The last images of the interviews show the 'real' Charles, sitting in a café, contemplating his text/image on the TV screen. He is embarrassed by the persona he presents, and when someone in the café recognises him, he leaves hurriedly; he no longer recognises himself in the words he is speaking. A brief scene of Pierre and his mother watching the same broadcast gives the impression that they would rather not recognise it either; decidedly Charles as he has translated into media text is appreciated by nobody.

In the brief interlude in the hotel which follows, Charles' refusal of his persona is put into concrete form; he gives a false name to the receptionist. This sequence is characterised by the great reduction of verbal text, without, however, a rich image coming to supplement it. Charles is still the centre of visual interest, the décor is drab, and long *plans-séquences* follow his actions in the style of the New Naturalism.

These two sections constitute an introduction to the film, and illustrate how naturalism and exploration of audiovisual language are both fundamental to Tanner's narrative. Translation of reality into broadcast media is a persistent theme; not only the television

---

[57] It was particularly the experience of *Dr. B., médecin de campagne* which led to this particular narrative device. See Dimitriu 1985: 37.

programme but also the radio present a version of Charles as text, given to 'read' by the outside world and also, as it happens, by himself. The radio's portrait of Charles is a strictly external one – the description of a missing person – and Charles is amused by it, but it also inserts him into a wider context, since he is one item among others in a news bulletin. The other main item – strictly equivalent textually to the description of Charles – is a report on the activities of a student group to which Marianne belongs. The connection is registered objectively, through the juxtaposition of the two texts, and subjectively through the concern with which Charles greets the news that there have been scuffles in which Marianne may have been involved. Charles and the Swiss news are connected in more ways than one.

Throughout the film the juxtaposition of non-naturalist text and naturalist image is consistent. Dialogue is only one small element of the verbal sound-track. Broadcast texts – particularly when the speaker is shown listening to them – have a significance more permanent and more distant. Other texts are read; this occurs for the first time in the first sequences, where an apprentice reads a speech, obviously detached from the words he is speaking. Later, in Paul's house, Charles reads aloud, or at least gives the impression of doing so; and in the final scene he reads a passage of his book to the indifferent ambulance drivers. Here, the fact that the text is not quite identified with the speaker gives it more value; it has a general significance outside its importance to the character who utters it. For this to be true it is not necessary to be sure that the text is read; a certain kind of utterance, the presence of a book are enough for the spectator to perceive the words as a text, relevant to the actor speaking it but having a prior existence and therefore a prior relevance. In the scene where Charles is reading in his room, his own situation (and the image) take on the role of illustration of the text, which *could* credibly be Charles' own thoughts.

The 'free text', made up of assorted quotations given originally by Marianne to Paul, takes the separation of individual and text even further. Although the individual quotations are sometimes ascribed an author – but as often as not they are anonymous – they take their value from their collective unity. For example, the juxtaposition of 'C'est seulement par ceux qui sont sans espoir que l'espoir peut nous être rendu. Walter Benjamin' (It is only through those who have no hope that hope can be returned to us) with 'Tout le monde ne peut pas être orphelin. Jules Renard' (Not everyone can be an orphan) creates a coherent text different from either of its separate components. Although Marianne supposedly chooses them, it is Paul who speaks them, and he has to rote-learn them prior to understanding them. The source of this text is therefore unidentified; the last quotation is a sub-title detached even from Marianne. It is treated very much as a theatrical script, rehearsed by Paul for the critical audience of Charles, subject to the whims of the actor (when Paul is angry, the attribution of a quote to Bakunin is fired out like an insult directed at Charles). The quotations also impose a structure on the film. They are closely linked to the progression of days, and each one is preceded by its position on a time-scale. The narrative itself gives very little idea of passing time, other than that it is not great, and so the 'free text' imposes a temporal order which is lacking. This gives it a more dominant position in the narrative than a random series of quotations could have.

Dimitriu (1985) suggests, quoting Gerhart Waeger, that the reception of these quotations by the audience was facilitated by the use that Godard made of a similar structure during the 1960s, but the graffiti-sensibility was also, as we have mentioned, a hallmark of 1968 and use and re-interpretation of quotations corresponds to the Situationist conception of 'détournement'. Many of the phrases Tanner uses were subversive originally, but not all.

There are also occasional song-texts in *Charles*, which fall into the same category in carrying external significance which the singer does not necessarily realise ('Elle est de retour le joli mois de mai') and one example of actual theatre, when Marianne and Charles 'perform' the end of a radical play at the dinner table for Paul and Adeline, who are totally confused until they realise that the text is prescribed. Although this text is presented as a theatrical tirade, it has evident relevance for a Swiss audience in 1970, especially when spoken by the student Marianne: 'We hear from beyond the mountains, the echoes of history reaching us. We often listen to them in the evenings ...'

Thus the separation of characters and text is a fundamental factor in the discourse of *Charles*. It is a process which seems to owe a good deal to Brecht and to the theatre. Even the dialogues which have no external source are not exempt from the same effect; there is scarcely any dialogue which sounds completely natural, and Charles particularly expresses himself in set-pieces. The audience is also kept at a distance by an inescapable vein of irony, in this case not purely verbal. Even if the image is never rich, visual gags are possible: the contrast between Charles in the kitchen, singing the index to a cookery book, or struggling with a sardine tin, and the dignified business leader of the first sequences, for example. The very barrenness of the image can be the source of irony, as in the desolate landscape which Paul and Adeline get out of the car to admire: 'It's our favourite spot'. The psychiatric nurses of the final scene, despite the near-tragic function which they have in the narrative, behave like a pair of clowns – but their farcical side does not prevent them from carrying a sense of menace. The detective is both ridiculous and ominous.

Many of these elements recur in Tanner's next film, *La Salamandre*, but the direct references to 1968 are absent. Tanner returns to direct reference in 1973 with *Retour d'Afrique*, conceived in some ways as a reaction to the previous two films, in terms of both Tanner's own preoccupations and the reception which they had received. In *Retour d'Afrique* he intended to give much greater priority to the film form; despite the formal innovations which can be discerned in *Charles* and *La Salamandre*, the story and its presentation are the priority, to which experiment – mostly textual – is subordinate. In *Retour d'Afrique*, Tanner declared his intention to start with the technique and to explore its possible effect. Also, confronted by the almost unanimous reception of *La Salamandre* as a comedy, Tanner turned against the use of humour, even in its bitterest form of caricature.

Retour d'Afrique concerns a young couple, Vincent and Françoise, who decide to leave Geneva for Algeria: Vincent has been promised work there and they see an opportunity to contribute to a 'real' revolution. The promised work falls through and the couple, having announced their departure and left their previous work, retreat into their flat. Nine months later, in the second part of the film, they have begun a new life in Geneva, living in an HLM[58] on the outskirts of the city, taking new jobs, and deciding to have a child.

---

[58] Habitation à Loyer Modéré: low-rent social housing, almost always in tower-blocks.

Retour d'Afrique contains a much more structured political discourse than Tanner's other films. Indeed, while *Charles* and *La Salamandre* were received as comedies, *Retour d'Afrique* was accused in Switzerland of being a political pamphlet, and Tanner, rather to his surprise, was attacked as a dangerous subversive in some quarters, although the film achieved a reasonable audience. The couple's progress is twofold. On the one hand, there is their changing perception of their place in society. At the beginning of the film, their rather sedentary leftism can only imply identification with a Revolution perceived from afar. It is distant in place and they see it as a coherent whole: in Algeria there is a revolution, and so in moving there they will, almost automatically, become part of that revolution. Implicit in their decision to move is the assumption that to be left-wing and active in Switzerland is impossible, of course. By the end of the film, they have come to believe that it is not only possible but necessary to act positively in Geneva; the next step is to recognise the possibility that the distant revolution can only be relevant if close at hand. At the same time, the couple's relationship evolves, as Françoise takes on more and more importance; at the end of the film she is both more lucid and more committed than Vincent.

Dimitriu considers that *Retour d'Afrique* has worn less well than any other of Tanner's films: 'You have to have lived through the period to be able to forget its weaknesses, the most important of which is transposing the spirit of May '68 into the 70s' (Dimitriu 1985: 50).[59] Which, apart from the value-judgement, begs the question of how the film relates to May '68, and what particular form 'l'esprit de mai' can be considered to take in it.

In this perhaps more than in any other of Tanner's films, it is necessary to take into account the involvement with, or detachment from, the events of May which Tanner's position implied. Vincent and Françoise progress from the desire to join a revolution which is at once very far away and already in progress, to the decision to remain in their own non-revolutionary country and attempt to bring about what changes they can. For their equivalents in 1968 the events in Paris fall neatly between these extremes: far away, and yet close enough for their approach to be

---

[59] 'Il faut avoir vécu l'époque pour faire abstraction de ses faiblesses, dont la plus importante est de transposer l'esprit de Mai 68 dans les années 70'.

envisaged; already in progress, yet with a very uncertain future. Thus the experience of May 1968 is a necessary stage in the development of Vincent and Françoise, even though unspoken. For the spectator, its memory validates their final decision to remain in Geneva, providing a historical precedent for the creation of a revolution within an equivalent city; while the memory of the Spanish Civil War, evoked by one of Vincent's fellow-workers, is the reminder of the failure of a historical effort to emigrate towards a revolution. The couple's model of revolutionary action develops, in fact, from one deriving from a time pre-1968 (from Spain through Cuba and Vietnam, the desire of Western leftists to identify with a struggle taking place elsewhere)[60] to one where events in Europe must be the guiding principle.

The change is presented as positive in more ways than one. In the first part of the film, the couple's relation to their ideas remains principally on the level of signs – the departure for Africa is as much a sign of their aspirations as a real potential action; the tree that Vincent and his colleagues plant is a symbol of liberty for the Spaniard Emilio, but when in the second part Vincent helps Emilio to fight his deportation he is engaged with reality. The spirit of May '68, in the film, implies not only the conception of a revolution in daily life, but the recognition, and the adoption, of effective practical action. The fact that the pointers to action are not invented by the couple themselves but provided by their contact with the world outside their middle-class shell is not only in the Brechtian tradition, as Guy Braucourt observed (Tanner 1973b: 30).[61] but rejoins the ideals of May and even more of June; it is Emilio's need which spurs Vincent to action, while the conversation of the postal workers who are Françoise's new colleagues in the second part of the film contributes both to the development of her feminist awareness and to the couple's final decision to have a child.

Much more than *Charles mort ou vif* or *La Salamandre*, the film engages with precise political or social issues. The restructuring of the couple, the situation of immigrant workers, the relation of the city to its inhabitants, even the function of the cinema, are all discussed. All these themes entered the French cinema in the

---

[60] This myth is treated satirically in *Valparaiso Valparaiso* (Pascal Aubier, 1971).

[61] 'Méthode qui relève du meilleur théâtre didactique de Brecht' ['A method derived from the best of Brecht's didactic theatre'].

1970s partly in response to the debates brought to light by May. The appearance of feminism in French cinema was just beginning in 1973,[62] and *Retour d'Afrique* even broke new ground in this respect.

However it is perhaps in the relation of *Retour d'Afrique* to the work of Godard that the film engages most clearly with post-'68 reflection on the cinema. This is the only film where Tanner's cinema engages with that of his fellow-countryman, but here the *rapprochement* is obvious and derives above all from a coincidence of themes. The reference to *La Chinoise* implied by the presence of Anne Wiazemsky and Juliet Berto gives to the whole film the sense of a *response*, to the French sense of May in general and to Godard in particular. In the first sequence of the film, Tanner, in voice-over, pronounces: 'To speak words may be an act in itself. It's also perhaps a substitute for action. Quoting other people's words can contribute to one's self-knowledge'.[63] The procedure is Godardian in the forcible reminder of the existence of a film-maker at work, the sentiments are even more so, and the first narrative sequence is a discussion of the revolutionary vocation of cinema. The image in *Retour d'Afrique* is even more austere, but 'cleaner' than that of the earlier films; the characters are framed against empty backgrounds, as in so many of Godard's films. The intrusive presence of the city and its sounds is reminiscent of the Godard of *Deux ou trois choses*.

But *La Chinoise*, a film which connotes 1968 to any spectator capable of taking the reference at all, is the principal and precise referent: and in *La Chinoise*, of course, we are still immediately prior to 1968, when events were still potential. Within the world of *Retour d'Afrique* (identified, at the beginning of the film, as Geneva,

[62] Films made by women in France from 1968 to 1973 numbered 19. From 1974 to 1979 there were 55. This is not, of course, a measure of an expression of feminism in the cinema, but it gives an idea at least of the increase in the female voice. Tanner remarked that 'Certaines amies du MLF me disent "Tu as fait un bout de chemin, mais tu n'as pas été assez loin". Je leur réponds que je suis un type et que si elles faisaient du cinéma elles-mêmes, cela pourrait aller plus loin' ['Some of my friends in the Women's Liberation Movement says, "You've come a step of the way, but not far enough". My answer is that I'm a guy and that if they got involved in cinema themselves, they could take things further'] (Tanner 1973a: 109). The statistics are some indication of a move in this direction.

[63] 'Dire des mots est peut-être un acte en lui-même. Cela est peut-être aussi un substitut à l'action. Citer les mots des autres peut contribuer à la connaissance de soi-même'.

1970) are to be found the same faces/factors/actors as those of *La Chinoise*, a film widely considered as foreseeing 1968. What is more, the procedure of the protagonists of *Retour d'Afrique* has borne some resemblance to that of their predecessors; both films are concerned with a period of isolation in a flat spent reflecting upon revolution. That period is the subject of *La Chinoise*, but in *Retour d'Afrique* it constitutes an absence in the film. There could not be a better illustration of the constructive use of reference. The importance of the couple's final decision to remain in Geneva depends on the realisation that their action there can have some effect; by recalling *La Chinoise* Tanner has turned the possibility that a potential for movement exists into a quasi-certainty, but that certainty has a purely cinematic existence. In the Geneva of *Retour d'Afrique* 1968 is lurking, but in the reality of Geneva 1973 there can be no such certainty. The reference increases the optimism of the film, which in any case ends on a positive note; at the end the couple have clear aims and a sense of direction. It also increases the spectator's awareness of participating in an artificial, cinematic world, where one text can be used in another to give it sense and the illusion of social action.

Le Milieu du monde, which shares with its immediate predecessor a preoccupation with the form of the film and a generally serious tone, is the most pessimistic of all Tanner's films regarding the chances of any change taking place in Switzerland, and the spirit of 1968 seems very distant from it. Its theme is clearly the insularity and immobility of a country presented as irredeemably 'middle-of-the road', and influences from across the borders are neutralised. Switzerland as an extreme case of a dominant ideology reigning through consensus is a constant metaphor for Tanner, and gives *La Salamandre* and *Charles mort ou vif* their character. They could be described as 'contes philosophiques'; Swiss society as an exemplar of consensual stasis no doubt contributed greatly to the films' force in France, where the very fact of 1968 meant that the dominant ideology was no longer so self-confident. In *Retour d'Afrique*, for once, the dominant ideology in Switzerland appears shakeable; although the film uses reference to 1968 to reinforce its message, its optimism is not dependent on the contingency of 1968. The situation in Switzerland is implicitly compared to that of France in 1967, and that comparison is in the nature of a hypothesis, a supposition that the same elements of dissent may exist in this exemplary example of political hegemony. *Le Milieu du monde* analyses the mechanics of the hegemony, but in doing so it can no longer concern itself directly with efforts to elude or break it. It is for this reason that the film seems more pessimistic than its predecessors (although the pessimism also corresponded to a real sense of disillusion on Tanner's part). It was conceived to function as a piece of analysis, and the continual reminders of the presence of the camera – unexpected movements, titles, shots inserted which break the time structure – serve to ensure that the audience reads it as such: 'it's a question of ... playing an eminently dialectical game between the traditional forms of cinema-as-spectacle and the methods which can throw them off balance, move the nerve-centre of the film from the question "What's going to happen?" to the question "Why do things happen like this?"' (Tanner 1974b: 47).[64]

Jonas qui aura 25 ans dans l'an 2000, which appeared in 1976 and was seen as summing-up the post-'68 experience, could not be more different in atmosphere. Tanner referred to it as a synthesis of all his previous work; although it is much nearer to the first two films than to the formal analyses more recently completed. The role of the décor, although greater than in *Charles*, is clearly subordinate to the characters. There is a return in force of humour and theatricality, and the theme of the individual in revolt also returns, multiplied by eight. The protagonists of the film represent eight different ways of articulating rupture with the Switzerland/dominant ideology which here has a shadowy existence, visible only through its direct effects on the 'eight little prophets'. Dimitriu describes *Jonas* as 'the film of abundance in all its forms: in terms of its themes, of the rich variety of ideas and metaphors and the multiple formal approaches' (Dimitriu 1985: 65).[65] Despite a fairly modest visual ambition, it is indeed abundance which remains as the overwhelming impression of Jonas.

The individuals who congregate around the smallholding belonging to Marguerite and her husband Marcel form a very

[64] 'il s'agit ... de jouer en somme un jeu éminemment dialectique entre les formes traditionnelles du cinéma-spectacle et les techniques pour les faire déraper, de déplacer le centre névralgique du film de la question "Qu'est-ce qui va se passer?" à la question "Pourquoi est-ce que ça se passe comme ça?".

[65] 'le film de l'abondance sous toutes les formes: thèmes traités, foisonnement d'idées et de métaphores et multiplication de principes formels'.

loosely structured collectivity, in no way isolated from the world outside, but their relative unity becomes a means of realising their dreams at least in part. Union never subsumes the individual projects of each member, but it is proof against their previous isolation, and the child conceived by Mathieu and Mathilde, the Jonas of the title, is at once the consecration of the union of all eight, and the vehicle for their diverse ideals.

Dimitriu calls this film 'at once an analysis and a synthesis of May '68' (Dimitriu 1985: 62)[66] (which captures the dichotomy of unity and diversity which is fundamental to it) and Serge Daney, reviewing it in *Cahiers du cinéma*, reads into the names of the eight, which all begin with Ma, a direct reference to MAi. Tanner neither confirmed nor denied this, but the group can certainly be read as incarnations of different possible discourses prolonging '68 into the 1970s. However, May '68 itself does not have a positive role. It constitutes a personal reference for only one of the protagonists, the journalist Max, and for him it means disillusion. Reference to 1968 demands that one looks to the past, and rather than being a valuable possession it is something that Max learns to overcome through his contact with the other members of the group. Tanner's interest was in the new possibilities which 1968 had provided for expressing dissent, and not in any concrete achievement:

> In the minds of many people, 68 was a political phenomenon, I mean politicians' politics. Party militants at the time, like the character Max in the film, believed that the institutions would undergo radical change. Their hopes were disappointed, and there was a huge dip which we're still living through now, an immense sense of disillusion. What interests me is what's left. Because some gates were opened, in terms of discourses, and individual and group action, outside the boundaries of the party system. The way that young people and women talk now is not at all the same as it was before 68. (Tanner 1977: 48)[67]

[66] 'en même temps l'analyse et le synthèse de mai 68'.

[67] Dans l'esprit de beaucoup de gens, 68 était un phénomène politique, au sens de la politique politicienne. Ceux qui militaient dans un parti, à cette époque, comme le personnage de Max dans le film, croyaient à un changement radical des institutions. Leur espoir a été déçu, et il y a eu un grand creux de vague, que l'on vit encore aujourd'hui, et qui constitue une énorme désillusion. Ce qui m'intéresse, c'est ce qu'il en reste. Car certaines vannes ont été ouvertes, au niveau du discours, au niveau d'actions individuelles ou de groupes, qui n'étaient pas insérées à l'intérieur d'un parti. La façon dont les jeunes ou les femmes parlent aujourd'hui n'est pas du tout la même que celle dont ils parlaient avant 68.'

The various characters of *Jonas* each represent one (or more) of the 'vannes ouvertes' and together they make up a flood of alternative discourse. They are united first in couples: in order of appearance, Mathieu and Mathilde, Marguerite and Marcel, Max and Madeleine, Marco and Marie. Mathieu comes from the world of organised labour, politicised and unionised, but out of work and attracted by the idea of a change of environment. He seeks out the smallholding in the hope of a job on the land, and gradually develops a passionate interest in alternative education, first in collaboration with the teacher Marco, then on his own initiative among the children of the smallholding. Mathilde, perhaps the least disaffected of the group, essentially wants only a happy life, identified as an uncomplicated relationship, material sufficiency, and, preferably, a child. The character came in for some feminist criticism, which Tanner acknowledged, but Mathilde plays a vital role in the constitution of the group. Expressive of a tendency towards stability without which any synthesis would be impossible, she finally embodies that synthesis by conceiving the 'communal child'.

Marguerite and Marcel, the smallholders, are of course both representative of a move back to the land, but are nonetheless diverse. Marguerite is the centre and hub of the group. She is an ambiguous figure; described by Marcel as a witch in spite (and because) of being unflinchingly down-to-earth, a mother-figure for the group (presiding over the smallholding/sanctuary and providing subsistence) but not the mother of Jonas nor conventionally maternal in her behaviour, at once empowering the group's various escapisms (she owns the land and sells the produce) and impatient with ideals that interfere with the necessities of the farm. Her practicality can approach the revolutionary, for example in the arrangement she has made to provide sexual services at a low price to the immigrant workers at a nearby hostel, an uncomplicated means of satisfying a mutual need simply ignoring the social taboos involved. Marcel expresses a poetic form of ecological sensibility; he is fascinated by all species of animals, giving his biological information symbolic value. The name of Jonas for the child, selected by Marcel, gives considerable final weight to his ecological symbolism, which clearly appealed to Tanner, but Marcel is essentially passive. He has little interest in or contact with the outside world, and Marguerite carries out the farm's links with the exterior. He sees her as a 'witch', translating her practical qualities into his eco-magical terms. The two are in many ways perfect complements.

Max and Madeleine are totally urban creatures. Max is a left-wing journalist continuing rather halfheartedly to sustain the ideals which he had hoped to see realised in 1968. Madeleine conceals her disaffection under the exterior of an elegant and efficient secretary, and fuels it from the mechanisms with which her work brings her into contact – she takes temporary jobs, and is familiar with a wide spectrum of commercial society. Her consolation is in other cultures; she practises tantrism, and leaves Switzerland for Asia when she can, working strictly to provide herself with the means of escape. Max calls her a 'hippy de luxe' and describes her behaviour as the worst kind of escapism; she is, however, capable of practical action in the Swiss present, and despite his mockery he learns from her. Tanner too indulges in a good deal of irony at the expense of both Max and Madeleine, and their words are accordingly rendered less powerful, but not invalidated.

Marco and Marie are not new characters in Tanner's work; in many ways they are transferred to *Jonas* from *La Salamandre*. Paul the writer has become Marco the history teacher, both played by Jacques Denis. Both characters channel their subversive ideas through the imagination and hope to impart them to 'pupils'. Marco's attempts to subvert the official education system by unorthodox explanations of Time and by the introduction into history classes of guest speakers who talk about their relationship with their environment (first Mathieu, then Marie, are thus invited to participate in the exercise of 'thinking themselves historically' in front of his class), are clearly derived from May, although he does not define himself in relation to it. His attitude at the outset displays a belief in the potential of his students to understand and sympathise with his stance, and perhaps to foster a Swiss 1968 – that non-existent event which obsesses Tanner. His procedures evoke many of the principal themes of May. The 'prise de parole' by the workers as exemplified by Mathieu and Marie works relatively well. The questions directed at Marie almost suggest that his students have understood the concept of history as forces acting on individuals, while Mathieu's Marxist analysis of recession introduces (in an appropriately basic manner) the political theories that were more or less taken for granted in 1968, applying them however to 1976. When Marco himself is teaching, he applies himself to making his points memorably and spectacularly, giving great importance to imagination and a sense of humour; again, factors important to the revolutionaries of May. His performance with a string of sausages during his first lesson is a kind of didactic theatre. His readiness to act the clown also destroys his position of authoritarian dispenser of knowledge; the hierarchy of the class is further subverted by the introduction of alternative teachers in his later classes. All these elements seem to embody positive ideas, and yet Marco is finally discredited. The students reject him; and while even Max still believes despite himself that his past ideals have relevance, and is prepared to wait for a future, however distant, when he can put his experience and his eloquence to use, Marco, in taking a job in an old people's home, abandons all attempts to project his ideas into the future through his pupils, and implicitly identifies himself and his anarchic form of disaffection with the past and the previous generation. He makes no attempt to direct Marie's revolt; she teaches him more than he teaches her, and finally his only influence on her is sexual.

Marie is similarly a version of the Rosemonde of *La Salamandre*: adolescent, working-class, holding a precarious position on the edge of the world of work which holds neither hope nor attraction; and, importantly, already of the post-'68 generation. Her action is a reaction to her own exploitation, although she is more consequent than was Rosemonde, and shows solidarity with the victims of a consumer society: working as a check-out girl, she systematically reduces the bills when she feels it desirable. She also maintains a direct connection with an earlier tradition, in the shape of an old railway-worker in whose (partly fantasised) past she actually participates through play/theatre.

These individuals together constitute an anthology – perhaps not exhaustive but certainly wide-ranging – of the possibilities for alternative thinking in the late 1970s. The disparate elements are re-synthesised through a unifying space – the smallholding – which is also a unifying cause; it is the need to save the land from developers which introduces Max and Madeleine to the group, although this is not presented as a major problem in the film. It is sufficient that Marguerite be forewarned, and that she refuse to sell, which of course she duly does. The film then presents a series of separate 'stories' linked by an ideal space which all the protagonists share; the synthesis is symbolically completed in the potential character Jonas. All the eight (although Marie is absent, her name is proposed) take part in the naming which confers identity on the as-yet anonymous child. This long scene is the most expressive in the film of the unity of the disparate group, even though in fact they are not all assembled. The eight are physically present together only once, and the scene, like that of the 'christening-meal' swiftly takes the form of an improvised celebration, which cements their unity.

The sense of community which we receive from *Jonas* does not, however, come solely from the two group scenes. The majority of the film is concerned with incidents involving only one or two of the characters in their own spaces.[68] The existence of a 'magnetic centre' is thus not sufficient to connect the eight; the consistency of tone across the various separate incidents is an extremely important factor. *Jonas* functions as a series of inter-linked sketches, clearly forming a unity through the correspondence of characters and the visual style. This latter marks a return to the earlier films in the importance given to the text; the image is largely unspectacular and 'naturalist', with the exception of the occasional black-and-white sequences entering the characters' imaginations. These rely on specifically cinematic codes (the change of colour, the monotonous music) to distinguish them. These apart, the text rules, frequently a consciously sententious text (we once again have the impression that the characters are quoting even when they clearly are not). At its most extreme this can be irritating; the conversations between Max and Madeleine seem to be entirely composed of enigmatic 'pearls of wisdom'. The importance of the text is, of course, theatrical, all the more since the manner of filming in very long sequence-shots, and Tanner's insistence on adhering to the prepared script, meant that the actors experienced the performance as theatrical rather than cinematic. Several sequences develop into impromptu performances (Dimitriu has emphasised the importance of the concept of performance in *Jonas*).

---

[68] The work-place is central in defining these characters. All are shown at work at some point in the film. Some (Marie, Madeleine) create their identity in antagonism to their work, some (Marco, Max, Mathieu) by attempting to redefine it, while Marguerite works to fulfil her identity – the assumed ideal situation.

The method reflects Tanner's assessment of 1968: '68 (or rather May '68) was a huge street theatre ... and the after-effects are what matters, much more than the events themselves, in exactly the same way that the theatre presents hopes and arouses hidden desires, which stay on the surface afterwards' (*Cahiers du cinéma* 1977: 42).[69] Tanner did not wish to make a film for the *génération 68* particularly – he had little interest in reviving memories, and we have already seen that Max's experience is now more a force for inertia than for action. The aim of the film is therefore to recreate the 'théâtre de rue' for a new audience: 'I wanted the lifestyles that I presented to speak to people other than those you call "the survivors of 68, the survivors of the shipwreck". First of all there was no shipwreck, at least not for those who weren't themeselves actors in the play, as was the case here' (*Cahiers du cinéma* 1977: 42).[70] Once again, 1968 is referred to as a play, and Tanner's return to his 'petit théâtre genévois' is clearly the most appropriate form for any film reassessing it. If the film represents a culmination of Tanner's reflection on the events, it does not only aim to establish an account of the state of what was 1968 in 1976. Its ambition is larger; that of a cinematic happening aiming to recreate, perhaps on a modest scale, something of the effect of liberation and of unity in protest which 1968 had on those who were witness to it. Many of the incidents in the film are in the nature not only of performance, but also of celebration: Marie's games with Charles-le-vapeur are a ritual, celebratory evocation of the past; the two occasions in which the group come together at the farm both become (in the case of the meal, are by definition) celebratory; Marguerite and Marcel receive the speculator with a mocking *mise-en-scène* which celebrates their independence at his expense, much as the street demonstrations of May treated authority figures, and so on. *Jonas qui aura 25 ans dans l'an 2000* is at once the child who synthesises the eight protagonists, the film that unites their interlinked discourses

[69] '68 (ou plutôt mai 68) fut un grand théâtre de rue ... et ce qui importe, bien davantage que les événements, ce sont les retombées, dans la mesure justement où ce théâtre mit en scène des espoirs et fit affleurer des désirs cachés, qui depuis sont demeurés à la surface'.
[70] 'J'ai souhaité que ces modes de vie mis en scène interpellent surtout d'autres que ce que tu appelles "les rescapés de 68, les rescapés du naufrage". D'abord il n'y a pas eu de naufrage, en tout cas pas pour ceux qui, comme ici, n'étaient pas directement les acteurs de la pièce'.

(lives and words) and also a first attempt to integrate those discourses into a performance which might find its parallel, on a larger scale, in the *théâtre de rue* of the dimensions of 1968.

Tanner, the passionate spectator of 1968, who 'was not himself an actor in the play' has here arrived at a synthesis of the poles of involvement and detachment at work in all his films. His previous film *Le Milieu du monde* had recorded the apparently inevitable erosion of dissent and of all tangible relics of 1968 after three films which had attempted to project the influence of the French revolt into Switzerland. *Jonas* represents the next step: to recreate the discourse of dissent in a new form, *freed* from the inhibiting force of 1968, its previous incarnation. *Jonas* is Tanner's 1968, in which he participates instead of watching admiring in the audience. Certainly, the underlying issues are not precisely the same. If the class struggle has its place – a privileged place, since it is Mathieu who has the last word – the film reflects the rising importance of a fledgling Green movement as a base for the alternative left. Mathieu returns to his previous place of work and of dissent while other elements of the group prepare to publish an 'environmentalist' journal. Tanner has updated the issues, therefore, and located this happening firmly in 1976.

His direction then changed. *Messidor* in 1979 marks a move in another direction, a bid for individual liberty which no longer seems to have much interest in solidarity. Marie and Jeanne, the two protagonists, embark on their flight by defining it, quite lucidly, as a game, although a serious game, which pits them against the rest of the world as a whole, no matter whether individuals are sympathetic or hostile. They do not have enemies so much as adversaries, which is to imply that they basically accept their situation – without adversaries there would be no game. Although still centred on life on the margins, *Messidor* presents it not as a potential force for change, but simply a free choice which carries with it its own modes of behaviour and its own risks. Six years later in France, Agnès Varda would carry that logic to its grim individual conclusion in *Sans toit ni loi* (1985).

Nonetheless Alain Tanner continued to reflect cinematically on the implications of May, and more particularly on the inherent needs that it expressed, for eight years. He was able to do this unhampered by whatever tangible results could in France impede progress by creating an illusion of change. Tanner, in unaffected

Switzerland, made of his perception of 1968 a series of 'contes philosophiques', culminating in a highly original *état des lieux* which makes some attempt to sketch what factors would enter into a recreation of such an outburst in the late 1970s. If any one film-maker could represent the cinematic inheritance of May, it seems that it would be Tanner. His work includes all the themes which we have identified as introduced to the cinema by the thinking of 1968, although he does not structure his work according to any defined political programme. Tanner's films may stand as a summary of the new thinking behind the cinema, and of the new themes and styles explored by it.

With the careers of these two film-makers, at the margins of French cinema and of French society and therefore observing the turmoil of May and its aftermath from a position which partakes both of the insider and of the outsider, many of the tensions which a certain French cinema of the 1970s faced are illustrated. Opposing notions of what constituted fidelity to the social reality of the material – documentary opposed to fiction, or understated, TV-influenced 'naturalism' as against carefully constructed arte-facts which declare their identity as filmic construct and as performance – create constructive tensions as they did in the overall cinematic debate in France. The delays and illogicalities of the Gaullist government's censorship system, of which *Mister Freedom* fell foul, mutate in Klein's later work into the recupera-tion of social and cultural tolerance by a political establishment still quite as wedded to repression. Both Klein and Tanner are faced with the direct issue of how to render an account of 1968 at the end of the decade, and in their different ways they resume effectively the changes in the use to which the discourse of the period was put, and the necessity of looking beyond mere memories of the past if the true ideals of the period are to have any meaning. They engage with the need for, and increasingly the existence of, outlets for the voices of those hitherto relatively silent in the cinema: women, rural and marginal communities, or the minority cultures of France, all of which greatly increased their cinematic presence in the 1970s.

In fact, with the turn of the decade, and the election of a Socialist government in 1981, the French cinema did turn its face away from the issues which had exercised the 1970s with unexpected firmness – a decision in which Tanner too participated. The popular genre cinema, which with the exception of the *série-Z* thrillers seemed to have remained relatively untouched by the debates shaking the *auteur* sector, had nonetheless been influenced by them, and when in the 1980s the popular cinema returned to the forefront of debate as a possible vehicle for confrontation with the ever-more-powerful American import, it was with a greater freedom to approach the social tensions of the country than it had ever enjoyed hitherto, as the rise of the 'social comedy' in the late 1980s and early 1990s (*Trois hommes et un couffin*, 1985) may illustrate. That the tensions of the 1970s had not been quite forgotten became evident in the political commitment and adventurous approach to the margins of the country shown by the dynamic young cinema of the late 1990s, which has brought the new rifts and tensions of a multicultural France to the screens. In the winter of 1996–97, the upsurge of civic protest against new and severe immigration laws was spearheaded by this 'young cinema', which took the initiative of a manifesto, the 'Appel des 59', calling for civil disobedience faced with what seemed to be a legal requirement on citizens to become informers. Such political outspokenness on the part of the industry seems not to have continued into the new millennium, but there is still a small and marginal, but well-received, vein of committed film within French production (examples are the work of the Dardenne brothers, Laurent Cantet, or Robert Guédiguian). As for the theoretical debates of the early 1970s, their influential impact on the general discourse of film studies is now generally acknowledged, and if their translation into cinematic practice was always limited to the intellectual margins of French cinema, the results in the following decade were nonetheless interesting and have considerable importance in the complex image of itself projected by the French cinema. The eager anticipation of a total change in cinematic practice, with which the Etats-Généraux du cinéma set out to rethink the industry and all film-production, was never, even for that year, a likely reality, but the demands which 1968 and its memory made on the screen reflection of the country did have their effect throughout the decade, and despite the apparent U-turn which the 1980s represented, they have never been entirely forgotten.

REFERENCES

Avant-scène (1970) Dossier *Charles mort ou vif*, *Avant-scène* 103, mai.

Bergala, Alain (1981) 'L'Oeil avale', *Cahiers du cinéma* 322, avril: xiv.

Boujut, Michel (1974) *Le Milieu du monde ou Le Cinéma selon Tanner*, Lausanne: L'Age d'Homme.

Cahiers du cinéma (1977) Dossier *Jonas qui aura 25 ans en l'an 2000*, *Cahiers du cinéma* 273, janvier–février: 38–50.

Dimitriu, Christian (1985) *Alain Tanner*, Paris: Henri Veyrier.

Held, Jean-François (1967) 'L'Anti-Godard', *Le Nouvel Observateur*, 24 mai: 32.

Klein, William (1968) 'William Klein: Mister Freedom ou l'effrayant guignol', interview with G. Braucourt, *Lettres françaises*, 31 décembre: 14, 19.

Klein, William (1969a) 'Tous des crapules', interview in *Nouvel Observateur* 218, 13–19 janvier: 27–9.

Klein, William (1969b) Interview in *Image et son* 226, mars: 79–84.

Klein, William (1970) Interview in *Cinéma 70* 151, numéro spécial Politique et cinéma, décembre: 64–6.

Klein, William (1971) Interview in *Image et son* 246, janvier: 51–60.

Klein, William (1975) Interview with Claire Clouzot in *Ecran 75* 38, juillet–août: 58–60..

Klein, William (1977) Interview with Jean Delmas, *Jeune cinéma* 100, février: 16–22.

Klein, William (1978) Interview in *Impact/Revue du cinéma direct*, mai, no. 8/9 (Cinémai 68): 40–1.

Klein, William (1983) Interview in *Art Press 69*, avril: 4–7.

Klein, William (1985) Interview in *Révolution* 278, 28 juin–4 juillet: 43–5.

Marker, Chris (1977–78) 'William Klein', *Graphis* 194(33): 486–99.

Serceau, Daniel (1983a) 'Du messianisme prolétarien à la transformation des consciences', *CinémAction* 25: 118–29.

Serceau, Michel (1983b) 'Un suisse au-dessus de toutes les utopies: Alain Tanner', *CinémAction* 25: 108–15.

Tanner, Alain (1970) Interview in *Télérama* 1044, 18 janvier: 60.

Tanner, Alain (1971) Interview in *Cinéma 71* 161, décembre: 111–16.

Tanner, Alain (1973a) Interview in *Cinéma 73* 180, septembre–octobre: 106–9.

Tanner, Alain (1973b) Interview with Guy Braucourt, *Ecran 73* 18, septembre–octobre: 23–30.

Tanner, Alain (1974a) Interview in *Revue du cinéma/Image et son* 280, janvier: 50–2.

Tanner, Alain (1974b) Interview with Noël Simsolo, *Ecran 74* 29, octobre: 45–7.

Tanner, Alain (1977) Interview in *Cinéma 77* 217, janvier: 46–53.

Filmography of principal directors discussed, 1968–80

RENÉ ALLIO

1969 *Pierre et Paul*, 90 min., col.

Production: Les Films de la Colombe, Madeleine Films, Polsim Productions, Productions de la Guéville
Producer: Claude Nedjar
Production Manager: Guy Blanc
Script: René Allio
Camera: Georges Leclerc
Editing: Chantal Delattre
Sound: Bernard Aubouy
Music: Jacques Dutronc
Principal Actors: Pierre Mondy (Pierre), Bulle Ogier (Martine), Madeleine Barbulée (Mathilde), Robert Juillard (Paul), Pierre Santini (Moran), Philippe Moreau (Trabon), Francis Girod (Levasseur)

1970 *Les Camisards*, 100 min., col.

Production: ORTF, Polfilm, Polsim Productions
Producer: Eric Geiger
Script: René Allio, Jean Jourdheuil
Camera: Denys Clerval, Jean-Paul Schwartz
Editing: Sylvie Blanc
Sound: Bernard Aubouy
Music: Philippe Arthuys
Production Design: Christine Laurent, Nicole Rachline
Costume Design: Christine Laurent
Principal Actors: Rufus (Jacques Combassous), Philippe Clévenot (Lafleur), Jacques Debary (Gédéon Laporte), Gérard Desarthe (Abraham Mazel), Dominique Labourier (Marie Bancilhon), François Marthouret (Lieut. François de la Fage), Gabriel Gascon (Capitaine Alexandre Poul), André Reybas (Baron de Vergnas), Hélène Vincent (Catherine de Vergnas), Christine Laurent (Marguerite Combes)

1973 *Rude Journée pour la reine*, 105 min., col.

Production: Citel Films, ORTF, Polsim Productions
Script: René Allio
Camera: Denys Clerval
Editing: Sylvie Blanc
Sound: Paul Lainé
Music: Philippe Arthuys
Costume Design: Christine Laurent

Principal Actors: Simone Signoret (Jeanne), Jacques Debary (Albert), Gérard
Depardieu (Fabien), Olivier Perrier (Julien), Orane Demazis (Catherine),
Christine Rorato (Mathilde), Arlette Chosson (Annie)

1976 *Moi, Pierre Rivière, ayant égorgé ma mère, ma soeur et mon frère...*, 130 min., col.
Production: Films Arquebuse, Polsim Production, Société française de produc-
tion, INA
Producers: René Féret
Production Director: Michèle Plaa
Script: René Allio, Pascal Bonitzer, Jean Jourdheuil, Serge Toubiana, after work
of Michel Foucault
Camera: Nurith Aviv
Editing: Sylvie Blanc
Production Design: Françoise Darne, François Vantrou, Denis Fruchaud
Costume Design: Christine Laurent, Agnès de Brunhoff
Sound: Pierre Gamet, Francis Bonfanti, Patricia Noïa
Principal Actors: Claude Hébert (Pierre Rivière), Jacqueline Millière (the
mother), Joseph Leportier (the father). Annick Gehan (Aimée), Antoine
Bourseiller (Judge Legrain), Jacques Debary (Dr. Bouchard)

1980 *Retour à Marseille*, 117 min., col.
Production: Action Films, Filmproduktion Janus, FR3
Production Director: Bernard Lorain
Assistant Directors: Xavier Castano, François Vantrou
Script: René Allio, Janine Peyre
Camera: Renato Berta
Editing: Sylvie Blanc
Production Design: Christine Laurent
Music: Lucien Bertolina, Georges Boeuf (Groupe de musique expérimentale de
Marseille), William Chamla.
Principal Actors: Raf Vallone (Michel), Andréa Ferréol (Cécé), Jean Maurel
(Charles), Gilberte Rivet (Jeanne), Paul Allio (le Mino), Ariane Ascaride
(Lydie), Philippe Caubère (M. André), Olivier Perrier (police chief).

YVES BOISSET

1970 *Cran d'arrêt*, 87 min., col.
Production: Francos Films, San Marco
Producer: Francis Cosne
Assistant Producer: Claude Othnin-Girard
Assistant Directors: Fabrizio Diotallevi, Jean-Philippe Mérand
Script: Yves Boisset, Antoine Blondin, François Cosne from novel by Georgio
Scerbanenco
Camera: Jean-Marc Ripert, Daniel Gaudry
Editing: Paul Cayatte, Béatrice Bellest
Costume Design: Jean de Vernant
Sound: Bernard Aubouy, Jean Nény
Music: Michel Magne
Principal Actors: Bruno Cremer (Duca Lamberti/Lucas Lamberti), Renaud
Verley (David Auseri), Marianne Comtell (Livia Ussaro), Rafaella Carrà (Alberta
Radelli), Rufus (photographer's assistant)

1971 *Un Condé, 95 min., col.*
Production: Empire Films, Stephane Films
Producer: Véra Belmont
Script: Yves Boisset, Sandro Continenza, Claude Veillot, from novel by Pierre Lesou
Camera: Jean-Marc Ripert
Editing: Albert Jurgenson (French version), Vincenzo Tomassi (Italian version)
Music: Antoine Duhamel
Principal Actors: Michel Bouquet (Inspector Favenin), Françoise Fabien (Hélène Dassa), Gianni Garko (Dan Rover), Michel Constantin (Viletti), Rufus (Raymond Aulnay), Bernard Fresson (Inspector Barnero)

1971 *Le Saut de l'ange, 90 min., col.*
Production: International Apollo Films, Lira Films, Océanic Films, SN Films
Script: Yves Boisset, Claude Veillot, Richard Winckler, from novel by Bernard-Paul Lallier
Camera: Jean Boffety
Editing: Albert Jurgenson
Music: François de Roubaix
Principal Actors: Jean Yanne (Louis Orsini), Senta Berger (Sylvaine Orsini), Sterling Hayden (Mason/Custer), Raymond Pellegrin (Diego Alvarez), Gordon Mitchell (Henry di Fusco), Daniel Ivernel (Commissioner Pedrinelli)

1972 *L'Attentat, 120 min., col.*
Production: AMLF, Corona Cinematografica, Sancrosiap, Terzafilm Produzione Indipendente, Transinter Films
Producers: Giuliano G. de Negri, Tullio Odevaine
Assistant Directors: Luigi Biamonte, Claude Othnin-Girard
Script: Jorge Semprun, Ben Barzman, Brasilio Franchina
Camera: Ricardo Aronovich
Editing: Albert Jurgenson
Production Design: Marc Desages
Music: Ennio Morricone
Principal Actors: Jean-Louis Trintignant (François Darien), Michel Piccoli (Colonel Kassar), Jean Seberg (Edith Lemoine), Gian Maria Volonté (Saddiel), Michel Bouquet (Maitre Lempereur), Bruno Cremer (Maitre Bourdier), Daniel Ivernel (Antoine Aconetti), Philippe Noiret (Pierre Garcin), François Périer (Rouannat), Jean Bouise.

1973 *R.A.S., 110 min., col.*
Production: Productions de Tana, Transinter Films
Producer: Dany Carrel
Assistant Director: Claude Othnin-Girard
Script: Yves Boisset, Claude Veillot, from story by Roland Perrot
Camera: Jacques Loiseleux
Editing: Albert Jurgenson
Music: François de Roubaix
Principal Actors: Jacques Spiesser ((Rémy March), Jacques Villeret (Private Girod), Jacques Weber (Alain Charpentier), Claude Brosset (Chief Adjudant Santoni), Roland Blanche (Sergeant Lebel)

1974 *Dupont Lajoie,* 100 min., col.
Production: Sofracima
Producers: Gisèle Rebillon, Catherine Winter
Assistant Directors: Jean-Claude García, Daniel Wührmann
Script: Yves Boisset, Jean-Pierre Bastid, Jean Curtelin, Michel Martens
Camera: Jacques Loiseleux
Editing: Albert Jurgenson
Sound: Raymond Adam, Patrick Bordes
Music: Vladimir Cosma
Principal Actors: Jean Carmet (Georges Lajoie), Pierre Tornade (Colin), Jean
Bouise (Inspector Boulard), Michel Peyrelon (Albert Schumacher), Ginette
Garcin (Ginette Lajoie), Jean-Pierre Marielle (Léo Tartaffione), Isabelle
Huppert (Brigitte Colin), Jacques Villeret (Gérald)

1975 *Folle à tuer,* 93 min., col.
Production: Lira Films, Produzioni Artistiche Internazionali
Producers: Ralph Baum, Jean Bolvary, Raymond Danon, Roland Girard
Production Management: André Hoss
Assistant Directors: Laurent Heynemann, Claude Othnin-Girard
Script: Yves Boisset from novel by Jean-Patrick Manchette
Camera: Jean Boffety
Editing: Albert Jurgenson
Set Design: Maurice Sergent
Sound: Raymond Adam
Music: Philippe Sarde
Principal Actors: Marlène Jobert (Julie), Tomas Milian (Thompson), Thomas
Waintrop (Thomas), Michel Peyrelon (Walter), Jean Bouise (Rosenfeld),
Michael Lonsdale (Stéphane Mostri)

1976 *Le Juge Fayard dit 'le Shérif',* 112 min., col.
Production: Action Films, Filmédis, Société française de production.
Producers: Yves Gasser, Yves Peyrot
Assistant Directors: Robert Boulic, Jean-Claude García, Sébastien Grall
Script: Yves Boisset, Claude Veillot
Camera: Jacques Loiseleux
Editor: Albert Jurgenson, Laurence Leininger
Production Design: Serge Sommier
Costume Design: Manuel Tortosa
Music: Philippe Sarde
Principal Actors: Patrice Dewaere (Judge Fayard), Aurore Clément (Michèle
Louvier), Philippe Léotard (Marec), Michel Auclair (Dr. Simon Pradal), Jean
Bouise (Public Prosecutor Arnoud), Daniel Ivernel (Marcheron), Marcel
Bozzuffi (Joanno), Myriam Mézières ('la belle Jenny')

1976 *Un taxi mauve,* 120 min., col.
Production: National Film Studios of Ireland, Rizzoli Film s.p.a., Sofracima,
Sphinx Films, TF1
Assistant Directors: Barry Blackmore, Jean-Claude García, Peter Holder
Producers: Peter Rawley, Catherine Winter
Script: Yves Boisset, Michel Déon from novel by Michel Déon
Camera: Tonino Delli Colli

Editing: Albert Jurgenson
Production Design: Arrigo Equini, Franco Fumagalli, Peter James
Art Direction: John Lucas
Costumes: Tanine Autré
Sound: Bernard Aubouy
Special Effects: Gerry Johnston
Music: Philippe Sarde
Principal Actors: Charlotte Rampling (Sharon), Philippe Noiret (Phillip), Peter Ustinov (Taubelman), Agostina Belli (Anne Taubelman), Fred Astaire (Dr. Scully)

1978 *La Clef sur la porte,* 102 min., col.

Production: Cinéproduction, Société française de production
Script: Yves Boisset, André Weinfeld, from novel by Marie Cardinal
Music: Philippe Sarde
Sound: Nadine Muse
Principal Actors: Annie Girardot (Marie Arnault), Patrick Dewaere (Philippe), Eléonore Klarwein (Charlotte), Malène Sveinbjornsson (Alice), Barbara Steele (Cathy)

1980 *La Femme flic,* 103 min., col.

Production: Films A2, Sara Films, Société Nouvelle Cinévog
Producers: Antoine Gannagé, Alain Sarde
Assistant Director: Jean-Claude Sussfeld
Script: Yves Boisset, Claude Veillot
Camera: Jacques Loiseleux
Editing: Albert Jurgenson
Production Design: Maurice Sergent
Costumes: Laure de Saboulin
Sound: Nadine Muse
Music: Philippe Sarde
Principal Actors: Miou-Miou (Inspector Corinne Lavasseur), Jean-Marc Thibault (Commissioner Porel), Alex Lacast (Inspector Simbert), Roland Blanche (Abbé Henning), Jean-Pierre Kalfon (Backmann), François Simon (Dr. Godiveau)

FRANK CASSENTI

1973 *Salut, voleurs!,* 85 min., col.

Production: R.O.C.
Principal Actors: Areski Belkacem, Jean-Luc Bideau, Anouk Ferjac, Jacques Higelin, László Szabó

1976 *L'Affiche rouge,* 90 min., col.

Production: INA, Z Productions
Producer: Jean-Serge Breton
Script: Frank Cassenti, René Richon
Camera: Philippe Rousselot
Editing: Annie M. Mercier
Production Design: Yves Oppenheim
Costumes: Josiane Balasko
Music: Carlos Carlsen, Juan Cedrón

Principal Actors: Roger Ibanez (Missak Manouchian), Pierre Clémenti (Marcel Rayman), László Szabó (Joseph Boczov), Malka Ribowska (Mélinée Manouchian), Julian Negulesco (Spartaco)

1979 *La Chanson de Roland,* 110 min., col.

Production: Aviva Film, FR3, Images du Monde, Z Productions
Executive Producer: Jean-Serge Breton
Production Manager: Jean-Marie Richard
Assistant Director: Claude Othnin-Girard
Script: Frank Cassenti, Michèle-Anne Mercier, Thierry Joly
Camera: Jean-Jacques Flori
Editing: Annie M. Mercier
Production Design: Renaud Sanson
Costume: Ghyslain Martin
Sound: Georges Prat
Music: Antoine Duhamel
Principal Actors: Klaus Kinski (Roland/Klaus), Alain Cuny (Turpin/the monk), Dominique Sanda (Anna), Pierre Clémenti (Olivier/ the clerk), Jean-Pierre Kalfon (Marsile/Turold/Charlemagne), László Szabó (Duke Naimes/ Hungarian knight), Jean-Claude Brialy (the Lord)

JEAN-LOUIS COMOLLI

1968 *Les Deux Marseillaises* (with André S. Labarthe), 110 min., col.

Production: Argos Films
Camera: Daniel Cardot, Jean-Yves Coic, Philippe Théaudière
Editing: Lise Beaulieu, Dominique Villain
Principal Actors: René Andrieu (himself), Albin Chalandon (himself), Claude Denis (himself), Roger Hanin (himself), Jean-François Revel (himself)

1976 *La Cecilia,* 113 min., col.

Production: Filmoblic, Saba Cinematografica
Producers: Fanny Berchaux, Claude Nedjar, Hubert Niogret
Script: Jean-Louis Comolli, Marianne di Vertimo, Eduardo de Gregorio
Camera: Yann Le Masson
Editing: Claudio Biondi
Production Design: Claudio Patrone
Sound: Tonino Testa
Music: Michel Portal
Principal Actors: Massimo Foschi (Giovanni Rossi), Maria Carta (Olimpia), Vittorio Mezzogiorno (Luigi), Mario Bussolino (Ernesto Lorenzini)

CONSTANTIN COSTA-GAVRAS

1969 *Z,* 127 min., col.

Production: Office national pour la commerce et l'industrie cinématographique (Algeria), Reggane Films, Valoria Films
Producers: Jacques Perrin, Ahmed Rachedi, Eric Schlumberger, Philippe d'Argila
Production Managers: Mourad Bouchouchi, Mohamed Ouled Moussa, Hubert Mérial

Assistant Directors: Ghaouti Bendedouche, Philippe Monnier
Script: Jorge Semprún from novel by Vassilis Vassilikos
Camera: Raoul Coutard
Editing: Françoise Bonnot
Production Design: Jacques d'Ovidio
Costume: Piet Bolscher
Sound: Michèle Boëhm, Sidi Boumedienne Dahmane, Jean Nény
Music: Mikis Theodorakis
Principal Actors: Yves Montand (Z), Irène Papas (Hélène), Jean-Louis Trintignant (the 'little judge'), Jacques Perrin (journalist), Charles Denner (Manuel), Marcel Bozzuffi (Vago), Renato Salvatori (Yago), Georges Géret (Nick), Magali Noël (Nick's sister), Jean Bouise (Georges Pirou), Jean Dasté (Illya Coste)

1970 *L'Aveu,* 135 min., col.
Production: Fono Roma, Les Films Corona, Les Films Pomereu, PIC, Selenia Cinematografica
Producers: Robert Dorfman, Bertrand Javal
Assistant Director: Alain Corneau
Script: Jorge Semprún from book by Artur and Lise London.
Camera: Raoul Coutard
Editing: Françoise Bonnot
Production Design: Bernard Evein
Sound: William Robert Sivel
Music: Giovanni Fusco
Principal Actors: Yves Montand (Anton Litvak), Simone Signoret (Lise), Gabriele Ferzetti (Kohoutek), Michel Vitold (Smola), Jean Bouise (Factory Boss), László Szabó (Secret Policeman), Antoine Vitez

1973 *Etat de siège,* 115 min., col.
Production: Cinema X, Dieter Geissler Filmproduktion, Euro International Film s.p.a., Reggane Films, Unidis
Producers: Jacques Henri Barratier, Léon Sanz, Jacques Perrin
Production Managers: Léon Sanz, Pascal Bazart
Assistant Directors: Christian de Chalonge, Eduardo Durán, Jorge Durán, Emilio Pacull, Pablo de la Barra
Script: Costa-Gavras, Franco Solinas from story by Franco Solinas
Camera: Pierre-William Glenn
Editing: Françoise Bonnot
Production Design: Jacques d'Ovidio
Sound: André Hervée, Michèle Boëhm
Music: Mikis Theodorakis
Principal Actors: Yves Montand (Philip Michael Santore), Renato Salvatori (Captain Lopez), O.E. Hasse (Carlos Ducas), Jacques Weber (Hugo), Jean-Luc Bideau (Este), Jacques Perrin (Telephone Operator)

1975 *Section spéciale,* 118 min., col.
Production: Goriz Films, Janus Film, Les Productions Artistes Associés, Reggane Films
Producers: Jacques Perrin, Giorgio Silvagni, Claude Heymann, Gérard Crosnier
Production Managers: Bernard Bouix, Gérard Crosnier
Assistant Directs: Denys Granier-Deferre, Jean-Michel Lacor

Script: Costa-Gavras, Jorge Semprún from book by Hervé Villeré
Camera: Andréas Winding
Editing: Françoise Bonnot
Production Design: Max Douy
Costume: Hélène Nourry
Sound: Harald Maury, Françoise London
Music: Eric Demarsan
Principal Actors: Louis Seignier (garde des Sceaux), Roland Bertin (Secretary-General, Justice Ministry), Michael Lonsdale (Interior Minister), Ivo Garrani (Admiral), Claude Piéplu (President of the 'Section Spéciale'), Michel Galabru (Président Cournet), Jean Bouise (Counsellor Linais), Bruno Cremer (Sampaix), Jacques Perrin (lawyer Lafarge)

1979 *Clair de femme,* 105 min., col.
Production: Corona Cinematografica, Iduna Film Produktiongesellschaft, Janus Film, Parva Cinematografica, Société des films Gibe
Producer: Georges-Alain Vuille
Assistant Directors: Jochen D. Girsch, Bernard Paul
Script: Costa-Gavras, Christopher Frank, Milan Kundera, from novel by Romain Gary
Camera: Ricardo Aronovich
Editing: Françoise Bonnot
Production Design: Mario Chiari, Eric Simon
Sound: Pierre Gamet
Music: Jean Musy
Principal Actors: Yves Montand (Michel), Romy Schneider (Lydia), Catherine Allégret (Prostitute), Daniel Mesguich (Police Officer), Roberto Benigni, Lila Kedrova, Heinz Bennent, Jean Reno

PHILIPPE DEFRANCE

1980 *Le Fou de mai,* 100 min., col.
Production: Les Films de 'Ga', Z Productions
Script: Philippe Defrance
Camera: Jean Monsigny
Editing: Joëlle van Effenterre
Sound: Georges Prat
Music: Jean-Marie Sénia
Principal Actors: Claude Lévèque (Pierre), Zorica Lozic (Anne), Coline Serreau (Josée), Philippe Defrance (Martin)

JACQUES DOILLON

1971 *L'An 01* (with Alain Resnais, Jean Rouch), 90 min., b/w and col.
Production: UZ Productions
Assistant Directors: Edward Folger, Jean-Jacques Schakmundès
Script: Gébé
Camera: Gérard de Battista, Michel Houssiau, William Lubtchansky, Jean Monsigny, Renan Pollès
Editing: Noëlle Boisson

Sound: Pierre Gamet et al.
Music: François Béranger, Jean-Marie Dusuzeau
Principal Actors: Romain Bouteille (Collector of banknotes), Coluche (office chief), Marcel Gassouk (his father), Miou-Miou (the woman who gets up at six), Albert Delpy (thief), Patrice Leconte (chauffeur), Josiane Balasko, François Cavanna, Professeur Choron, Christian Clavier, Gérard Depardieu, Delfeil de Ton, Gébé, Jacques Higelin, Gérard Jugnot, Nelly Kaplan, Thierry Lhermitte

1974 *Les Doigts dans la tête*, 104 min., b/w
Production: UZ Productions
Producer: Jacques Doillon
Script: Jacques Doillon, Philippe Defrance
Camera: Yves Lafaye
Editing: Noëlle Boisson
Production Design: Manuel Durouchoux
Principal Actors: Christophe Soto (Christophe), Olivier Bousquet (Léon), Roselyne Vuillaume (Rosette), Ann Zacharias (Liv)

1975 *Un sac de billes*, 105 min., col.
Production: AMLF, Les Films Christian Fechner, Renn Productions
Producer: Pierre Grunstein
Production Manager: Jérôme Kanapa
Assistant Directors: Lionel Bernier, Anne Pamuzac
Script: Jacques Doillon, Denis Ferraris, from novel by Joseph Joffo
Camera: Yves Lafaye
Editing: Noëlle Boisson
Production Design: Christian Lamarque
Costumes: Mic Cheminal
Sound: Michel Fauré
Music: Philippe Sarde
Principal Actors: Richard Constantini (Joseph), Paul-Eric Shulmann (Maurice), Joseph Goldenberg (Father), Reine Bartève (Mother)

1978 *La Femme qui pleure*, 90 min, col.
Production: La Guéville, Lola-Films, Renn Productions
Producers: Danièle Delorme, Yves Robert
Production Managers: Philippe Lièvre, André Mennecier
Script: Jacques Doillon
Camera: Yves Lafaye
Editing: Isabelle Rathery
Sound: Michel Kharat
Principal Actors: Dominique Laffin (Dominique), Haydée Politoff (Haydée), Jacques Doillon (Jacques), Lola Doillon (Lola)

1979 *La Drôlesse*, 90 min., col.
Production: La Guéville, Lola-Films
Producers: Danièle Delorme, Yves Robert
Assistant Directors: Dominique Besnehard, Guy Chalaud
Script: Jacques Doillon
Camera: Philippe Rousselot

Editing: Laurent Quaglio
Costume: Mic Cheminal
Sound: Michel Viharat, Michel Kharat
Special Effects: Jean-Pierre Lelong, Claude Villand
Principal Actors: Madeleine Desdevises (Mado), Claude Hébert (François),
  Paulette Lahaye (Mado's mother), Juliette Le Cauchoix (François' mother),
  Dominique Besnehard (the schoolteacher)

CLAUDE FARALDO

1971 *Bof, anatomie d'un livreur,* 110 min., col.
Production: Albina Productions S.a.r.l., Filmanthrope, Marianne Productions
  S.A.
Script: Claude Faraldo
Camera: Sacha Vierny
Music: Jean Guérin
Principal Actors: Marie Dubois (Germaine), Marie-Hélène Breillat (Nana), Paul
  Crauchet (Paolo), Julian Negulesco (the Son)

1972 *Themroc,* 110 min., col.
Production: Filmanthrope, Les Productions FDL
Producers: François de Lannurien, Hélène Vager
Script: Claude Faraldo
Camera: Jean-Marc Ripert
Editing: Noun Serra
Sound: Dominique Hennequin, Harald Maury
Music: Harald Maury
Special Effects: André Trielli
Principal Actors: Michel Piccoli (Themroc), Béatrice Romand (sister), Marilú
  Tolo (secretary), Francesca Romana Coluzzi (neighbour), Coluche (neighbour/
  worker/policeman), Patrice Dewaere (builder), Miou-Miou (neighbour).

1973 *Tabarnac*
Camera: Armand Marco
Principal Actors: the group 'Offenbach' (Gerry Boulet, Johnny Gravel, Michel
  Lamothe).

1976 *Les Fleurs du miel,* 96 min., col.
Production: Contrechamp, Dimage
Script: Claude Faraldo
Camera: Jean-Marc Ripert
Editing: Anna Ruiz, Juliane Ruiz
Sound: Antoine Bonfanti, Auguste Galli
Music: Jefferson Starship
Principal Actors: Brigitte Fossey (woman), Gilles Ségal (husband), Claude
  Faraldo (delivery man), Mireille Pame (maid)

1980 *Deux lions au soleil,* 110 min., col.
Production: Basta Films, FR3
Producer: Stéphane Tchalgadjieff

Assistant Directors: Patrick Grandperret, Vincent Lombard
Script: Claude Faraldo
Camera: Bernard Lutic
Principal Actors: Jean-François Stévenin (Paul), Jean-Pierre Sentier (René), Catherine Lachens (Babette), Jean-Pierre Tailhade (Le volviste)

RENE GAINVILLE

1968 *Le Démoniaque,* 90 min., col.
Production: CEPC
Principal Actors: Anne Vernon (Sophie), Claude Cerval (Joe Kerr), François Gabriel (Joy), Genevive Grad (Lise), Jean-Paul Belmondo

1969 *Un jeune couple,* 84 min., col.
Production: Entervolve, Films de l'Epée, Terra Film
Producer: Jacques Bar
Camera: Roger Fellous
Principal Actors: Jean-François Calvé (Charles), Alain Libolt (Gilles), Anny Duperey, François Gabriel

1970 *Alyse et Chloé,* 95 min., col.
Production: Films de l'Epée, Productions F.D.L.
Script: René Gainville adapted from Marie-Louise de Villiers
Camera: Roger Fellous
Editing: Monique Kirsanoff
Production Design: Robert Luchaire
Principal Actors: Catherine Jacobsen (Alyse), Michèle Girardon (Chloé), Karyn Balm (Marthe), Christine Kerville (Luc Bordier), Pierre Arditi

1974 *Le Complot* (with Agnieszka Holland), 120 min., col.
Production: 14 Luglio Cinematografica, Eguiluz Films, F.D.L., Productions Simone Allouche
Producers: Simone Allouche, Lela Milcic
Script: Salvator A. Crocella, Jean Laborde, Miguel Rubio
Camera: Etienne Szabo
Editing: Monique Kirsanoff
Music: Riz Ortolani, Michel Magne
Principal Actors: Michel Bouquet (Lelong), Michel Dechaussoy (Leblanc), Raymond Pellegrin (Paraux), Jean Rochefort (Dominique), Marina Vlady (Christiane)

1979 *L'Associé,* 94 min., col.
Production: FR3, Magyar Televízió, Maran Film
Script: René Gainville, Jean-Claude Carrière from novel by Jenaro Prieto
Camera: Etienne Szabo
Editing: Raymonde Guyot
Art Direction: Sydney Bettex
Music: Mort Shuman
Principal Actors: Michel Serrault (Julien Pardot), Claudine Auger (Agnès Pardot), Catherine Alric (Alice Duphorin), Judith Magre (Mme. Brézol)

JEAN-LUC GODARD

1968 *Le Gai Savoir,* 95 min., col.
Production: Anouchka Films, Bavaria Atelier GmbH
Script: Jean-Luc Godard adapted from Jean-Jacques Rousseau
Camera: Georges Leclerc
Editing: Germaine Cohen
Principal Actors: Juliette Berto (Patrice Lumumba), Jean-Pierre Léaud (Emile Rousseau), Jean-Luc Godard (Narrator).

1968 *One Plus One* (*Sympathy for the Devil*), 100 min., col.
Production: Cupid Productions
Producers: Eleni Collard, Michael Pearson, Iain Quarrier
Production Manager: Tim van Rellim
Script: Jean-Luc Godard
Camera: Colin Corby, Anthony B. Richmond
Editing: Agnès Guillemot, Kenneth F. Rowles
Sound: Arthur Bradburn
Music: The Rolling Stones
Principal Actors: The Rolling Stones (Mick Jagger, Keith Richard, Brian Jones, Bill Wyman, Charlie Watts), Marianne Faithfull, Anita Pallenberg, Anne Wiazemsky (Eve Democracy)

1968 *Cine-tracts,* c. 30 min., b/w

1968 *Un film comme les autres* (with Groupe ARC), 100 min., b/w and col.
Script: Groupe ARC
Camera: Jean-Luc Godard
Editing: Groupe ARC

1968 *One American Movie* (One A.M.) (incomplete)
Production: Leacock-Pennebaker Inc.
Script: Jean-Luc Godard
Camera: D.A. Pennebaker, Richard Leacock
Principal Actors: Rip Torn, Jefferson Airplane, Eldridge Cleaver, Tom Hayden, Le Roi Jones

1969 *British Sounds* (with Jean-Henri Roger), 52 min., col.
Production: Kestrel Productions
Script: Jean-Luc Godard, Jean-Henri Roger
Camera: Charles Stewart
Sound: Fred Sharp

1969 *Pravda* (with Groupe Dziga-Vertov), 60 min., col.
Production: C.E.R.T.
Producer: Claude Nedjar

1969 *Vent d'est* (with Groupe Dziga-Vertov), 100 min., col.
Production: Kuntz Films, Poli-Film, Anouchka-Films
Script: Jean-Luc Godard, Daniel Cohn-Bendit, Sergio Bazzini
Camera: Mario Vulpiani

Editing: Jean-Luc Godard, Jean-Pierre Gorin
Principal Actors: Gian-Maria Volonté (Northern Ranger), Anne Wiazemsky
(revolutionary), Paolo Pozzesi (revisionist), Christiana Tullio Altan (young
bourgeoise), Daniel Cohn-Bendit, Marco Ferreri, Glauber Rocha

1969 *Luttes en Italie* (with Groupe Dziga-Vertov), 76 min., col.
Production: Cosmoseion
Principal Actors: Christiana Tullio Altan, Anne Wiazemsky, Jérôme Hinstin,
Paolo Pozzesi

1970 *Jusqu'à la victoire* (with Groupe Dziga-Vertov) (incomplete)

1971 *Vladimir et Rosa* (with Groupe Dziga-Vertov), 103 min., col.
Production: Télé-Pool, Grove Press
Principal Actors: Anne Wiazemsky, Jean-Pierre Gorin, Jean-Luc Godard, Juliet
Berto, Claude Nedjar

1972 *Tout va bien* (with Jean-Pierre Gorin), 95 min., col.
Production: Anouchka-Films, Vicco-Film, Empire-Film
Production Manager: Alain Coffier
Script: Jean-Luc Godard, Jean-Pierre Gorin
Camera: Armand Marco
Editing: Kenout Peltier
Sound: Bernard Orthion, Armand Bonfanti
Production Design: Jacques Dugied
Principal Actors: Yves Montand (him), Jane Fonda (her), Vittorio Caprioli
(boss), Jean Pignol (C.G.T. representative), Anne Wiazemsky (leftist)

1972 *Letter to Jane* (with Jean-Pierre Gorin), 60 min., b/w and col.
Production: Jean-Luc Godard, Jean-Pierre Gorin
Script: Jean-Luc Godard, Jean-Pierre Gorin

1974 *Ici et ailleurs* (with Anne-Marie Miéville), 50 min., col.
Camera: William Lubtchansky

1975 *Numéro Deux*, 88 min., col.
Production: Sonimage, Bela, S.N.C
Script: Jean-Luc Godard, Anne-Marie Miéville
Camera: William Lubtchansky
Sound: Jean-Pierre Ruh
Music: Léo Ferré
Principal Actors: Sandrine Battistella (Sandrine), Pierre Oudry (husband),
Alexandre Rignault (grandfather), Rachel Stefanopoli (grandmother)

1975 *Comment ça va*, 78 min., col.
Production: Sonimage, Bela, S.N.C.
Script: Anne-Marie Miéville, Jean-Luc Godard
Principal Actors: M. Marot, Anne-Marie Miéville

1976 *Six fois deux (sur et sous la communication)*, 600 min., col.
Production: I.N.A., Sonimage

Script: Jean-Luc Godard, Anne-Marie Miéville
Camera: William Lubtchansky, Dominique Chapuis

1977–78 *France tour détour deux enfants*, 312 min., col.
Production: I.N.A., Sonimage
Script: Jean-Luc Godard, Anne-Marie Miéville
Principal Actors: Camille Virolleaud, Arnaud Martin (the children), Betty Barr, Albert Dray (presenters)

1979 *Sauve qui peut (la vie)*, 87 min., col.
Production: Sara Films, MK2, Saga Production, Sonimage, C.N.C., Z.D.F., S.S.R.O.R.F.
Producers: Alain Sarde, Jean-Luc Godard
Script: Anne-Marie Miéville, Jean-Claude Carrière
Camera: William Lubtchansky, Renato Berta, Jean-Bernard Menoud
Editing: Anne-Marie Miéville, Jean-Luc Godard
Art Direction: Romain Goupil
Sound: Jacques Maumont, Luc Yersin, Oscar Stellavox
Music: Gabriel Yared
Principal Actors: Isabelle Huppert (Isabelle Rivière), Jacques Dutronc (Paul Godard), Nathalie Baye (Denise Rimbaud), Roland Amstutz (client)

GERARD GUERIN

1971 *Lo Païs*, 90 min., col.
Production: Laura Productions
Producers: Vera Belmont, Gérard Guérin
Script: Jean-Pierre Bastid, Gérard Mordillat
Camera: Jean Monsigny
Music: Gilles Servat
Principal Actors: Olivier Bousquet (Gaston), Anny Nelsen, Gilles Servat, Nada Strancar

MARIN KARMITZ

1968 *Sept jours ailleurs*, 100 min., b/w
Production: MK2 Productions, Productions de La Guéville
Production Managers: Jean Lavie, Daniel Riché
Script: Marin Karmitz, Catherine Martin
Camera: Alain Derobe
Editing: Roger van Leyden
Sound: Bernard Aubouy
Music: Jacky Moreau
Principal Actors: Jacques Higelin (Jacques), Catherine Martin (Catherine), Michèle Moretti (Michèle)

1969 *Camarades*, 80 min., col.
Production: La Guéville, Les Films 13, MK2 Productions, Reggane Films
Producer: Daniel Riché

Camera: Pierre-William Glenn
Principal Actors: Yan Giquel (Yan), Juliet Berto (Juliette), Dominique Labourier (Jeanne), Gilette Barbier

1971 *Coup pour coup*, 86 min., col.
Production: Cinema Services, MK2 Productions, Westdeutscher Rundfunk
Principal Actors: Simone Aubin, Jacqueline Auzellaud, Elodie Avenel, Anne-Marie Bacquié, Marin Karmitz et al.

WILLIAM KLEIN

1968 *Mister Freedom*, 95 min., col.
Production: Films du Rond-Point, O.P.E.R.A.
Producers: Guy Belfond, Christian Thivat, Michel Zemer
Script: William Klein
Cinema: Pierre Lhomme
Editing: Anne-Marie Cotret
Art Director: Jacques Dugied
Costumes: Janine Klein
Sound: Antoine Bonfanti
Music: Michel Colombier, Serge Gainsbourg
Principal Actors: Delphine Seyrig (Marie-Madeleine), John Abbey (Mr. Freedom), Donald Pleasance (Dr. Freedom), Jean-Claude Drouot (Dick Sensass), Serge Gainsbourg (M. Drugstore), Rufus (Freddy Fric), Philippe Noiret (Moujik Man), Sami Frey (Christ), Jean-Luc Bideau (fighter), Daniel Cohn-Bendit (himself), Yves Montand, Simone Signoret

1969 *Eldridge Cleaver Black Panther*, 75 min., col.
Production: O.N.C.I.C.
Principal Actors: Eldridge Cleaver, Kathleen Cleaver (themselves)

1969–74 *Muhammad Ali, the Greatest*, 120 min., b/w and col.
Production: Films Paris-New York, Delpire Advico
Camera: William Klein, Etienne Becker
Sound: Harald Maury
Music: Mickey Baker
Principal Actors: Muhammad Ali, George Foreman, Sonny Liston, Malcolm X, the Beatles, Joe Louis, Mobutu Sese Seko

1976 *Le Couple Témoin*, 100 min., col.
Production: Film Paris-New York, Artco Genève
Producer: Jeanne Klein
Script: William Klein
Camera: William Klein, Philippe Rousselot
Editing: Valérie Mayoux
Music: Michel Colombier
Principal Actors: André Dussollier (Jean-Michel), Anémone (Claudine), Zouc (psychologist), Jacques Boudet (psychologist), Eddie Constantine (Dr. Goldberg)

1977 *Hollywood, California: a Loser's Opera*, 60 min., col.
Production: OKO
Camera: Igor Luther
Editing: Ragnar, Nelly Quettier

1978 *Grands soirs et petits matins*, 105 min., b/w
Production: Films Paris New York
Camera: William Klein, Bernard Zitzerman
Editing: Catherine Binet, Valérie Mayoux, Nelly Quettier, Ragnar
Sound: Harald Maury
Principal Actors: Daniel Cohn-Bendit, Alain Krivine etc.

1978 *Music City, USA*, 75 min., col.
Production: OKO
Camera: Igor Luther
Editing: Ragnar, Nelly Quettier

1980 *The Little Richard Story*, 90 min., col.
Production: OKO
Camera: Igor Luther
Editing: Ragnar, Nelly Quettier

CHRIS MARKER

1974 *La Solitude du chanteur de fond*, 60 min., b/w and col.
Camera: Pierre Lhomme
Editing: Chris Marker
Principal Actors: Yves Montand, Chris Marker

1977 *Le Fond de l'air est rouge*, 240 min., b/w and col.
Production: Dovidis, ISKRA, INA
Script: Chris Marker
Camera: Pierre-William Glenn, Willy Kurant
Editing: Chris Marker
Music: Luciano Berio
Principal Speakers: François Maspéro, Yves Montand, François Périer, Jorge Semprún, Simone Signoret

JEAN-PIERRE MOCKY

1969 *La Grande lessive*, 95 min., col.
Production: Balzac Films, Firmament Films, Méditerranée Cinéma, Océanic Films
Producers: Georges Cheyko, Jean-Pierre Mocky
Production Manager: Pierre Saint-Blancat
Script: Jean-Pierre Mocky, Alain Mour, Claude Penn
Camera: Marcel Weiss
Editing: Marguerite Renoir
Production Design: Pierre Tyberghein
Sound: René Sarazin

Music: François de Roubaix
Principal Actors: Bourvil (Armand Saint-Just), Francis Blanche (Dr. Loupiac),
    Roland Dubillard (Missenard), Jean Tissier (Benjamin), Michael Lonsdale
    (Delaroche), Jean Poiret (Jean-Michel Lavalette)

1970 *Solo,* 83 min., col.

Production: Balzac Films, Cine Eclair, Showking Films, Société Nouvelle Cinévog
Producers: Jean-Pierre Mocky, Jérôme Goulven, André Weis
Production Manager: Gilbert Marion
Assistant Directors: Luc Andrieux, Jacques de Chavigny, Pierre Drouot
Script: Jean-Pierre Mocky, Alain Moury
Camera: Marcel Weiss
Editing: Marguerite Renoir
Sound: Séverin Frankiel, Lucien Yvonnet
Music: Georges Moustaki
Principal Actors: Jean-Pierre Mocky (Vincent Cabral), Sylvie Bréal (Micheline),
    Anne Deleuze (Annabel), Denis LeGuillou (Virgile Cabral)

1970 *L'Etalon,* 90 min., b/w and col.

Production: Balzac Films, CCFC, Filmel
Producer: Jean-Pierre Mocky
Production Manager: Gilbert Marion
Script: Jean-Pierre Mocky, Alain Moury
Camera: Marcel Weiss
Editing: Marguerite Renoir
Production Design: Jacques Flamand
Music: François de Roubaix
Principal Actors: Bourvil (William Chaminade), Francis Blanche (Dupuis),
    Jacques Legras (Pointard), René-Jean Chauffard (Finus), Michael Lonsdale
    (Both)

1971 *Chut!,* 88 min., col.

Production: Balzac Films
Producer: Jean-Pierre Mocky
Production Manager: Marcel Mossotti
Assistant Directors: Luc Andrieux, Edgar Baum, Loïc Pichon, François Pradeau
Script: Jean-Pierre Mocky, Raphaël Delpard
Camera: Marcel Weiss
Editing: Jean-Pierre Mocky, Marguerite Renoir
Production Design: Jacques Flamand
Sound: Séverin Frankiel
Music: François de Roubaix
Principal Actors: Jacques Dufilho (Fritz Ducharrel), Michael Lonsdale (Sergel),
    Henri Poirier (lawyer), Maurice Vallier (Henri Butin)

1972 *L'Albatros,* 92 min., col.

Production: Balzac Films, Belstar Productions, Profilm
Producer: Jean-Pierre Mocky
Production Manager: Marcel Mossotti
Assistant Directors: Luc Andrieux, Jean-Marie Ghanassia, Francis Guesweiler,
    Léonard Guillain, Iosko Heterovitch, Francis Hylari

Script: Jean-Pierre Mocky, Raphaël Delpard, Claude Veillot
Camera: Marcel Weiss
Editing: Marie-Louise Barberot
Production Design: Jacques Dor, Jacques Flamand
Sound: Séverin Frankiel
Music: Léo Ferré
Principal Actors: Jean-Pierre Mocky (Stef Tassel), Marion Game (Paula Cavalier), André Le Gall (Councillor Lucien Grimm), Paul Muller (President Ernest Cavalier)

1974 *L'Ombre d'une chance*, 95 min., col.
Production: Balzac Films
Producer: Jean-Pierre Mocky
Assistant Directors: Luc Andrieux, Patrick Le Bohec, Frédéric Le Pinday
Script: Jean-Pierre Mocky, Alain Moury, André Ruellan
Editing: Marie-Louise Barberot, Michel Saintourens
Production Design: Jean-Claude Riedel
Sound: Séverin Frankiel
Music: Eric Demarsan
Principal Actors: Jean-Pierre Mocky (Mathias Caral), Robert Benoît (Michel Caral), Jenny Arasse (Sandra), Agnès Desroches (Huguette)

1975 *L'Ibis rouge*, 90 min., col.
Production: Les Films de l'Epée, M Films
Producers: Jean-Pierre Mocky, Jean-Claude Roblin
Production Manager: Robert Paillardon
Assistant Directors: Luc Andrieux, Jean-François Villemer
Script: Jean-Pierre Mocky, André Ruellan from novel by Fredric Brown
Camera: Marcel Weiss
Editing: Delphine Desfons, Michel Saintourens
Production Design: René Loubet, Jean-Pierre Mocky
Costumes: Rosine Lan
Sound: Séverin Frankiel
Music: Eric Demarsan
Principal Actors: Michel Simon (Zizi), Michel Serrault (Jérémie), Michel Galabru (Raymond Viliers), Jean Le Poulain (Margos)

1975 *Un linceul n'a pas de poches*, 125 min., col.
Production: Balzac Films, S.N. Prodis
Producer: Jean-Pierre Mocky
Production Manager: Robert Paillardon
Assistant Directors: Luc Andrieux, Eric Ferro
Script: Jean-Pierre Mocky, Alain Moury from novel by Horace McCoy
Camera: Marcel Weiss
Editing: Marie-Louise Barberot
Production Design: René Loubet
Sound: Séverin Frankiel
Music: Paul de Senneville, Olivier Toussaint
Principal Actors: Jean Carmet (Commissioner Bude), Michel Constantin (Culli), Michel Galabru (Thomas), Daniel Gélin (Laurence), Michael Lonsdale (Raymond), Jean-Pierre Marielle (Dr. Carlille), Jean-Pierre Mocky (Michel

Dolannes), Michel Serrault (Justin Blesh), Myriam Mézières (Mira Barnowski), Sylvia Kristel (Avril)

1977 *Le Roi des bricoleurs, 80 min., col.*

Production: M. Films
Producers: Jean-Pierre Mocky, Maurice Saccardi
Production Manager: Robert Paillardon
Assistant Directors: Luc Andrieux, André Heinrich, Alain Lévy, Nathalie Perrey
Script: Jean-Pierre Mocky, André Ruellan, Michel Saintourens
Camera: Marcel Weiss
Editing: Jean-Pierre Mocky, Nathalie Perrey, Michel Saintourens
Production Design: René Loubet
Costumes: Rosine Lan
Sound: Séverin Frankiel, Pierre Lay
Music: Eric Demarsan
Principal Actors: Sim (Malju), Michel Serrault (Bordin), Pierre Bolo (Goumic), Paulette Frantz (Anne Goumic)

1979 *Le Témoin, 90 min., col.*

Production: Belstar Productions, M. Films, Multimedia, Produzioni Atlas Consorziate
Producer: Robert Dorfmann
Production Managers: Teodoro Agrimi, Henri Baum
Assistant Directors: Tony Aboyantz, Mario Maffei, François Pecnard
Script: Jean-Pierre Mocky, Sergio Amidei, Augusto Caminito, Jacques Dreux, Rodolfo Sonego, Alberto Sordi from novel by Harrisson Jude
Camera: Sergio d'Offizi
Editing: Michel Lewin
Production Design: Carlo Leva
Costume: Bruna Parmesan
Sound: Roberto Alberghini, Louis Hochet, Antonio Pantano
Music: Piero Piccioni
Principal Actors: Alberto Sordi (Antonio Berti), Philippe Noiret (Robert Maurisson), Roland Dubillard (Commissioner Guérin), Gisèle Préville (Louise Maurisson)

1980 *Le Piège à cons, 90 min., col.*

Production: Audiphone, M. Films, Sève
Producer: Jean-Pierre Mocky
Production Manager: Robert Paillardon
Assistant Directors: Jean-Paul Durand, Lâm Lê, Etienne Méry, Gaspard de Chavagnac
Script: Jean-Pierre Mocky, Patrick Granier, Jacques Dreux
Camera: Marcel Weiss
Editing: Annabel Le Doeuff, Catherine Renault
Production Design: Lâm Lê, Etienne Méry
Sound: Louis Hochet
Music: Stéphane Varègues
Principal Actors: Jean-Pierre Mocky (Michel Rayan), Catherine Leprince (Francine Vanneau), Bruno Netter (Séverin Lanier), Jacques Legras (Commissioner Roubert)

ALAIN TANNER

1969 *Charles mort ou vif*, 93 min., b/w
Production: Le Group 5, Schweizerische Radio- und Fernsehgesellschaft
Producer: Alain Tanner
Script: Alain Tanner
Camera: Renato Berta
Editing: Silva Bachmann
Sound: Paul Girard
Principal Actors: François Simon (Charles Dé), Marcel Robert (Paul), Marie-Claire Dufour (Adeline), André Schmidt (Pierre Dé), Maya Simon (Marianne Dé), Jean-Luc Bideau (ambulance driver)

1971 *La Salamandre*, 125 min., b/w
Production: Filmograph S.A., Forum Films, Svocine
Producer: Gabriel Auer
Script: Alain Tanner, John Berger
Camera: Sandro Bernardoni, Renato Berta
Editing: Marc Blavet, Brigitte Sousselier
Music: Patrick Moraz
Principal Actors: Bulle Ogier (Rosemonde), Jean-Luc Bideau (Pierre), Jacques Denis (Paul), Véronique Alain (Suzanne)

1973 *Le Retour d'Afrique*, 110 min., b/w
Production: Groupe 5 Genève, SSR, Filmanthrope, Nouvelles éditions de films
Producer: Alain Tanner
Assistant Directors: Michel Schopfer, Bertrand van Effenterre
Script: Alain Tanner
Camera: Renato Berta, Carlo Varini
Editing: Brigitte Sousselier, Marc Blavet
Production Design: Yanko Hodjis
Principal Actors: Josée Destoop (Françoise), François Marthouret (Vincent), Juliet Berto, Anne Wiazemsky

1974 *Le Milieu du monde*, 115 min., col.
Production: Citel Films, Action Films, SSR
Produvers: Yves Gasser, Yves Peyrot
Production Manager: Bernard Lorain
Assistant Directors: Michel Schopfer, Nicolas Philibert
Script: Alain Tanner, John Berger
Camera: Renato Berta
Editing: Brigitte Sousselier
Production Design: Serge Etter
Sound: Pierre Gamet
Music: Patrick Moraz
Principal Actors: Olimpia Carlisi (Adriana), Philippe Léotard (Paul), Juliet Berto (Juliette), Denise Perron (widow Schmidt), Jacques Denis (Marcel)

1976 *Jonas qui aura 25 ans en l'an 2000*, 116 min., col.
Production: Action Films, Citel Films, Société Française de Production, SSR
Producers: Yves Peyrot, Yves Gasser

Production Manager: Bernard Lorain
Assistant Directors: Laurent Ferrier, Anita Peyrot, Alain Klarer
Script: Alain Tanner, John Berger
Camera: Renato Berta
Editing: Brigitte Sousselier
Sound: Pierre Gamet
Music: Jean-Marie Sénia
Principal Actors: Jean-Luc Bideau (Max), Myriam Mézières (Madeleine), Rufus (Mathieu), Myriam Boyer (Mathilde), Roger Jendly (Marcel), Dominique Labourier (Marguerite), Jacques Denis (Marco), Miou-Miou (Marie)

1979 *Messidor,* 128 min., col.
Production: Citel Films, Action Films SSR
Producers: Yves Gasser, Yves Peyrot
Production Manager: Bernard Lorain
Assistant Directors: Xavier Castano, Alain Klarer
Script: Alain Tanner
Camera: Renato Berta
Editing: Brigitte Sousselier
Sound: Pierre Gamet
Music: Arie Dzierlatka
Principal Actors: Clémentine Amouroux (Jeanne), Catherine Rétoré (Marie)

Index of film titles

Note: numbers in italics refer to illustrations; n after a page number refers to a note on that page.

Index of names and subjects

Note: numbers in italics refer to illustrations; n after a page number refers to a note on that page.